THE TRANS-APPALACHIAN WARS, 1790-1818:

Pathways to America's First Empire

By:

John Eric Vining

Order this book online at www.trafford.com
or email orders@trafford.com

Most Trafford titles are also available at major online book retailers.

Printed in Victoria, BC, Canada.

ISBN: 978-1-4269-2341-8 (sc)
ISBN: 978-1-4269-2342-5 (dj)

Library of Congress Control Number: 2009913324

*Our mission is to efficiently provide the world's finest, most comprehensive book publishing
service, enabling every author to experience success. To find out how to publish your book, your
way, and have it available worldwide, visit us online at www.trafford.com*

Trafford rev. 01/19/2010

 www.trafford.com

North America & international
toll-free: 1 888 232 4444 (USA & Canada)
phone: 250 383 6864 ♦ fax: 812 355 4082

Dedication

This book is dedicated to *Alan J. Vining*. His outstanding effort to create the maps contained within the book have gone far to make it a solid contribution to the historical record. Thanks, Al, for your many hours spent in front of the computer!

CONTENTS

Part 3 *Aftermath of Conflict: The Fruits of Empire*

Part 4 *Close-up: Details Relating to the Trans-Appalachian Wars*

ACKNOWLEDGEMENTS
And
Pre-Text Notes

(1)

The author desires to relate that the basic foundational structure of this book is predicated on the concept that the historical facts and phrases stated in the book are drawn from previous historical works developed and published by research historians. The author fully and humbly acknowledges his immense debt to these historians.

To enhance the readability of the text, the author has chosen to use contemporary writing and noting techniques utilized by modern historical authors. These methods do not include the use of quotation marks within the body of the work on every fact, phrase, or idea drawn verbatim from another text. Quotation marks within the main body of the text are basically reserved for verbatim quotations of human beings.

The author wishes to state that every effort has been made to fully document all facts, phrases, ideas, and quotations of other historians and writers in the endnotes. In those endnotes, verbatim facts and the first few words of verbatim phrases are enclosed in quotation marks, and followed by a full documentary note. Direct quotations from humans follow the same structuring convention, but the first few words of the phrase are *italicized*. Paraphrased ideas follow the same conventions as facts and phrases, but are not enclosed in quotation marks and are not italicized. The author strongly encourages all readers to rigorously examine these endnotes and consult the original texts to confirm the veracity of the facts, phrases, ideas, and quotations contained in this work.

(2)

The author intends no disrespect by the use of the masculine pronouns *he* and *him* or the feminine pronouns *she* and *her* to refer to sovereign nations or departments of these nations. This device was used to promote consistency between quotes from earlier references, when this convention was considered standard and acceptable, and the current, modern portions of the text.

(3)

The terms *Native American* and *Indian* are used interchangeably throughout this text. The author intends no disrespect to the original inhabitants of the Americas through the use of either term.

Similarly, the term *Negro* was used in the common vernacular of the period in which this text is set. It was used as noun and as an adjective, even to the extent of given names of structures and installations, such as the *Negro Fort* on the Apalachicola River, Florida. The author wishes to maintain historical accuracy. At the same time, the author intends no disrespect to the African-American community through the use of the term.

INTRODUCTION

Many years ago, I read an outstanding book by Byron Farwell entitled, The Great War in Africa, 1914-'18. Farwell made a comment in the foreword of that book that always stuck with me: "...interest in a war should not be gauged by the size of the butcher's bill."

The American Woodland Wars of the 1790s, the War of 1812 in the west, and the First Seminole War epitomize this thought. In terms of political ramifications and intrigues, military strategies and tactics, and interactions between different entities and individuals, these campaigns rank high on the scale of complexity and interest. Particularly in the Old Northwest and Southern areas, "ya needed a scorecard to keep track a' the teams." If you look closely at the campaigns and battles, you can see the influence of Braddock, Napoleon, and Wellington. Look deeper and you see the strategies and tactics that will evolve and play on a so much bigger scale in the Mexican and Civil Wars. Look backward and you see the ghost of the Revolutionary War still haunting the corners of the theaters. (Please see Appendix A for a short history of the Revolutionary War and its aftermath in the Old Northwest.)

Because they are so related, I have chosen to link the struggles in the Old Northwest, Old Southwest, and Old South from 1790 to 1818 together as The Trans-Appalachian Wars. One might question the label "Trans-Appalachian," particularly in reference to the struggle for the Floridas in 1817-'18. The Appalachian Mountains sweep from northeast to southwest through Georgia and Alabama: thus, depending on your point of reference, even Florida can be "over the mountains" geographically.

Still, the term "Trans-Appalachian" is simply a convenient geographical heading to group a set of related, but not necessarily well-understood, conflicts. These conflicts basically had a common thread that united them: they served as political/military vehicles for the expansion of the territory of the United States: in other words, they served to foster "empire building." In each, the struggle against the nature of the land itself was nearly as great as that against human enemies. The strategies, tactics, and infrastructures developed to cope with these foes are as fascinating as any "war stories" ever told.

This book is intended to explore the theme that the purpose of these wars was "empire building." It is also intended to serve as an educational primer for some of the most interesting, yet possibly least documented (at least in flowing narrative form) and understood struggles which ever occurred the North American continent.

John Eric Vining

THE MIAMI VALLEY /
Great Black Swamp Corridor

CHAPTER 1

Prologue –

The First American Empire: Ohio in the Old Northwest Territory

Americans have an interesting trait as a people that is somewhat amusing for a historian to stand back and objectively view. We find it very easy to condemn and see the evil in colonialism, hegemony, and the empires of the past. From the time we are young, reaching back in books to the beginning of recorded history, we read of the great Middle Eastern and Western empires and perhaps unconsciously applaud their demise. The Assyrians, the Babylonians, the Medes, the Persians, Alexander, the Romans, the Ottomans, Napoleon, the Third Reich, the British, the Soviet Union – all rose and fell in the blink of an eye in our short span of recorded consciousness. Some we see as evil; some we see as at best benevolently despotic; virtually none are viewed positively. Americans are free: Americans are democratic; the power is with the people. How very curious that we cannot see that our entire society west of the Appalachian Mountains was built on the very concept we silently despise!

Surely this cannot be true! Why, we *NEVER* were an imperial power – well, OK. At the very end of the Nineteenth Century, we did win a war with Spain and inherit a few unwanted islands. But we only kept them long enough to set them up as democracies just like us, then set them free…

What is an *"empire,"* anyway? Webster's dictionary defines it as *"Supreme power in governing; region over which dominion is extended."*

Think of the Russian empire – not the Soviet Union, but the original Russian Siberian/Asian empire – or perhaps the British Empire in Africa or India. How did Russia or Britain acquire and administer these lands? By conquering the indigenous inhabitants of the land, then warding off other imperial powers that wanted a piece of the conquest, and finally introducing infrastructures to economically exploit the conquered territory.

Ask the modern western Native American if his nation has been conquered by an imperial power...

Ask the British, French, or Spanish if they still have a colonial empire in western or southern North America. If they had an empire then and don't have it now, who controls it? If it was an empire under their control then, is it any less of one under our control now?

This book is based on the premise that the western United States (basically the area west and south of the Appalachian Mountains) is an empire America wrested from the indigenous Native American tribes and from European colonial powers, who from the Sixteenth through the Nineteenth Centuries sought to control it. (I view the original thirteen colonies as established by imperial Europe.) If this is so, then the original "colonial war" in which the fledgling United States engaged was the Northwestern "Indian War" of the 1790s (which stretched into the War of 1812 in the Northwest Territory, with an uneasy approximate 15-year interlude). This colonial war conceptually can include its related struggles, the Patriot War, the Creek War, the Southwestern Theater of the War of 1812, and the First Seminole War. From a Midwestern viewpoint, these southwestern conflicts served to protect the Old Northwest from further threats of Native American interdiction or physical/economic hegemony from the old European colonial powers. The security thus provided allowed vast streams of immigrant settlers (or if you will, colonists) to enter the Old Northwest and capitalists to invest in the first colonial infrastructures to exploit the newly conquered territory. This in turn created the first commercially viable imperial area of the new country – the agricultural garden that became Northwest and West Central Ohio.

Once the concept is accepted that Western America, and particularly northern/western Ohio, is an imperial holding, it becomes interesting to visualize the axis of advance utilized to conquer and exploit it. For example, Alexander marched east through Asia Minor to conquer the Middle East. European Russia moved east, conquering the trackless steppe mile by mile in establishing its Siberian empire. Britain marched northeast from Cape Colony through the Vaal to establish the Union of South Africa.

A new concept I will introduce in this book is that the United States utilized a definite strategic geographical route in conquering its first imperial area – a route I entitle "The Miami Valley / Great Black Swamp Corridor." Repeated studies of the path to empire in the Old Northwest during the period 1790 – 1845 show that this strategic corridor was used time and again to first militarily conquer, then economically conquer, America's first imperial holding.

Before we can move on, however, we must establish the definition of a term that has developed a negative connotation in modern America – *"exploitation."* Again referring to Webster, "exploitation" is a neutral concept: the *"successful application of industry on any object, as land, mines, etc."* To *exploit* is *"to make use of; to work."* To appreciate the activities, which occurred after the military conquest of Ohio, we must see the exploitation of the natural resources of the region as beneficial to the growth of America as we know it today.

This book is not intended to be overly critical of the growth process of the United States from its earliest days as a nation. What is done is done. As Barbara Hershey's character stated in the movie *The Last of the Dogmen*, "What happened was inevitable; the way it happened was unconscionable"- a simple, moving commentary on the inexorable westward movement of European/American civilization and its clash with the existing Native American civilization. Rather, the intent is to see events in the context in which they actually occurred and provide an understanding for the animosities that still remain as a result of our imperial struggles. I thus hope to provide an objective view of a tremendously interesting period in and geographical area of our history, and in some small way to help heal the wounds that still have not closed with the passage of time.

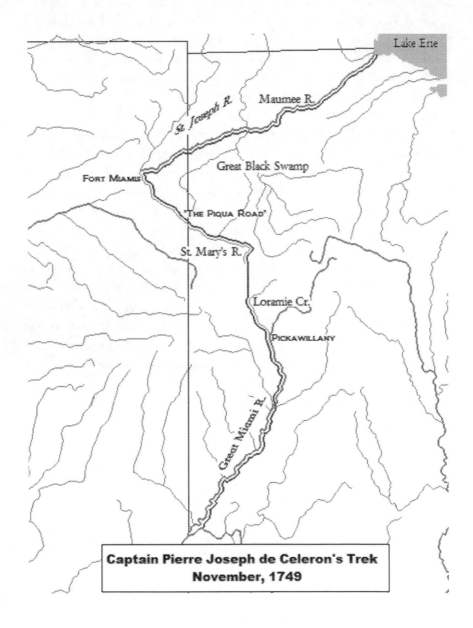

Lake Erie

St. Joseph R.

Maumee R.

Great Black Swamp

FORT MIAMIS

"THE PIQUA ROAD"

St. Mary's R.

Loramie Cr.

PICKAWILLANY

Great Miami R.

**Captain Pierre Joseph de Celeron's Trek
November, 1749**

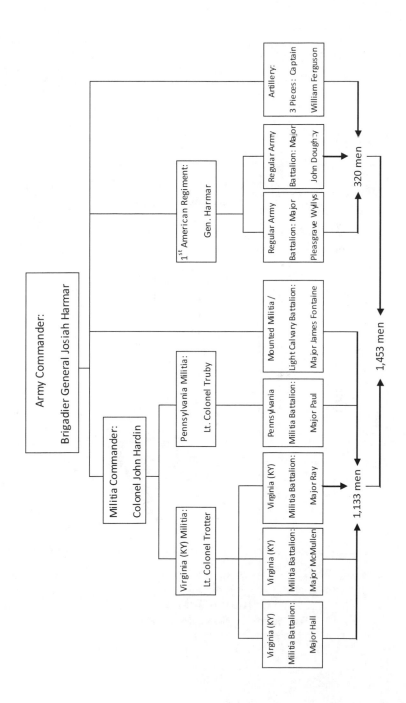

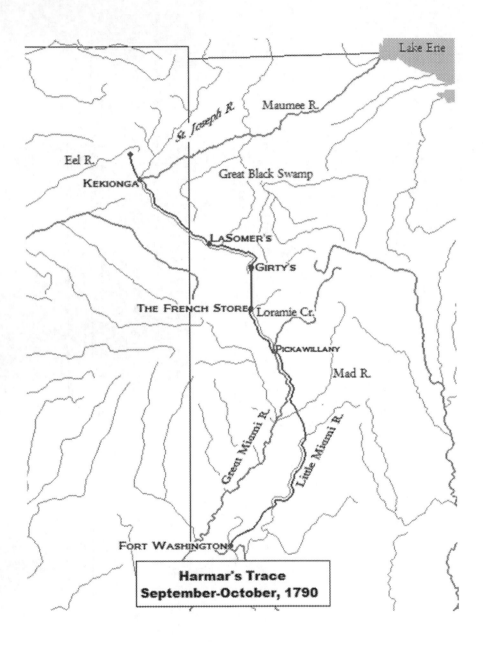

Lake Erie

Maumee R.

St. Joseph R.

Eel R.

KEKIONGA

Great Black Swamp

LASOMER'S

GIRTY'S

THE FRENCH STORE Loramie Cr.

PICKAWILLANY

Mad R.

Great Miami R.

Little Miami R.

FORT WASHINGTON

**Harmar's Trace
September-October, 1790**

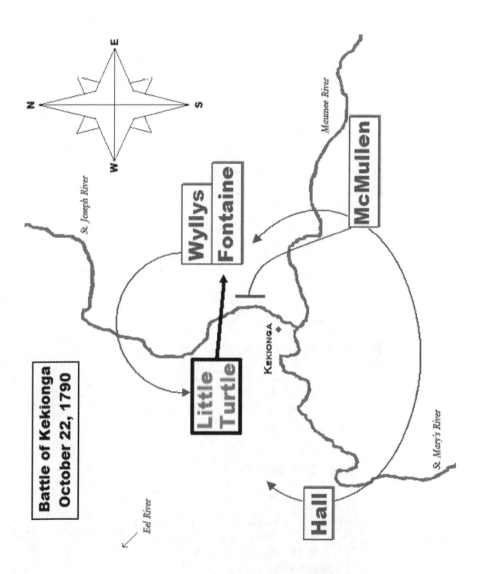

Battle of Kekionga
October 22, 1790

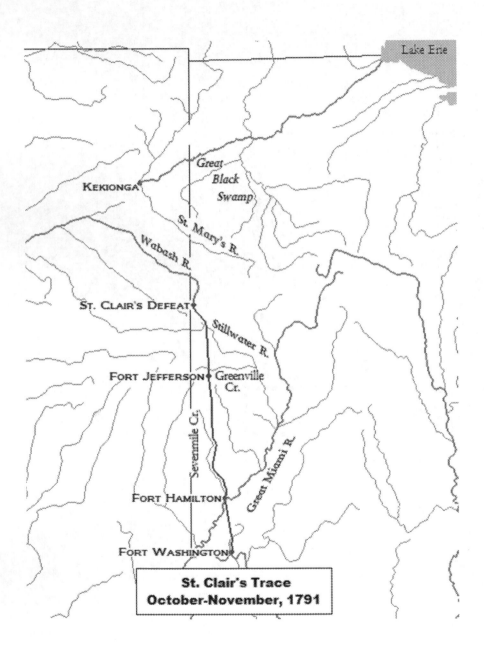

Lake Erie

Great
Black
Swamp

KEKIONGA

St. Mary's R.

Wabash R.

St. Clair's Defeat

Stillwater R.

Fort Jefferson Greenville
Cr.

Sevennile Cr.

Great Miami R.

Fort Hamilton

Fort Washington

**St. Clair's Trace
October-November, 1791**

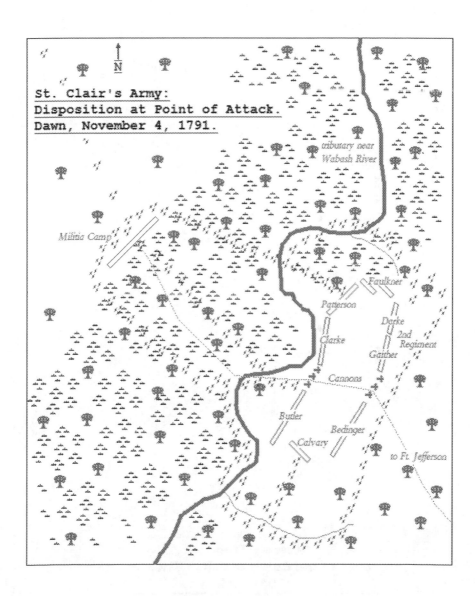

St. Clair's Army:
Disposition at Point of Attack.
Dawn, November 4, 1791.

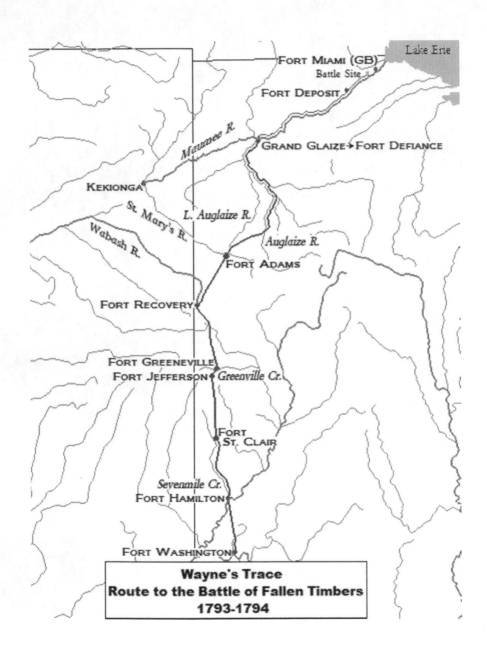

Wayne's Trace
Route to the Battle of Fallen Timbers
1793-1794

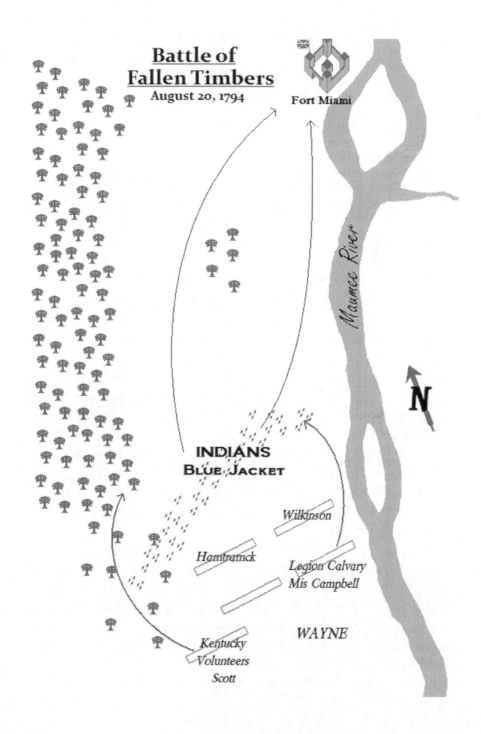

Battle of
Fallen Timbers
August 20, 1794

Fort Miami

Maumee River

N

INDIANS
BLUE JACKET

Wilkinson

Hamtramck

Legion Calvary
Mis Campbell

WAYNE

Kentucky
Volunteers
Scott

CHAPTER 2

The Collision of Empires: Prelude to Imperial War

Few people traveling through the serene farmland of the northwest quadrant of Ohio would view the area as a flash point of evolving empires – a place where various civilizations clashed in a violent interface with the frontier. Yet, in the late Eighteenth and early Nineteenth Centuries, this was exactly the case. European empires fought for control of the land. A budding new nation had dreams of empire, and was composed of the rugged individualists to make this dream a reality. In the middle were the Native Americans,* inhabiting the land and confused by the laws, greed, and customs of the white invaders – both American colonists and European imperialists. The volatile, inflammatory mix of European imperialism, American westward-looking "Manifest Destiny," and Indian mysticism fueled a conflict in precisely this area where cattle now peacefully graze and gentle breezes ruffle the leaves of growing crops. America's first foray into its western empire began with its move into what is now the Northwest Ohio/Northeast Indiana area.

Allan W. Eckert captured the spirit of this confusing caldron of imperialistic clashes and Native American defense in his book, **Wilderness Empire***:*

*"Only a handful of white men were here now. In fact, only a handful had **ever** been here since the Jesuit father Jacques Marquette had established his mission called St. Ignace (the site of present St. Ignace, Michigan) on the north side of the strait, across from Michilimackinac. That year – 1671 – had been a proud one for France. It was on June 14 that Sieur de St. Lusson had stood on the banks of the Sault Sainte Marie some fifty miles north of here with his arms upraised in rather grandiose gesture and made his impressive declaration in a loud voice.*

"I hereby take possession for France,' he had said, 'of lakes Superior and Huron and of all other countries, streams, lakes and rivers contiguous and adjacent – those already discovered as well as those yet to be discovered – which are bounded on one side by the seas of the North and of the West, and on the other side by the South Sea, and in all their length and breadth!'

"The three Jesuit priests and sixteen other French and Canadians behind him nodded and murmured smiling approval at the well-rehearsed speech. The several hundred Indians in a semicircle behind them took this as a cue and they, too, nodded and smiled and murmured, even though uncomprehending of what was occurring here. It was well for the white men that these assembled Ottawas, Chippewas, and Hurons did not understand. The claim was highly audacious in several respects – mainly in that it ignored the fact that not only did Spain and Great Britain have similar claims on this same vast territory, but that it was in reality a territory owned and occupied by a large number of Indians of native Great Lakes tribes, along with the remnants of other tribes defeated, dispossessed and dispersed by the fierce Iroquois warrior far to the east of here decades ago."

In 1749, the Marquis de la Gallissoniere, the governor of New France, realized that several treaties between the colonial powers contesting the Great Lakes region had failed to settle the boundary questions which vexed the European powers. He set in motion a plan to fix the boundaries in the Old Northwest in France's favor. Summoning Captain Pierre Joseph de Celoron de Bienville and a detachment of French troops, Gallissoniere ordered them to circumnavigate a huge circular route from Lake Ontario to and down the Ohio River, through the rivers of the Old Northwestern wilderness, and back to Lake Erie, burying at various points along this great watercourse leaden plates bearing the following inscription (river names adjusted for location):

Year 1749
This in the Reign of Louis Fifteenth
King of France

We, Celoron, commanding the detachment sent by the Marquis de la Galissoniere, Commander-General of New France, to restore tranquillity in certain villages of these cantons, have buried this plate at the confluence of (La Belle Riviere and the Kanaougon, this 29th July), as a token of renewal of possession heretofore taken of the aforesaid (Riviere LaBelle), of all streams that fall into it, and all lands on both sides of the source of the aforesaid streams, as the preceding Kings of France have or ought to have enjoyed it, and which they have upheld by force of arms and by treaties, notable those of Ryswick, Utrecht, and Aix-La-Chapelle.

In due course, and after the placing of several of these lead plates, Celoron de Bienville came to the confluence of the Ohio and Great Miami Rivers. Eckert describes Celoron's northward passage:

[November 20, 1749 – Monday]

"The journey up the Great Miami River had been a strenuous one for the expedition under Captain Pierre Joseph de Celoron de Bienville. Time after time the river shallowed to such extent that it ran only an inch or two deep over rocks and gravel and the canoes had to be laboriously dragged across such riffles. They sprang leaks, becoming constantly wet and decidedly unsafe. And the riffles became even more numerous after they had passed a place where within one mile two major rivers and a smaller creek joined the Great Miami (present Dayton, Ohio). Without the water those three streams had provided, passage became even harder.

"It took thirteen days for them to reach…{the} principally Miami village of Pickawillany (also known as "New Chillicothe," present Piqua, Ohio), near the mouth of that muddy little creek (Loramie Creek) which joined the Great Miami."

After a stay at Pickawillany, Celoron continued his journey north-northwest:

"Following the rough map provided for him by the governor, they left the larger river and now paddled up the muddy creek until they could go no further. Here they unloaded the canoes a final time, stacked them all in a great pile and burned them (at present Fort Loramie, Ohio). The remaining supplies were divided among them into shoulder packs and

they set off afoot along the portage trail which led to the headwaters of the St. Mary's River. When they came to that stream they followed the Indian path which paralleled it (known for many years as "The Piqua Road") and moved downstream until they came to where this stream met the St. Joseph River to form the Maumee River or, as the Indians called it, the **Omee**.

"Located here was Fort Miamis (now Fort Wayne, Indiana), which was presently under the command of Lieutenant de Raimond. {Raimond had} a large collection of bark and wooden dug-out type canoes to which Celoron and his party were welcome. Celoron bade farewell to Lieutenant Raimond, thanked him for the boats and started his party on the float down the Maumee River to Lake Erie."

Gallissoniere and Celoron could not have known that they had laid out the soon-to-be United States' first path to empire. This gateway would provide a route to the battle sites of two wars, provide a path for five American armies, and forge a trail whose course would be used build three different types of public transportation infrastructures.

Before all this could happen, American title to the area must be secured (at least in the Western European sense). Spain had never renounced her claims to the entire Mississippi and Ohio Basins, but as the Eighteenth Century wore on, her ability to enforce these claims or prevent others from enforcing their claims grew weaker and weaker. She had been ceded the west bank of the Mississippi River by France in 1763 and East and West Florida by Great Britain in 1783. Spain maintained garrisons at St. Louis, Natchez, New Orleans, Mobile, and Pensacola. She thus had the nominal ability to block the movement of goods and passengers on the Mississippi, jealously guarding her threat to economically strangle the Old Northwest Territory or project power from the Floridas. In fact, Spain's power in the Western Hemisphere was waning due to a weakening of her homeland, and as the Nineteenth Century dawned, the Spanish Empire definitely was facing a setting sun.

The French had a formidable empire in North America during the early to mid Eighteenth Century, particularly in Canada and the far northern and western fringes of European civilization in North America (what is now the Upper Peninsula of Michigan, the shorelines of Lake Michigan, Wisconsin, and Illinois). However, the French and Indian War of 1754-'63 cost France most of her "middle western" and northern possessions; France ceded them to Great Britain as part of the war-ending treaty. France would later completely sell her North American possessions to the fledging United States and her far-sighted leader, Thomas Jefferson, in the Louisiana Purchase of 1803.

The most enduring imperial presence to the north and west of the American colonies was the colonies' own master. Great Britain held Canada and nominal control over the Old Northwest between 1763, the end of the French and Indian War, and 1783, the conclusion of the American Revolutionary War. At the end of this war, England made the stunning cession of the Old Northwest to the newly forming United States. Clearly, the gift was a Trojan Horse, as Britain had no real intention of giving permanent control of the area to the U.S. Britain maintained garrisons in disputed territories such as Dutchman's Point, Point-au-Fer, Oswegatchie, Oswego, Niagara, Mackinac, and Detroit, even though these points were well south of the line established by the 1783 Treaty of Paris. From these outposts, Britain fomented trouble by sending agents among the Indians to arouse hostility against the mountain-bursting, now-encroaching American hordes. Certainly, the plan was to bleed the financially weak United States by causing it to have to conquer and defend the vast Old Northwest Territory area. Spain refused to recognize the ceding of these territories by Great Britain to the United States (with the full approval of France, who also noted Spain's fading imperial abilities and viewed Spain as but a temporary caretaker of her North American possessions). Thus, Spain's moral high ground from which to fan the flames of conflict in the wilderness was enhanced.

Upon taking office as President of the United States, George Washington, with his western experiences in the French and Indian War and his lifelong interest in the frontier, was determined to hold the West at every risk short of war with the European colonial powers. However, to do this he was confronted with a series of complex and critical problems. Not only was the international situation thorny, as outlined above, but there were difficult domestic issues as well. First among these was the geographical split of the growing country. Most of the new nation's population was on the east side of the Appalachian Mountains, and that population cared little for the problems of the West. Most Easterners thought if the fledgling settlements of southwestern Pennsylvania, eastern and north central Tennessee, north central Kentucky, and the north bank of the Ohio were to survive at all, they must do so as protectorates of Spain, France, or Britain. The Easterners had almost no common interests or causes with the Westerners.

Secondly, if Washington was to hold the Old Northwest for the new United States, he would have to do this with a minimum of what we now call infrastructures. Only one road – of dubious quality - ran as far west as Pittsburgh. The only other track crossing the mountains, the Wilderness Road, was merely a horse trail. In the Old Northwest itself, most passages were similar to, for example, the Piqua Road (an Indian path between villages) or portages between shallow, sometimes swift-running rivers.

By far the most difficult problem was the conflict between the Algonquin (Midwestern forest-dwelling) tribes of Native Americans and the onrushing western settlers. The new United States Congress developed a plan to meet the nation's war debts through the sale of western lands to settlers. In order to obtain this land, Congress attempted to persuade the indigenous Native American tribes to cede the land to the U.S. via treaties (i.e.: "land for trinkets"). At the same time it was negotiating with the Indians, the government was sending surveyors to lay out townships in 640-acre sections in present day Ohio. This dual deception immediately led to conflict.

Several of the tribes (notably the fierce Shawnees) refused to have any part in negotiating away their ancestral lands. They and several other tribes were adamant in their position that the boundary line between the U.S. and the Indian territory must be the Ohio River. Secondly, the non-divisible 640-acre plots were priced for Eastern investors, available at essentially closed auctions. This process put the price of land out of reach to all but land speculators. Thus, large numbers of squatters simply ignored the process and staked out the land they wanted. For well over a decade, the settlers poured into the Old Northwest, grabbing Indian land as well as treaty land. They then fought with unmitigated savagery to maintain it, building increased enmity with the Easterners. Because of this enmity, the settlers were left to shift for themselves for years, with little moral, financial, or military help from their Eastern counterparts. In their poverty and isolation, they resolved that fighting for themselves for their own best interests was their only recourse. The urge to secede became stronger and bitterer as time progressed.

In the Twenty-first Century, it is hard to imagine that the threat of the Old Northwest Territory seceding was real. Yet, several the territory's most famous leaders of the era – those whose counsel and leadership many of the settlers might have followed – advocated some sort of political union with Spain in order to secure the passage of trade down the Mississippi. Some were engaged in dialog with either the Spanish or the British agents who were freely circulating throughout the western area, asking for aid in defense and trade. James Wilkinson had taken an oath of allegiance to Spain. Dr. James O'Fallon was openly negotiating with the Spanish to form an independent colony near Natchez, while his brother-in-law George Rogers Clark contemplated Spanish citizenship.

The Native American tribes of the Old Northwest added misery and desperation to the settler's sense of poverty and isolation. The Indians, even though their veil of confusion, saw one thing clearly: settlers and speculators alike were gobbling their land up at an alarming rate. They fought with savagery equal to that of the settlers to save their homelands, committing unspeakable outrages against the westerners. The budding Shawnee-Delaware-Wyandot-Miami confederacy, supplied and encouraged by the British in Detroit, and led by such redoubtable leaders as Little Turtle, Blue Jacket, and a rising power by the name of Tecumseh, exacted a fearful toll on the bloodied Ohio settlers. A smaller southern alliance of Creeks and Cherokees, supplied and encouraged from the Floridas by the Spanish, threatened to add to the conflagration. Meanwhile, in retribution for real or alleged atrocities, tribe after tribe of Indians were attacked by white raiding parties bent on revenge for these Native American depredations. In 1780, '82, and (by proxy, under his top lieutenant Benjamin Logan,) '86, George Rogers Clark used the Miami Valley corridor among other routes to lead privately financed militia and volunteers in campaigns against Indian towns in Ohio and other areas in the Northwest Territories.

In short, raids and counter raids kept this seething caldron that was the Old Northwest at a boil. The settlers' squatting isolated the westerners from any sympathy from the East, and the Native Indians became more and more obstinate and violent in their refusal to negotiate with the United States government over the cession of Native American territory.

Into this churning maelstrom in 1789 strode President George Washington. He recognized that three immediate goals must be met: 1) the western settlements must be kept from seceding, 2) the European powers must be shown that the fledgling United States could possess and defend its territory, and 3) the Native Americans must be impressed with the United States government's ability to enforce its will in Ohio.

Washington realized that one action was most likely to have the desired effect on all three constituencies involved: a military expedition deep into the heart of the Northwest Territory. This first and foremost would address the settlers' most bitter complaint: that they had no assistance in the unremitting Indian warfare. The expedition would show the settlers that the United States was genuinely interested in their welfare and they were not merely pawns in an international power struggle. A strong show of force would show Britain that its interference with American affairs on American soil was doomed to failure (although formal assurance must be given that the Americans would not directly threaten the British garrison in Detroit). Finally, the destruction of a major Indian village deep in Native American territory would impress upon the Native Americans the ultimate futility of their failure to negotiate the cession of a part of Ohio to the powerful federal government. The expedition was duly authorized.

The federal infrastructure to support the expedition was developed. A war department was organized. A regiment of regular troops from the several states was raised, sworn in, equipped, and paid with the meager military equipment, supplies, and finances available. Brigadier General Josiah Harmar, a veteran of the Revolutionary War, was named the Federal commander and directed to prepare plans for a military expedition into the Old Northwest Territory. The expedition's objective was to compel the Indian tribes to recognize

America's preponderant interests in that area and to cease and desist from their attacks upon the white settlers. Northwest Territorial Governor Arthur St. Clair, also a Revolutionary War veteran, was authorized to call out the western militia to reinforce Harmar's regulars. Dark war clouds loomed to the northwest as the 1780s became the 1790s.

* The terms Native Americans and Indians are used interchangeably throughout this book. No disrespect is intended to the original inhabitants of the Americas through the use of either term.

CHAPTER 3

Bloody Trek to Defeat:
Harmar's Old Northwest Campaign of 1790

In 2002, Max Boot wrote a book entitled _The Savage Wars of Peace: Small Wars and the Rise of American Power._ In it, Boot spoke of a "...tradition in U.S. military history – a tradition of fighting small wars...pursuing limited objectives with limited means. These are the nonwars that Kipling called 'the savage wars of peace' and that a modern author, Bob Shacochis, has evocatively described as 'a foggy, swamp-bottomed no-man's land...an empty space in an army's traditional reality, where there are no friends and no enemies, no front or rear, no victories and, likewise, no defeat, and no true endings.'"

Boot discussed "...fascinating stories – tales of blunders and bravery, low cunning and high strategy, nobility and savagery – involving forgotten heroes of American history." He limited his book to foreign small wars, and specifically excluded "the many wars against Native Americans, the primary occupation of the U.S. Army until 1890." However, had he chosen, Boot's above descriptions of small wars could have easily encompassed the struggle in the Old Northwest Territory between 1790 and 1813.

The situation in the Old Northwest during the 1780s was tangled, to say the least. Britain had ceded the Northwest Territory to the fledgling United States, but maintained strategic outposts within and in close proximity to the area. From these outposts, they sent agents among the settlers and Native Americans in the Old Northwest to foment unrest. The Spanish in the Mississippi Valley and the Floridas did the same in the South. Many settlers were ready to secede from the United States and cast their lot with the very foreign empires they had so recently fought in order to protect their hard won land. Native Americans fought settlers with zeal, seemingly assured of European backing in their quest to re-conquer and retain their homelands. The settlers antagonized Eastern power brokers with their squatting, in defiance of Eastern monetary hegemony. The struggling new government wished to raise money from the sale of large blocks of Ohio to the old Eastern moneyed elite, hoping to pay war debts, but antagonized both the surging settlers and the incumbent Indians in the process.

The government's first plan to retrieve the situation in the Northwest Territory was to negotiate with the Native American tribes of Ohio, basically hoping to swindle the Indians out of vast territories for very small sums of goods and money. (After all, the Creator certainly could not have intended for vast tracks of some of the richest land on earth to be inhabited and controlled by a relative handful of backward aboriginal tribes, the government reasoned.) The government made a determined effort at the treaty process, concluding treaties with some or all of the Algonquin tribes of Ohio at Fort McIntosh, January 20th, 1785; Fort Finney (soon to be replaced by Fort Washington), January 3rd, 1786; and Fort Harmar (now Marietta, OH), January 9th, 1789. All failed through the treachery of one or another of the parties to the treaties. The peace following the final treaty at Fort Harmar lasted only a few months. By the summer of 1790, Native American depredations north of the Ohio became unbearable to both the settlers and the federal government.

President Washington, in consultation with Territorial Governor Arthur St. Clair and U.S. Army Commander Josiah Harmar, decided on a new course of action. He reasoned the only way to stop the secession of the Northwest, inhibit European interference in American territory, and coerce the Native Americans into submission was to send an American army deep into the Northwest Territory and execute a successful campaign of destroying Indian villages. General Harmar was authorized to draw on the regular army troops of the First American Regiment located west of the Appalachian Mountains, which he estimated to be approximately 400 soldiers (100 scattered in commands throughout Indiana and Illinois; 300 available to constitute a mobile force in Ohio). Governor St. Clair was vested with the power from Washington to call out the militias of Virginia (of which Kentucky was then a part) and Pennsylvania.

Altogether, it was planned that 700 Virginia/Kentucky and 500 Pennsylvania militia would assemble, to compliment the 300 regular U.S troops converging on Fort Washington (modern Cincinnati, OH).

When General Harmar saw the condition of the militia gathering at Fort Washington, his heart must have sunk. *Major William Ferguson* made this observation of the militia:

> "Amongst the Militia were a great many hardly able to bear arms, such as old infirm men, and young boys. They were not such as might be expected from a frontier country, viz. The smart active woodsmen, well accustomed to arms, eager and alert to revenge injuries done them and their connections: No, there were a great number of them substitutes who probably had never fired a gun. Major Paul of Pennsylva (sp) told me that many of his men were so awkward that they could not take their gun locks off to oil them and put them on again, nor could they put in their Flints so as to be useful…"

> *Lieutenant Ebenezer Denny* added:

> "Kentucky seemed as if she wished to comply with the requisitions of Government as ineffectually as possible, for it was evident, that about two-thirds of the men served only to swell their number."

Historian *Howard H. Peckham* summarized the above important facts, which would become crucial to the success or failure of the campaign:

> "They were boys, old men, drunkards, minor fugitives from justice, men without jobs or money, and the like – all the undesirable, restless, and unsuccessful element that is churned out of an established society and thrown to the frontiers. The motley rabble alarmed General Harmar because he had almost no time to train them. They numbered 1133, of which Harmar said 'at least 200 are good for nothing.' He added 320 regulars to the militia which made a total force of 1453 men."

Washington, St. Clair, and Harmar determined that Native American resistance was centered at a group of allied Indian villages located at the confluence of the St. Joseph, St. Marys, and Maumee Rivers, collectively known as Kekionga (and colloquially known as "Miamitown", currently Ft. Wayne, IN). This group of seven Miami, Shawnee, and Delaware villages (with another large Miami village 15 miles to the northwest of Kekionga) was alleged to be the vortex of the Native American maelstrom in the Northwest. Leaders such as the Miami Michikinikwa (Little Turtle), the Shawnee Blue Jacket, and Buckongahelas of the Delawares were thought to meet there regularly to reconfirm the alliance between their tribes and plan united efforts against the encroaching white settlers.

Harmar surveyed the wilderness to the north, and decided the best route to Kekionga was that followed by the French Captain Pierre Joseph de Celoron de Bienville 41 years before. The route, utilizing the valleys of the Miami Rivers, Loramie Creek, and the St. Marys River, was relatively flat, well-watered, and promised good grazing for the pack animals and cavalry. The United States would attempt to establish and consolidate its initial empire using the Miami Valley – Great Black Swamp Corridor into the forests of western Ohio.

The manuscript journal of Captain John Armstrong of the U.S. Regulars, as well as that of General Harmar, gives a detailed day-by-day account of the army' journey up the valleys of western Ohio toward its dates with destiny. The army started its movement on September 30th, 1790, leaving Fort Washington and moving along the valley of the Little Miami River. The army averaged about 10 miles per day during the campaign, and remained in this river valley or its tributaries through October 6th, staying on what General Harmar termed *Clark's Old Trace*, the route of one of George Rogers Clark's militia raids to Pickawillany. On October 7th, the army bore slightly to the northwest, crossed the Mad River, and moved into the valley of the Great Miami River, following this river northeastward until it reached Pickawillany on the 10th. The army turned slightly and moved due north up a tributary of the Great Miami, called Loramie Creek. Near the northernmost apex of Loramie Creek, at the point where it curved sharply to the northeast, the army reached a place General Harmar termed *The French Store*, later to be named Fort Loramie after French trader Pierre Loramie. Harmar's army then moved onto a short, ancient Indian portage route, reaching the headwaters of the St. Marys River in one day and camping just past *Girty's House* (named for half-breed renegade Simon Girty – present St. Marys, OH) on October 12th. The portage became the old Indian trace that paralleled the St. Marys River, eventually to be known as the *Piqua Road*.

As Harmar followed the trace north to the point where it veered to the northwest, he must have hesitated. Approximately 45 miles due north of this point, another large concentration of hostile Indian villages (collectively known as the Grand Glaize) was located at the confluence of the Auglaize and Maumee Rivers. Between Harmar and these Indian villages lay the forbidding and inhospitable Great Black Swamp. As much as marching to the northwest with the Grand Glaize on his right flank must have given him pause, Harmar certainly must have feared being caught by a Native American ambush in the Black Swamp even more. He avoided the Black Swamp by marching on toward Kekionga along the swamp's southwestern border.

Harmar's army followed the Piqua trail northwest, on the 13th reaching *La Somer's House* (renamed Shane's Crossing, present Rockford, OH). At La Somer's House, a Shawnee warrior was captured. Several of Harmar's men spoke the Shawnee language. The warrior freely volunteered that the Indians at Kekionga were in great consternation at the army's advance, and were abandoning the village to scatter to the northwest. Harmar conferred with his subordinates, and determined that a smaller, faster moving unit under the command of Colonel John Hardin should quickly move to Kekionga to there capture or destroy as many Indians as remained. By moving quickly, there was the possibility that the Native Americans, in their state of great confusion, might be easily defeated. Therefore, on the morning of October 14th, one company of Regulars and several of militia were detached from the main body for this move (about 600 men, or roughly 40% of the entire force). The move ultimately failed in its mission, as the Indians eluded even this fast moving force, which arrived at Kekionga on early on October 17th.

The main body continued it's pace on the Piqua Road and reached the confluence of the St Marys and St. Joseph Rivers (combining to form the Maumee River), where Kekionga was located, between 12:00 and 1:00 PM on October 17th, 1790. The invaders found the village virtually abandoned, but still containing vast quantities of vegetables and perhaps 10,000 to 20,000 bushels of ear corn. The army spent the next several days destroying corn, vegetables, supplies, and 300 buildings, moving among the seven villages to burn and loot. However, the army suffered a major loss on the night of the 18th when Native American raiders captured or destroyed many of the expedition's horses and pack animals.

The officers determined that an eighth village, located approximately 15 miles northwest on the Eel River, might contain many of the fugitives from Kekionga. On October 19th, Col. Hardin received command of a mixed group of about 210 soldiers (roughly 25 Regulars and 185 militia) to move on to this village via an Indian trace later known as the *Goshen Road* (present U.S. Hwy. 33), kill or capture its inhabitants, and destroy it. The officers failed to take into account their wily foe, Little Turtle, who drew the detachment toward the villages, then attacked in ambush at a narrow defile in the deep woods near the Eel River. At the first crash of gunfire, most of the militia turned and fled without firing a shot, scarcely stopping at Kekionga – 15 miles away. This left the small number of Regulars and a handful of the stauncher militia to face perhaps 100 to 150 skilled Native American warriors alone. They fought valiantly, but were virtually annihilated, 20 to 24 being killed; only eight officers and men of those who stood and fought escaped the carnage to reach the main army camp at Kekionga that evening.

The demolition of the Maumee villages by Harmar's main force continued throughout the 20th and during the early morning of the 21st. At approximately 10 AM, the army, having completed the destruction, formed to begin its movement back toward Fort Washington, moving seven to nine miles south along the Piqua Road.

On the evening of October 21st, Harmar's officers once again conferred. The officers determined that a swift retrograde movement back to Kekionga might catch the main body of the Indians returning to the village, destroy it in battle and yet salvage the campaign, or at least ease the army's withdrawal southward. Thus, at 9:00 PM on the night of the 21st, a substantial force of 340 militia and 60 Regulars was detailed under Regular Army Major Pleasgrave Wyllys to return to the Indian villages before daybreak and surprise any Native Americans found there.

Ensign D. Britt of the 1st U.S. Regiment gave what he felt was the reasoning for the retrograde movement:

> "The motive which I conceived led to the detaching of the party under Major Wyllys on the 21st Were that the Indians having avoided engaging the whole army, would collect at their Towns and harass the rear and flanks, as much as possible on its return; and a Stroke at them before they could assemble in large bodie (sp) would prevent their doing it with much effect."

Lieutenant E. Denny of the 1st U.S. Regiment expanded on the explanation of the reasoning:

> (The army was) "...intending to surprise any parties that might be assembled there, supposing that the Indians would collect to see how things were left. The General had felt the enemy, knew their strength, & calculated much upon the success of this enterprise."

The plan of battle was for a fairly straightforward enveloping flank attack. Reviews of contemporary accounts of the battle indicate that General Harmar retained overall command of the mission, but delegated to Major Wyllys the operational deployment of troops. Major Hall was to take his battalion of militia in a looping route to the south, then west and north of the Indians to provide one jaw of the surrounding vice. Major Wyllys' battalion of Regulars and Major Fontaine's mounted infantry/light cavalry would cross the Maumee moving north, then loop west and south to provide the other jaw. Major McMullen's battalion would remain east of the confluence of the rivers, pinning the Native Americans in place by initiating the battle after the flanking troops were set.

Almost from the beginning, things went wrong. Due to the halting progress of the militia during the night, the army detachment arrived at the towns not just before daylight, but sometime after sunrise. Then Major Hall's militia battalion, having gained its position to the south and west unnoticed, violated its orders by firing on a single Indian who approached its positions. Thus alerted, parties of Native Americans began scattering in various directions. McMullen's and Fontaine's undisciplined militia could not be restrained, pursued these scattering Indian bands, and dissipated the entire detachment's cohesion and strength. As a consequence, Major Wyllys' Regulars and the relatively small number of more disciplined militia that rallied with them were struck by a superior force of Native Americans led by Little Turtle, shortly after Wyllys' unit emerged from the river crossing. Wyllys' command was badly cut up; approximately 160 soldiers were killed (Major Wyllys and Major Fontaine among the dead) and many wounded. Little Turtle, although outnumbered by two-to-one at the beginning of the battle, was able to mass this number of warriors against that part of Harmar's army that stood and fought. His warriors paid a dear price in the vicious fighting, as perhaps 100 to 120 were killed.

The Miami Confederation had broken the back of the campaign. The October 22nd battle at the confluence of the three rivers had cost Harmar his best soldiers – many of the Regulars buried at the ford of the Maumee had marched with Washington and Gates in the Revolutionary War. Buried there also were the staunch among the militia troops. Harmar's command was left to straggle back to Fort Washington along the pathway on which it had approached Kekionga, its ranks filled with wounded struggling on foot because many of the draft animals had been killed or severely wounded by the Indians. Legends state that Indian scouts shadowing the retreating army could follow the progress of its retreat by the trail of blood it left along the trail.

Brigadier General Josiah Harmar proclaimed the expedition success, in that it completed it's primary missions; the destruction of the villages at Kekionga, the killing of approximately 120 Indians, and the destruction of the food and shelter the remaining Indians must rely upon in the coming winter. Evidently, he thought the cost of 183 dead and 37 wounded a reasonable price to pay for this destruction. However, the authorities viewing the bedraggled and bloody expedition re-entering Fort Washington felt differently, and General Harmar certainly got wind of the not too subtle official criticism of the conduct of the 1790 campaign. Secretary Knox let Harmar know of President Washington's disappointment in his failure to subdue the Indians and the high cost of the invaluable Regular Army soldiers.

On March 4, 1791, this subtle criticism became official, as President Washington relieved Harmar from command of the army and appointed Territorial Governor Arthur St. Clair as Major General and commander of the army. Colonel Richard Butler was promoted to Brigadier General and placed second-in-command.

General Harmar, stung by the criticism of his conduct of the campaign, demanded an official Court of Inquiry. This was granted by the new Commander in Chief, Major General St. Clair. The members of the Court were General Butler and Colonels Darke and Gibson. The Court convened on September 15, 1791. After several days of examining testimony, the court rendered a finding that was highly honorable to General Harmar. The findings fully exonerated Harmar from any blame for the conduct of the campaign. The testimony of the principal witnesses to the Court attributed the failure of the campaign to the weakness and insubordination of the militia.

Nevertheless, General Harmar refused to participate in a second expedition under General St. Clair in 1791, and resigned from the Army in 1792. His military career was finished, forever tarnished by his "successful" 1790 military campaign along the Miami Valley–Great Black Swamp Corridor. The plain facts were that as a direct result of the expedition, Little Turtle's reputation was enhanced and all the western tribes made resistance to the white encroachment a common cause with the Miamis. The Native Americans were encouraged by their two victories at the Eel River and Kekionga to make renewed attacks upon outlying white settlements.

The baton was passed to 55-year-old Major General Arthur St. Clair. *His* reputation would now rise or fall on the bloody path to America's first empire.

CHAPTER 4

Unremitting Fury:
St. Clair's Defeat at the Headwaters
of the Wabash–1791

Those readers familiar with the late-Twentieth / Early-Twenty-first Century political process will be very familiar with the concept of political "spin": the practice of casting a positive light on a less than positive event, in an effort to cause minimal damage to the responsible parties' reputations and future prospects. Many think this is a relatively new phenomenon, brought about by the glare of modern rapidly disseminated mass media. However, a review of historical records shows this to be an old practice in the political-military arena. Take for instance this passage from *General Josiah Harmar's* journal of the Western Ohio / Eastern Indiana campaign of 1790 against the Miami Indian confederation (contemporary racial bias noted beforehand):

> *Friday, Octr. 22nd.* – "Fine weather. The detachment under Major Wyllys and Col. Hardin performed wonders, although they were terribly cut up. Almost the whole of the Federal troops were cut off, with the loss of Major Wyllys, Major Fontaine, and Lt. Frothingham – which is indeed a heavy blow. The consolation is, that the men sold themselves very dear. The militia behaved themselves charmingly. It is supposed that not less than 100 warriors of the savages were killed upon the ground. The action was fought yesterday morning" (evidently Harmar actually made the entry on the 23rd, but dated it the 22nd) "near the *old fort* & up the river St. Joseph. The savages never received such a stroke before in any battle that they have had. The action at the Great Kanhawa, &c. was a farce to it."

In reality, the campaign was an unmitigated disaster for the fledgling United States. The Native Americans soundly defeated the American army in the two battles of the campaign, chiefly due to the unreliability and insubordination of the "charmingly behaved" militia. The Indians had whipped the army and knew it, and were emboldened to commit new depredations and atrocities in the Northwest Territory in defense of their homelands. In spite of his spin, General Harmar's military career was ruined, and the United States would have to attempt a second military expedition into the Northwest in 1791.

United States President George Washington cast about for a suitable replacement for General Harmar as commander of the army in the Northwest. He found such a man already in the Northwest – Territorial Governor Arthur St. Clair. St. Clair was a Major General in the Revolutionary War and a hero of that conflict. He had participated valiantly in several battles, playing substantial roles in the victories at Trenton and Princeton. A pall was cast over his military career when St. Clair failed to defend Fort Ticonderoga, abandoning it to the British in 1777. He was strongly criticized for this and was recalled from active service.

Upon the successful completion of the Revolutionary War, victories were celebrated and failures overlooked. War hero Arthur St. Clair won a seat in the transitional Congress of the Confederation, representing the Commonwealth of Pennsylvania. In 1787, he became president of that body, and late in the year was appointed governor of the Northwest Territory.

With St. Clair's accomplishments as a subordinate military commander and a solid political background, President Washington had confidence in the old warrior. St. Clair was commissioned Major General and commander of the United States Army on March 4th, 1791. General Harmar, upon hearing the news of St. Clair's appointment, resigned from the Army.

Events would prove that President Washington's confidence in General St. Clair was not enough. St. Clair faced tremendous problems on two fronts, either of which alone would have been enough to create defeat for the American cause. Together, these problems were a recipe for disaster.

The first major problem was a "stab in the back" from his peers and superiors in the area of logistics. The Secretary of War, Major General Henry Knox, was in overall charge of outfitting the expedition for war. He appointed his friend, William Duer, as chief government agent for supporting the quartermaster of the army with supplies and arms. Instead of discharging their duties in the best interests of the country, Knox and Duer stole $55,000 of the $75,000 allocated for the army to buy supplies and arms and used it for land speculation.

This left newly-appointed Army Quartermaster Hodgdon with less than a third of the funds originally allocated to outfit the army. Hodgdon let out contracts for supplies to low bidders in order to stretch the available dollars. As a consequence of this expedient, the troops got tents that leaked, clothing that wore out quickly, and shoes that were so flimsy they were considered "vile in the extreme." Duer sent stale, reprocessed gunpowder to the army. The result was that bullets would only carry a short distance. One soldier subsequently reported that his musket balls bounced off his Native American foes during the battle.

The army faced almost 200 miles of howling wilderness, through which it must cut a path for artillery and supply pack trains, plus build defensive fortresses. Yet, it was supplied with a total of 15 hatchets, 18 axes, 12 hammers, and 24 handsaws.

The army developed a serious deficiency in pack animals and horses for transport and attack. The quartermaster staff failed to supply enough sustenance for the animals for the expedition. The politically-appointed horsemaster "had never been in the woods in his life," according to one soldier. Hundreds of pack horses were injured fighting for food that was improperly scattered. Valuable cavalry horses were allowed to wander off in the night without hobbles or bells, with the result that many were lost or stolen by Indian scouts shadowing the army.

St. Clair's second major problem had to do with the nature of the militia assigned to his army. The authorities learned a lesson in Harmar's campaign, in which too few Regular Army troops had been assigned to the expedition. A second Regular Army regiment was raised, outfitted, and assigned to the Northwest. The First American

Regiment, which had suffered heavily from casualties in Harmar's campaign, was reconstituted with professional soldiers and staffed with experienced officers. The First was considered the best unit in the Army. However, the two professional regiments together were still too small to present an overwhelming force before the Native Americans, although they were considered militarily sound.

The militia raised to fill out the ranks was another story. Lieutenant John Armstrong stated they were from "the prisons, wheelbarrows, and brothels of the nation." They were "the worst and most dissatisfied troops I ever served with." The militia was "badly clothed, badly paid, and badly fed." The insubordination and lack of discipline of the militia would once again contribute heavily to the undoing of the campaign.

If the militia was difficult to handle in camp, it would prove to be virtually unmanageable on the march into the Northwest Territory. Washington, Knox, and St. Clair had once again determined that the Miami Villages at the confluence of the St. Marys, St. Joseph, and Maumee Rivers (collectively known as Kekionga) would be the target of this second expedition into the heart of the Old Northwest. St. Clair decided that the Miami River valleys would provide the initial corridor into the Northwest. However, he developed another strategy for the move toward Kekionga after using the Miami Rivers in the initial stages of the march. On September 17th, 1791, St. Clair marched approximately 20 miles in two days, from Fort Washington to the Great Miami River, and there built a substantial bastion which he named Fort Hamilton. From this intermediate base, St. Clair intended to strike out to the northwest over the high ground of a midwestern "continental divide." As he advanced, those rivers to his left would drain first into the Ohio River and eventually into the Gulf of Mexico via the Mississippi River. Those rivers to his right, including those in the pivotal Great Black Swamp, the true key to the Old Northwest, would drain into the Maumee River, thence into the Great Lakes, and eventually into the Atlantic Ocean via the St. Lawrence River. St. Clair's clear intention was to give the Black Swamp, with its unknown diseases and terrors, a wide berth.

In retrospect, St. Clair may not have made a totally bad decision in this regard. It was September 21st when he began to move, and the infamous Midwestern fall weather was about to break. The 55-year-old St. Clair suffered from gout, a severe inflammation of the joints, particularly those of the feet. The prospect of freezing weather in a flooded Great Black Swamp with hostile confederation forces on either flank (Kekionga on the left and the Grand Glaize to the right) could not have been appealing to the army commander had he chosen to strike out due north directly through the Black Swamp. In fact, the weather did break early in the fall of 1791, partially vindicating his decision.

St. Clair moved forward, the army traveling 45 miles northwest along one of the higher plateaus in the territory. Within 10 miles of the highest point in Indiana Territory (at 1,257 feet above sea level, near current Lynn, Indiana), St. Clair established a second advanced base on the Ohio side of the line, naming it Fort Jefferson. Jefferson was a well-placed, but rather small fort.

After completing and garrisoning Fort Jefferson, St. Clair began moving north again on October 21st. Although still early fall, St. Clair's undisciplined militia faced a cold front moving in from the north during the march, with freezing rain and snow. Quartermaster Hodgdon was doing his best for the army; during the march, flour and beef, as well as 60 militia reinforcements, joined the march on October 22nd, and more food and reinforcement was to arrive on the 27th. Nevertheless, the combination of bad weather, poor clothing and shelter, difficult carpentry work in erecting two forts, and an uncertain food supply took its toll on the army. Desertion among the militia was high from the beginning of the campaign.

As the march north progressed, General St. Clair made several tactical mistakes, and at least two of the more costly of these mistakes involved the handling of the unruly militia. Chief Payomingo and 20 Chickasaw warriors joined the army on the move north on October 27th. On October 29th, St. Clair detached these 21 fighters plus Captain Sparks and four top riflemen on a murky assignment to the distant flanks of the army to capture prisoners. What value these prisoners would have added to the expedition is questionable. On the other hand, 26 scouts fanning out in advance of the army might have given St. Clair valuable information on the size and location of his adversaries, of which he knew virtually nothing. In contrast, a young

Shawnee warrior named Tecumseh was in charge of shadowing the advancing American army. He provided the Miami Little Turtle and the Shawnee Blue Jacket, co-leaders of the confederation forces, with highly accurate information as to the size and composition of the army, plus valuable opinions on the best times and places for an attack. The difference between the two forces in terms of enemy intelligence gathering could not have been in greater contrast.

Second, approximately 60 of the militia deserted *en masse* on October 30th. St. Clair decided to detach the officers and men of the First American Regiment, under the command of the western veteran Major Hamtramck, to squelch this dangerous precedent by retrieving the deserters. Since the rumor was sweeping the army that the militia intended to plunder a supply convoy headed for Fort Jefferson, Hamtramck was also to guard the supply train to its destination, then rejoin the main force. The decision to detach 300 of the army's most able soldiers on an extended disciplinary and escort mission while in the immediate vicinity of the enemy is perplexing, to say the least. These two detachments, plus various other desertions, dropped St. Clair's force to approximately 1,400 soldiers. This very day, Little Turtle and Blue Jacket left Kekionga and moved south with approximately 1,000 to 1,040 warriors, the numerical odds tilting ever closer to parity as the day of battle drew nearer.

Third, St. Clair made a geographical mistake as he approached what would become the battle site. In his journal, he stated that he had reached the St. Marys River on the evening of November 3rd. In reality he was encamped on a small tributary near the headwaters of the Wabash River, at least 20 to 25 miles further south-southwest of the St. Marys. St. Clair's belief that he was much closer to his enemies than he really was makes his decision to detach his best regiment that much more perplexing.

Fourth, even though he thought he might be within 35 miles of Kekionga, General St. Clair decided *not* to build breastworks and emplacements upon making camp that evening. His journal stated his "men are much fatigued," and being that he felt he was so close to the enemy, he determined to rest them that night, then start early the next morning and march directly to attack the Miami confederation villages.

Next, St. Clair and his second-in-command, Major General Richard Butler, were barely on speaking terms by the evening of November 3rd, 1791. Perhaps the pressures of pursuing a late season campaign with unruly soldiers while St. Clair was personally ill created problems between Butler and St. Clair. However, St. Clair's failure to maintain a working relationship and a line of communication with his top subordinate was inexcusable.

Finally, General St. Clair made the momentous mistake of encamping a large portion of the militia up to a quarter of a mile in advance of the main army on the evening of November 3rd. The deployment represented on page 11 matches descriptions in St. Clair's personal journal of the campaign. His reason for detaching the militia so far in advance of his main body of troops has never been satisfactorily explained. A reason given for deploying these troops in such an advanced position was to keep the army from being surprised. If so, St. Clair scarcely could have picked worse troops for the job. A more likely reason probably was to keep the boisterous and undisciplined militia from disturbing the sleep of the remainder of the army. A very small detachment of Regulars under Captain Slough camped in advance of the militia, serving as pickets.

Throughout the night, Captain Slough became more and more aware of the advance of Native Americans along his front and flanks. Slough became so concerned that he notified his superior, General Butler, that a large number of the enemy was massing before him. Butler, his relations strained with St. Clair, chose not to correspond with the army's commander and provide this important piece of intelligence to him. It was a mistake that cost Butler his life, and contributed mightily to the defeat of St. Clair's army.

The confederacy's scouts readily identified the troops camped in the exposed location as mainly militia. Little Turtle, as at Kekionga a year before, was presented with an opportunity to mass a superior force against a small portion of the American army. The results would be even more spectacular this time.

As had been his practice throughout the march, General St. Clair had reveille beaten on the drums approximately one hour before sunrise, November 4th, 1791. The troops were assembled, then paraded, inspected, and dismissed approximately one-half hour later. Almost immediately after the soldiers reached their tents, a howling Native American charge broke into the exposed militia encampment. The militia quickly loosed a ragged, ineffectual volley in the direction of the onrushing Indians, but it was too little, too late. The athletic, fanatical warriors were already bounding among the milling militia soldiers, hacking and slashing with their deadly tomahawks. The terrified and demoralized militia broke and ran directly toward friendly lines, frantically seeking the safety of the regulars' gunfire. The militia was so thoroughly infiltrated with confederation warriors and the disorganized melee fell upon the main battalion lines so quickly that the troops of Majors Butler and Clarke could not fire and were themselves almost immediately broken into a disorganized mob. The Native Americans seemed cognizant of the importance of officers to the unity of both militia and Regular units, for they struck down the officer corps of the army with an even greater frequency than that administered to the general troops. This lack of unit leadership added to the terror and slaughter. Major General Butler, Lt. Colonel Oldham, and Major Butler all were quickly killed in the fierce hand-to-hand combat, and their units reduced to flight.

As the mob broke upon Lt. Colonel William Darke's Second American Regiment, General St. Clair ordered a bayonet charge by this unit directly into the milling, slashing tide about to wash over it. The charge was initially successful, and the Indians driven back three to four hundred yards by Darke's Regulars. However, more Indians appeared on the flanks of this charge. It was apparent the Native Americans were on the battlefield in great force, and superbly led. The Regulars had to retreat to their original lines to avoid being cut off and destroyed. As they retreated, the more valiant soldiers of Butler's and Clarke's harried battalions formed to support them. Several times the combined units of Darke, Butler, and Clarke charged in different directions with their slashing bayonets to meet different crises: each time the result was identical to that of the first charge. During the three hours of the battle, the gunfire and charges from the Indians increased incrementally in intensity on all sides of the surrounded American Army.

The American Army was in danger of complete and total annihilation. In desperation, General St. Clair ordered the exhausted troops of Darke's combined command to make one last bayonet charge in the direction of Fort Jefferson. Darke did so and opened a hole in the Native American lines, through which the surviving remainder of the army passed. Major Clarke and the battered remnant of his battalion covered the retreat - really a rout which did not stop until the army reached Fort Jefferson, 29 miles away, at sunset. Clarke was materially aided by the greed of the Indian warriors, who could not be persuaded by Little Turtle and Blue Jacket to delay the looting of the captured army encampment long enough to completely destroy the demoralized and rapidly fleeing American army.

The campaign was over. The tattered remains of the army reached Fort Washington on the Ohio River on November 8th, 1791. The official records vary as to the exact numbers of killed and wounded. By any reckoning, the battle was a complete disaster for the United States. The total dead of the army has been variously reported as 618, 630, or 637, including between 39 and 68 officers, which was up to four-fifths of the officer corps. The wounded has been reported as between 214 and 300. Only 500 of the original 1,400 soldiers left the field unwounded. Over 65% of the army was destroyed, including three-quarters of the Second American Regiment. The United States was virtually left without an army for two years. Included among the lost were approximately 150 women – wives who accompanied the army northward. Fifty-six were killed and the rest were captured to face a fate possibly worse than death. The Native American confederacy forces lost 21 killed and 37 to 40 wounded.

Material losses were almost as crippling to the fledgling American Army. The army lost 8 cannon, 1,200 muskets, and nearly $33,000 in war supplies – wagons, horses, pack animals, ammunition, and other accoutrements of war. The defeat has been characterized as the worst defeat ever suffered by any American army on any battlefield in any war.

The political result of the military disaster to General St. Clair was remarkably similar to that which befell General Harmar. An investigative committee established March 27, 1792, by the House of Representatives exonerated General St. Clair, and he was allowed to continue as Territorial Governor of the Northwest Territory. But behind the scenes, President Washington forced the resignation of his old friend and military subordinate Arthur St. Clair as commander of the American Army on April 7, 1792.

The search was on for a successor to the sad legacy established by Generals Harmar and St. Clair. But a very different general waited in the wings to assume the mantle of commander of the United States Army, and a new chapter was about to be written in the growing history of the Miami Valley / Great Black Swamp Corridor.

CHAPTER 5

The March to Immortality: "Mad Anthony" Wayne's Conquest of the Old Northwest–1794

What makes a successful military commander? In the 1790s, President George Washington had twice picked successful subordinates from his Revolutionary War experiences to lead the American army. Twice the result had been tremendous disasters for the United States in its war against the Algonquin tribes of Native Americans (and their British sponsors) in the Old Northwest Territory.

Beven Alexander wrote a book entitled *How Great Generals Win.* In the introduction to this work, he laid out several major principles that all great commanders follow to lead their forces to success:

> -Great generals do not repeat what has failed before. On the contrary, great generals strike where they are least expected against opposition that is weak and disorganized.

> -General Nathan Bedford Forrest said the key to victory is "to get there first with the most." However, "there" must be a point that is vital or at least extremely important to the enemy. To get "there," the leader must be able to "mystify, mislead, and surprise" the enemy, in the words of General Thomas J. "Stonewall" Jackson.

> -The great captain of arms will move so as to make the opposing general think he is aiming at a point different from what he is actually aiming at.

> -Practically all of the great generals' moves throughout history have been made against the enemy's flank or rear – either actual or psychological. It is only the unusual

general who can separate his primeval desire to confront his enemies directly from the need to disguise and hide his actions so as to catch his enemies off guard and vulnerable.

-The great general realizes that the purpose of war is not battle at all. It is a more perfect peace. To attain peace, a belligerent must break the will of the enemy people to wage war. Therefore, the purpose of military strategy is to diminish the possibility of resistance.

-The British military philosopher Basil H. Liddell Hart summarized the above strategies and tactics: "The successful general chooses the line or course of least expectation and he exploits the line of least resistance."

Alexander did not include Major General Anthony Wayne in his pantheon of great military captains. Yet, his above descriptions of great generalship could have been used as the defining logic behind Wayne's campaign against the Miami-Shawnee-Delaware-Wyandot confederation in 1793-'94.

Major General Arthur St. Clair resigned as commander of the United States Army on April 7, 1792. The dual defeats of Generals Harmar and St. Clair had subsequently left the Northwest Territory aflame. The Native Americans, bolstered by their successes, redoubled their efforts to push the settlers south across the Ohio River. The Miami Indians, in particular, moved some of their strength eastward to the villages at the confluence of the Maumee and Auglaize Rivers (known as the Grand Glaize) to signify their commitment to their allies in Ohio. The British, convinced the fledgling United States could not effectively occupy and defend the Old Northwest, accelerated moral and material support to the Indians. Once the U.S. was pushed out of the Northwest Territory, Britain would deal with her soon-to-be erstwhile Indian allies and rebuild her Northwestern empire.

President Washington chose another Revolutionary War subordinate, Anthony Wayne, as St. Clair's successor in mid-1792. Washington initially feared Wayne's well-earned reputation for rashness in battle, but an aggressive spirit was now needed. Wayne inherited the battered and demoralized remnant of St. Clair's army, then based in Pittsburgh, PA. But he also was to be the beneficiary of a new spirit manifested by the federal government. Twice, the government had saddled army commanders with ill-trained and ill-supplied recruits, then ordered them into battle prematurely. No one had the nerve (even had they been so disposed) to try this tactic on the fiery General Wayne.

Secretary of War Henry Knox and Wayne dubbed the new command *The Legion of the United States*. Wayne surveyed the levies which recruiters were gathering to reconstitute the army at Pittsburgh. They were the same felons, drifters, and bar flies which had been drawn to the previous two armies in search of food and clothing. One disgusted officer summed them up: "The offscourings of large towns and cities; enervated by Idleness, Debaucheries and every Species of Vice." Wayne had no intention of throwing these men, and his reputation, immediately into the Miami Valley / Great Black Swamp meat grinder, as had his two predecessors. He immediately changed the base of operations from Pittsburgh, with its allures of vice and drink, to a point 22 miles down the Ohio River. General Wayne began getting the recruits into physical shape by having the army wield axes and saws to build "Legionville," the army's first training base.

After construction of the base, the budding Legion was subjected to endless hours of foot drill, target practice, and instruction in the use of the bayonet. General Wayne was a believer in the employment of various weapons in battle. Many of his incoming Kentucky militia were riflemen mounted on horseback, sometimes known in other armies as "light cavalry" or "mounted infantry." Wayne knew these soldiers had both advantages and drawbacks. The long rifles of the day fired tight-fitting, .45 caliber soft lead balls. As the gun fired, the balls expanded to "fit" the barrel rifling, thus creating spin on the projectile. Because the projectiles were tight fitting, a rifleman could jam in and fire only one to two rounds per minute. But because the balls had spin, they flew in a flat trajectory, and were accurate and deadly over long distances (perhaps 150 to 200 yards or more). Many of these militia were experienced horsemen, and therefore could load and shoot rifles from horseback. Wayne realized this gave mounted infantry unusual flexibility. The mounted riflemen could ride quickly to the scene of battle, dismount, and fight as infantry to plug a breach in the line of battle. Or they could remain mounted and exploit a breach in the enemy's line. Finally, they could range far afield to offensively raid the enemy or defensively protect the army.

A second arm Wayne developed for the Legion was the regular cavalry. The main weapon of cavalry was the saber, a heavy, curved sword with a razor-sharp cutting edge. Some horse soldiers were additionally armed with short, single-shot carbines or pistols. Cavalry's main use on the field of battle was to serve as "shock troops," rousting the enemy from its firing positions, creating confusion and terror, and exploiting any kind of line breach or undisciplined retreat by attempting to turn it into a rout.

Artillery was a fine weapon upon the open plains of Europe. However, in the tangled forests and swamps of the Old Northwest, it served mostly as a defensive weapon to protect the rough-hewn forts. These forts in turn protected the army's line of supply and communication.

Wayne's favorite arm of the military was the infantry. He was determined to turn the "felons, drifters, and bar flies" mustered into the Legion into resolute infantry, willing to follow any order and press any advantage as a result of intense drilling, strict discipline, and unthinking adherence to commands. Infantry of the day was armed with muskets and bayonets. The musket was a fearsome weapon at short range. While its barrel had no rifling, it did fire a self-contained paper cartridge containing a powder charge, a .70 caliber round projectile, and three large "00" lead buckshot. The lack of rifling made the musket inaccurate at ranges greater than 80 yards, but the looser fitting and self-contained paper cartridge allowed the infantryman to fire three to four rounds per minute. The large caliber, soft lead projectiles created ghastly, incapacitating wounds at short range.

Further, the muskets of the day could be fitted with bayonets, on which Wayne placed great faith. The bayonet was an approximately two-foot long, double-edged blade attached to the barrel of the musket. A dense, resolute mass of bayonet-armed infantry charging an enemy could cause that enemy to break and run, at which time the cavalry could enter the fray, then shatter and devastate the enemy.

As Wayne intensely drilled his four martial arms at Legionville during the fall and winter of 1792, he studied the strategies and tactics of his predecessors. He was not above using what had worked for others, while discarding that which failed. He decided the routes chosen by Harmar and St. Clair had both good and bad points. The Miami Valleys were certainly the best route for beginning the move to the north, and the bastions created by St. Clair (Forts Hamilton and Jefferson) were well placed along mid-route. However, the distance between Hamilton and Jefferson was too far to be traversed in one day's travel, and Jefferson itself was too small. Further, both generals had failed to build protected encampments after each day's march, which exposed them to surprise attacks.

Wayne determined what he felt to be two of Harmar's and St. Clair's biggest mistakes. Both had made Kekionga the obvious objective of their moves, but Kekionga itself was the improper target. Even if Kekionga was destroyed by frontal assault, as Harmar had undoubtedly done, the Indians occupying the villages were merely forced backward onto their own territorial ground. Wayne studied the maps of what is now northern Ohio and determined that the Grand Glaize, north and east of the Great Black Swamp at the confluence of the Maumee and Auglaize Rivers, was the key to the conquest of the Northwest Territory. An attack on the Grand Glaize would split the confederacy by flanking Kekionga, present the opportunity to destroy vast Native American fields and gardens along the Auglaize and Maumee Rivers, and push the Indians toward the British on Lake Erie. This would force Britain to make a choice under the eyes of her Native American allies: defend those allies by fighting a large and well-trained Legion, or retreat and abandon them.

Further, both Harmar and St. Clair had feared and avoided the Great Black Swamp as being "the enemy's territory," from which the Indians could spring in ambush and destroy their armies at any moment. Wayne embraced the Black Swamp as a shield for his army, difficult for his army to traverse, but even more difficult for his enemy to conduct reconnaissance and attacks. The Legion was to emerge at the northern apex of the watery triangle formed by the Auglaize

River on the east, the Maumee River on the northwest, and the St. Marys River on the southwest, directly into what Wayne considered "the grand emporium of the hostile Indians of the west." Wayne would then destroy the confederation's housing and sustenance there at the Grand Glaize.

All through the winter of 1792 and into the first half of 1793, Wayne drilled his 3,000- man Legion and General Charles Scott's 1,500-man Kentucky mounted militia, while negotiators dealt with the Native Americans. During the early spring, a confident Indian congress meeting at the Sandusky Peninsula, with tribes represented from as far away as the Gulf of Mexico, the Great Plains, and Canada, sent word to Washington that the Ohio River was the only acceptable boundary between the United States and the Indian nations. In July, a separate commission, sent from the United States to Detroit to negotiate with the Algonquin tribes and traveling under the protection of the British, was treated to the same message.

By early August, 1793, Major General Anthony Wayne knew that negotiations had failed and the United States would once more be involved in a military expedition into the Northwest Territory. Wayne knew it was too late in the season for an upland campaign – he would not make the same mistake Harmar and St. Clair had made. However, he did want to establish his presence in the Old Northwest. Wayne moved the Legion from Legionville to Fort Washington, then up the Miami Valleys to Fort Hamilton. Indian scouts began shadowing the force immediately, but noticed a distinct difference between the Legion and the earlier armies. Never had they seen soldiers so disciplined and responsive to orders. Never had they seen an army move so resolutely and remorselessly, each night's bivouac protected by a sturdy fortified encampment. The Legion refurbished Fort Hamilton, then moved about 20 miles north up Sevenmile Creek to a recently constructed intermediate bastion, Fort St. Clair. After garrisoning St. Clair, the Legion once again ponderously and irresistibly moved toward Fort Jefferson. Wayne liked the location of Jefferson: it hinted at a move toward Kekionga, it was on a high-and-dry route, and it left room for feinting and maneuver. However, it was far too small for the 3,000-man Legion. Wayne moved another five miles northeast and built a mighty 53-

acre stronghold named Fort Greeneville, which became his advanced base for the move into the deep Northwest. He then settled down into another winter of relentless drilling and practicing.

The Indians who had been shadowing the army were stupefied by the prodigious effort expended to build Fort Greeneville. They were further alarmed and provoked as "Mad Anthony" Wayne added psychological warfare to his bag of tricks. In the late fall of 1793, General Wayne ordered eight companies of troops to move to the site of St. Clair's defeat. They were ordered to bury the bones of the dead soldiers, and there directly on the battlefield at the headwaters of the Wabash River build a strong satellite fortress, deliberately and strategically named Fort Recovery. It was garrisoned; then Wayne cocked his ear to hear the enemy's response. Wayne and Washington knew the Native American boundary dispute served as a smoke screen for the deeper issue: Great Britain's desire and will to reacquire the Old Northwest. Such a provocative move as the presence of Fort Recovery could not go unanswered by the Indians...or the British.

The reply was not long in coming. In February, 1794, Lord Dorchester, Governor General of Canada, issued the following proclamation, to be published and distributed to the Algonquin tribes:

> "Children, from the manner in which the people of the United States push on and act and talk, I shall not be surprised if we are at war with them in the course of the present year; and if so a line must then be drawn by the warriors. We have acted in the most peaceable manner and borne the language and conduct of the people of the United States; but I believe our patience is almost exhausted."

To add emphasis to this proclamation, British Lord Dorchester ordered Governor Simcoe to the foot of the Maumee River rapids (near current Toledo, Ohio) to there erect Fort Miami, in clear violation of the territorial sovereignty of the United States. This fort became a storehouse and distribution center for British rifles, gunlocks, gunpowder, and other war supplies for the Miami Confederation forces.

Duly bolstered, the confederation prepared to strike at the source of its provocation. Approximately 1,500 to 2,000 warriors converged on Fort Recovery at dawn on June 30th, 1794. This force attacked a supply train whose drivers had imprudently been allowed to leave Fort Greeneville for Recovery before the column's escort was ready. Fort Recovery's commander called out 140 dragoons and riflemen to come to the column's rescue, and in a fierce battle only 1,000 feet from the fort, 21 officers and soldiers were killed and 360 pack horses captured, at the cost of 3 dead warriors. The column fought its way into the fort, and 250 defenders braced for an Indian attack. Throughout the evening and into the night, the Native Americans assaulted the fort across the open ground surrounding the battlements, sustaining 40 dead and 20 wounded, while killing 22 defenders. Although the attack was pressed with fanatical savagery, the combination of disciplined riflemen and dragoons defending a professionally designed fortress proved too much for the Indians. Before first light on July 1st, the Native American forces melted silently away to the north, their confidence shaken by their defeat at Fort Recovery.

Anthony Wayne wasted little time pressing the advantage gained at Fort Recovery. General Charles Scott's rifle-armed Kentucky mounted infantry, which had trained with Wayne at Legionville, rode north to join the Legion at Fort Greeneville. Pushing these and his main infantry forces up from Greeneville to reunite with the rifles and cavalry at Fort Recovery, Wayne advanced not northwest toward Kekionga, but northeast toward the upper St. Marys River valley. By August 1st, on the St. Marys near the point where Harmar had veered northwest toward Kekionga in 1790, the Legion stopped. Wayne ordered the construction of a small fortification, Fort Adams, and from Adams spread conflicting rumors that he planned to move east and west in order to confuse the Indians. The deception was completely successful, as for two crucial days in early August while Wayne moved steadily north into the Great Black Swamp, the Indian scouting force lost contact with the Legion. On August 4th, Wayne crossed the Little Auglaize River and the nearby ancient glacial moraine, moving deep into the Black Swamp. The Delaware scouts once again discovered the Legion as it approached the Auglaize

River and was engaged in laying waste to the vast tribal corn and vegetable gardens in that area.

The Legion of the United States now moved further north to the ultimate confederacy stronghold - the Grand Glaize, which General Wayne ordered to be burned. Once more, Wayne added psychological provocation to his inexorable movement. He ordered that another strong fortification be built directly upon the site of the Grand Glaize, and named it Fort Defiance. The now-experienced soldiery quickly built the fort; the shaken Indians fell back northeastward toward British Fort Miami in confusion.

But the retreat did not last long. The Shawnee Blue Jacket, now the war faction leader (Little Turtle had fallen from favor after the loss at Fort Recovery), picked a strong site along the Maumee River only seven miles southwest of British Fort Miami. The site was an area where a long-past tornado had broken off many huge trees about chest high. The Indians strengthened this natural fortress by cutting off the second-growth saplings that had grown among the trunks and turning their sharpened ends toward the advancing Legion. Even if the Legion should somehow evict the 1,300-man confederation force from Fallen Timbers, the Indians could quickly retreat into the waiting arms of their allies, the British, in close proximity at Fort Miami. The British would surely defend them, as they had all but promised in February, 1794.

Anthony Wayne and his superbly trained Legion followed the Native Americans down the Maumee. At a point part way between Fort Defiance and Fort Miami, Wayne built small Fort Deposit, designed as a storehouse for the supplies and miscellaneous accoutrements of the soldiers. The general wanted his men to be lean and unencumbered for the climatic battle he saw rapidly approaching.

General Wayne's Legion approached Fallen Timbers on August 18th, and Wayne conducted a two-day reconnaissance of the strong fortification. After evaluating the enemy's position, he issued final dispositions and orders for the battle. Captain Robert MisCampbell and 400 saber-wielding regular cavalrymen would occupy the right flank along the Maumee River. They were to sweep the enemy's left flank and pinch it into the center. General Scott with 1,500 mounted riflemen, split into two brigades, would do the same on the left flank. Wayne's prized infantry, 2,100 soldiers strong and organized into four sublegions, would occupy the center. The Legion was given strict orders: they were to charge into the twisted fortress with bayonets only, enduring the first volley of fire from the confederation. Using bayonets to pry the Native Americans from their positions, they were to discharge the deadly projectiles from their muskets only when they could fire their weapons into the backs of their fleeing enemies at short range.

On a drizzling dawn, August 20th, 1794, the Legion of the United States executed General Wayne's plan to perfection at the Battle of Fallen Timbers. The overwhelming combination of the slashing sabers and pounding hooves of the plunging horsemen, in concert with the flashing bayonets and murderous discharges of the relentless infantry, routed the Miami Confederation forces in a forty-minute battle. The Legion lost between 33 and 44 killed and approximately 100 wounded in the short, savage charge into the woodland fastness, but repaid the confederation two to three times over in dead and wounded during the desperate rout of the Indians that followed.

But the Native Americans' greatest disaster still awaited them. As they fled to Fort Miami, they watched the British gates swing shut before them and the cannon portals and rifle loopholes remain empty. The British would not risk war with the United States to rescue their so-recently-embraced allies. At its leisure, and in full view of the nearby Indians, Wayne's Legion moved within pistol range of Fort Miami, tauntingly inspected its ramparts, and burned Indian and British outbuildings adjacent to its walls.

Wayne spent the next two months moving up and ravaging the Maumee Valley, destroying all buildings, plus all the acres upon acres of crops his Legion could not consume on its journey. He moved to Kekionga, burned the village, and once more erected a bastion on the ruins of a once-powerful Native American stronghold - this one triumphantly named Fort Wayne.

The Indians were shattered, both physically and psychologically. Forsaken by their allies, their will to resist destroyed by the bold tactics of General Wayne, they humbly answered his beckon to a conference at Fort Greeneville. On August 3rd, 1795, they signed the Treaty of Greeneville, ceding all but the northwest corner of Ohio to the United States. The Treaty was to buy a kind of uneasy peace in the eastern portion of the Northwest Territory for approximately 15 years – until another Native American confederacy and another great leader once again rose to contest the Miami Valley / Great Black Swamp Corridor one last time.

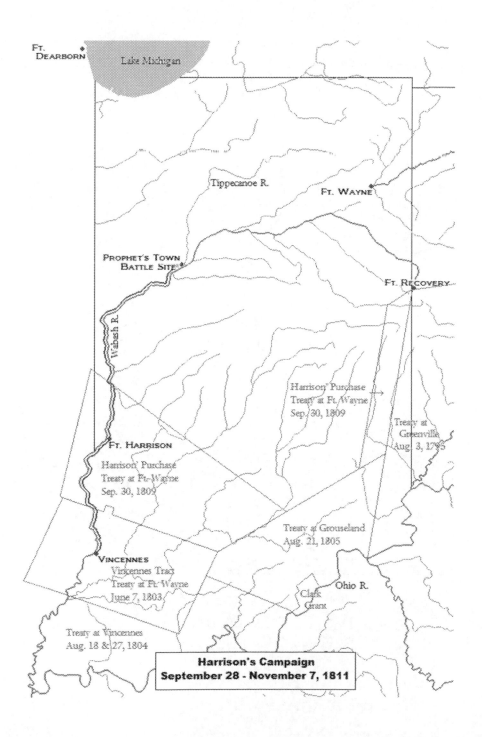

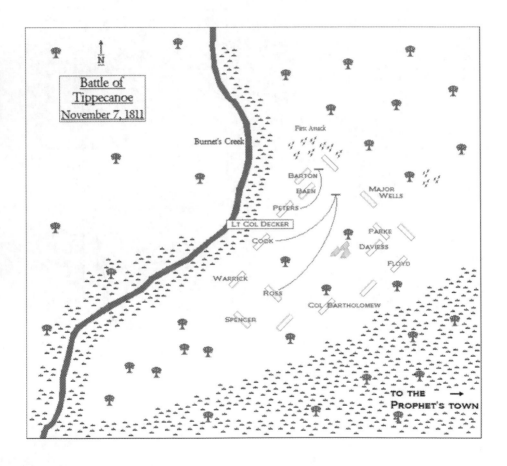

Battle of
Tippecanoe
November 7, 1811

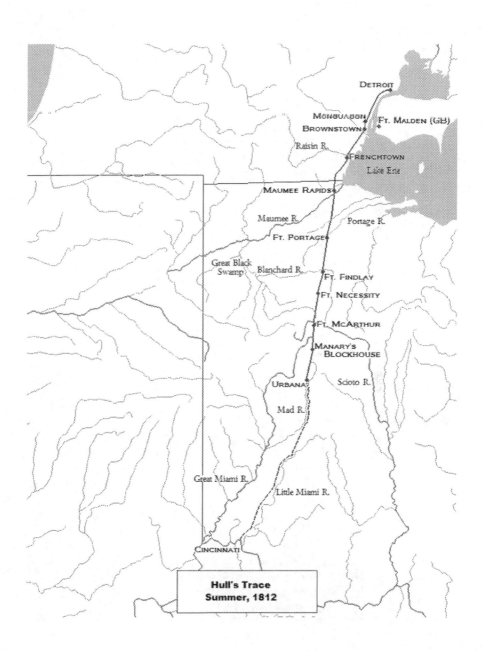

Hull's Trace
Summer, 1812

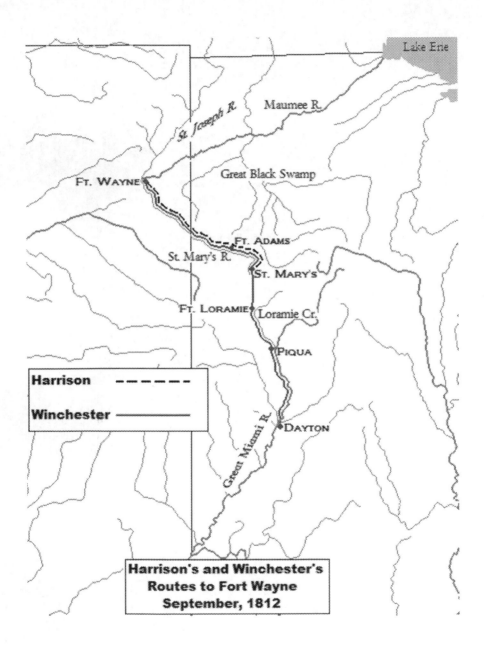

Harrison's and Winchester's
Routes to Fort Wayne
September, 1812

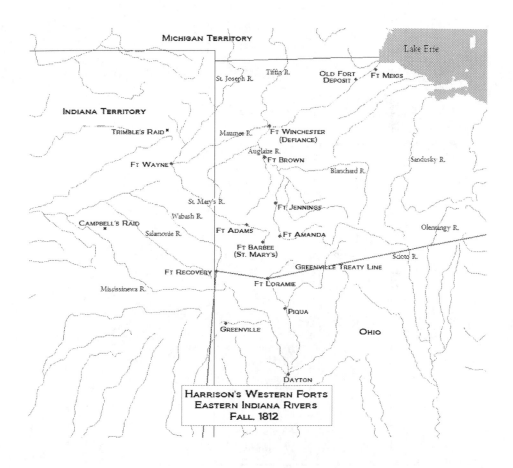

MICHIGAN TERRITORY

Lake Erie

Tiffin R.

St. Joseph R.

OLD FORT
DEPOSIT

FT MEIGS

INDIANA TERRITORY

TRIMBLE'S RAID

Maumee R.

FT WINCHESTER
(DEFIANCE)

Auglaize R.

Sandusky R.

FT WAYNE

FT BROWN

Blanchard R.

St. Mary's R.

FT JENNINGS

Wabash R.

CAMPBELL'S RAID

Salamonie R.

FT ADAMS

FT AMANDA

Olentangy R.

FT BARBEE
(ST. MARY'S)

GREENVILLE TREATY LINE

Scioto R.

FT RECOVERY

FT LORAMIE

Mississinewa R.

PIQUA

GREENVILLE

OHIO

DAYTON

HARRISON'S WESTERN FORTS
EASTERN INDIANA RIVERS
FALL, 1812

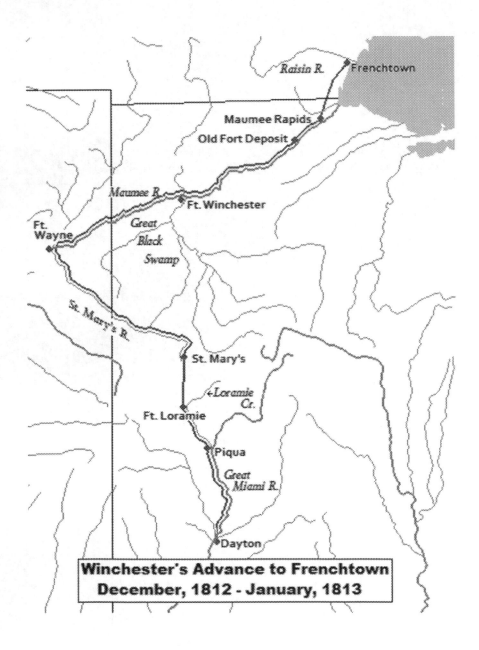

Winchester's Advance to Frenchtown
December, 1812 - January, 1813

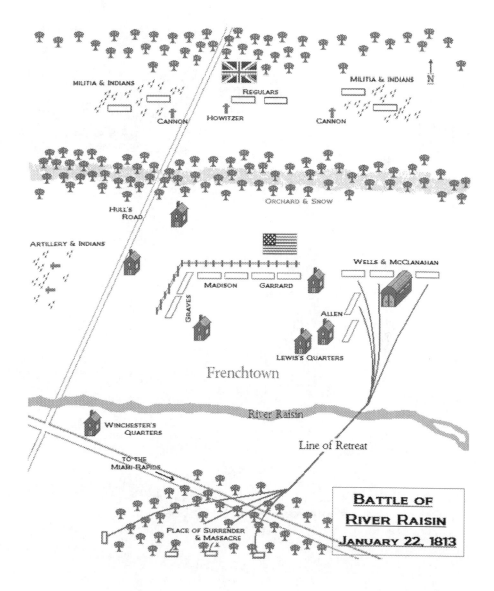

MILITIA & INDIANS

REGULARS

MILITIA & INDIANS

N

CANNON   HOWITZER   CANNON

ORCHARD & SNOW

HULL'S ROAD

ARTILLERY & INDIANS

WELLS & McCLANAHAN

MADISON   GARRARD

GRAVES

ALLEN

LEWIS'S QUARTERS

Frenchtown

River Raisin

WINCHESTER'S QUARTERS

Line of Retreat

TO THE MIAMI-RAPIDS

PLACE OF SURRENDER & MASSACRE

BATTLE OF RIVER RAISIN
JANUARY 22, 1813

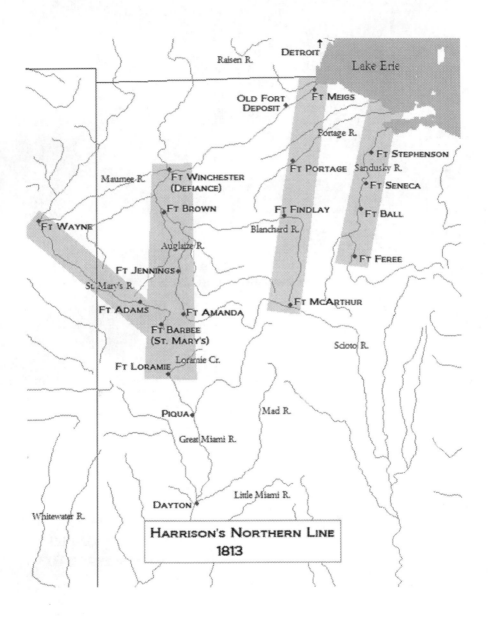

Raisen R.

DETROIT

Lake Erie

OLD FORT
DEPOSIT

FT MEIGS

Portage R.

FT STEPHENSON

Maumee R.

FT WINCHESTER
(DEFIANCE)

FT PORTAGE

Sandusky R.

FT SENECA

FT BROWN

FT FINDLAY

FT BALL

FT WAYNE

Blanchard R.

Auglaize R.

FT FEREE

FT JENNINGS

St. Mary's R.

FT ADAMS

FT AMANDA

FT McARTHUR

FT BARBEE
(ST. MARY'S)

Scioto R.

FT LORAMIE

Loramie Cr.

PIQUA

Mad R.

Great Miami R.

Little Miami R.

DAYTON

Whitewater R.

**HARRISON'S NORTHERN LINE
1813**

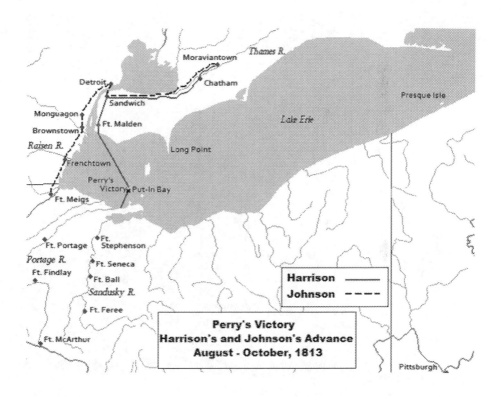

Perry's Victory
Harrison's and Johnson's Advance
August - October, 1813

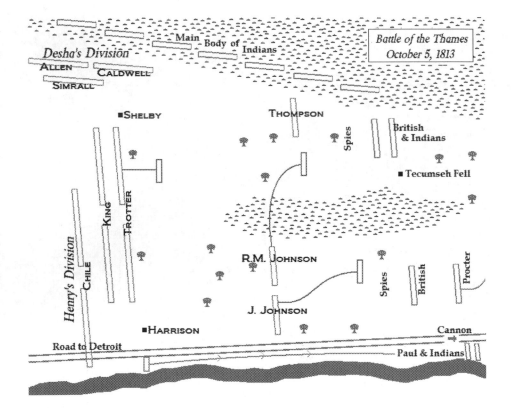

Desha's Division
ALLEN
CALDWELL
SIMRALL

Main Body of Indians

Battle of the Thames
October 5, 1813

■SHELBY

THOMPSON

Spies

British
& Indians

■ Tecumseh Fell

Henry's Division
CHILE
KING
TROTTER

R.M. JOHNSON

Spies

British

Procter

J. JOHNSON

■HARRISON

Cannon

Road to Detroit

Paul & Indians

CHAPTER 6

The Empire Contested:
The War of 1812 in the Old Northwest

1812: The Paths to Defeat

Of all the methods the United States used to build its first empire in the Old Northwest Territory, perhaps none was as insidious as the treaty process in which it engaged with the Native American inhabitants of the area. The Americans took full advantage of Native American unfamiliarity with the European concept of private land ownership, to the detriment of the Indians. This unfamiliarity with the concept bred confusion and anger among the Native American tribes. The entire process basically guaranteed that any peace based upon these negotiations was doomed to failure and conflict sooner or later. The early history of the Miami Valley / Great Black Swamp Corridor is virtually a case study in this phenomenon.

The United States / Native American campaigns of the 1790s were ended by the Treaty of Greeneville, August 3rd, 1795. In this document, the Native Americans agreed to forfeit all claims to territory south and east of a boundary line that ran south from the mouth of the Cuyahoga River to Fort Laurens, then southwest to Fort Loramie, northwest to Fort Recovery, then south to the Ohio River. In return for these tens of thousands of acres of prime land, the U.S. government agreed 1) to relinquish all claims to land north and west of the line (except for certain well-established posts, such as Detroit and Ft. Wayne), 2) to give the Indians $20,000 worth of goods upon signing the treaty, plus 3) to give an additional $9,500 in goods as an annuity each year thereafter. This treaty was very essence of the concept of "land for trinkets." Grossly one-sided, the Treaty of Greeneville still should have provided years of stability to Ohio, Indiana Territory, and Michigan Territory. It might have done so but for two factors: the continued presence of British/Canadian colonials across the river from Detroit (in Upper Canada), and the United States' appointment of William Henry Harrison as Governor of Indiana Territory.

The British never really gave up hope of regaining the Northwest Territory for the Crown. They maintained a malevolent presence at Fort Malden, Upper Canada, at the turn of the century, always willing to support destabilizing influences in the Old Northwest. A major destabilizing influence arose in the early 1800s with the revival of the Miami-Shawnee-Delaware-Wyandot *et. al.* confederacy, now headed by Shawnee leader Tecumseh and his mystic brother, Tenskwatawa ("The Prophet").

Meanwhile, in this same period, twenty-seven-year-old William Henry Harrison assumed the mantle of Governor of Indiana Territory in 1800. One of Harrison's primary goals as territorial governor was to expropriate the title to as much land as possible from the resident Native Americans in the territory. Harrison was extraordinarily successful in this endeavor, concluding land-grabbing treaties with various groups of Indians at Fort Wayne (June 7th, 1803), Vincennes (August 18th & 27th, 1804), Grouseland (August 21st, 1805), and again at Fort Wayne (September 30th, 1809). Each concession progressively increased the anger of Tecumseh, who held that no one group or multiple groups of tribes had the right to cede land that in reality belonged to all Indians. Tecumseh and his followers had never agreed to any cessions.

The last straw was the 1809 Treaty of Fort Wayne. This cession alienated up to one-fourth of the present state of Indiana to the United States. Tecumseh, accompanied by armed warriors, conducted acrimonious confrontations with Harrison in both August, 1810 and July, 1811. After this last conference, Tecumseh made it clear he was headed South to expand the confederacy by recruiting southern tribes such as the Creeks and Cherokees into his union.

Harrison, warily viewing this turn of events, now took advantage of the first of what would be several opportunities in the next three years. While Tecumseh was in the South during the fall of 1811, Harrison marched north with a force of approximately 1,000 soldiers to the center of the confederacy's movement, Prophet's Town, on the

Tippecanoe River in north-central Indiana. The Prophet, noting Harrison's hostile advance, decided to strike the army first. At dawn on November 7th, 1811, Tenskwatawa attacked the American army just outside Prophet's Town. Perhaps remembering old legends of bullets bouncing off soldiers at Fort Recovery 20 years before, Tenswatawa assured his warriors this would once again be the case. It was not so. Although they were taken by surprise, Harrison's regulars and militia rallied, the accuracy and lethality of their fire devastating the Native Americans in the improving sunlight. The Native American forces suffered a terrible defeat – psychologically as well as physically. The Prophet's influence as a religious mystic was permanently shattered, and Tecumseh's leadership was weakened. The confederacy forces faded away to the north even as Tecumseh returned to the destroyed Prophet's Town.

The Battle of Tippecanoe was arguably the first battle in what would become the War of 1812 in the Old Northwest. Certainly it created ramifications that affected the Miami Valley / Great Black Swamp Corridor during the War. Tecumseh, realizing his dream of a great standalone Indian confederacy was destroyed with the defeat at Tippecanoe, decided the only way to salvage any part of the dream was to throw his lot in with the British. He moved the remnant of his forces to Fort Malden, Upper Canada. This assured that in any coming conflict, the Detroit-Northern Ohio area would be a front line theater of battle.

Ostensibly caused by the British impressment of American sailors onto English ships to be used in Britain's effort to combat Napoleon in Europe, the War of 1812 was declared by the United States on June 18th, 1812. Perhaps this might have been the government's reason for declaring war, but in the Southern and Western parts of the country, the attitude of the citizens might be more represented by the slogan of "On to Canada." The westerners were once again tired of British war mongering and interference in Northwest Territory affairs, and determined to capture or destroy the source of that interference. In 1812, a major three-pronged effort was launched to capture Canadian territory. In the east, an ultimately unsuccessful offensive was launched north up the Lake Champlain corridor. In the central theater, an American army crossing the Niagara River was turned back at the Battle of Queenston Heights. The westernmost invasion involved utilizing Detroit's proximity to the Upper Canadian area as the jumping-off point for the third attempt to capture Canadian soil.

President Madison cast about for a commander for the western offensive, and finally settled on the territorial governor of Michigan, ailing 59-year-old William Hull. Although he was a Revolutionary War hero, the years and attendant physical infirmities had sapped Brigadier General Hull of his vigor and aggressiveness; he was now sluggish and inordinately cautious. Hull moved to the southern Ohio area and began building an army to move to Detroit. Hull gathered 1,200 Ohio militiamen and 800 Regular Army soldiers of the Fourth U.S. Infantry under Lt. Col. James Miller at Urbana, Ohio, just south of the 1795 Treaty of Greeneville Line.

Hull next began planning his route to Detroit. As he concentrated his forces in Urbana, it was clear to Hull that the Miami Valleys would provide the trunk of his army's supply line from Cincinnati to Urbana. However, looking north from centrally-located Urbana, Hull (like Harmar and St. Clair before him) failed to recognize the strategic significance of the western half of the Great Black Swamp, through which the Auglaize River flowed. He looked for high ground which would minimize the amount of time he would have to spend in the Swamp, and found such a route on another continental divide *east* of the forbidding Auglaize Valley. Hull's Trace cut north, close to the highest point in Ohio (near present Bellefontaine, Ohio) then slowly descended toward the Maumee Rapids (now Perrysburg/Toledo, OH) at a relatively narrow portion of the Black Swamp. Although Hull needed to build a log-corduroy road over this route, he still felt safer using this supply umbilical than a potential one through the Auglaize Valley. As he advanced toward Detroit, he fortified the trace with blockhouses, including Manary's Blockhouse, Fort McArthur, Fort Necessity, Fort Findlay, Fort Portage, and a blockhouse at the foot of the Maumee Rapids. En route to Detroit, Hull sent his personal effects ahead by boat, including his official papers. Unfortunately, unknown to Hull, war was declared between the United States and Britain during this period (June 18, 1812), and the ship on which this valuable intelligence was placed was captured by the British.

Hull reached Detroit on July 5th, 1812, and immediately began making plans for the conquest of Amherstberg and Fort Malden, Upper Canada. Colonel Lewis Cass, commander of the Third Ohio Regiment, moved his forces into Canada on July 12th and subsequently had success in forcing the British back into Upper Canada. However, General Hull became greatly concerned about his spread-out army and his supply route along the western shore of Lake Erie, and recalled Cass's command.

Hull then sent armed detachments back along the trace to assure the security of the route along the Detroit River and west coast of Lake Erie. This resulted in two battles, neither reassuring to the now increasingly frightened Hull. In the Battle of Brownstown (August 5th, 1812), a substantial 200-man detachment of U.S. Army soldiers under Major Thomas Van Horne was forced back to Detroit after advancing south along Hull's Trace. At the Battle of Monguagon (August 9th, 1812), another detachment of 600 soldiers under Lt. Col. James Miller defeated a smaller mixed force of British and Indians under Captain Adam Muir and Tecumseh south of Detroit. Although the battle was tactically a victory, the U.S. force suffered many casualties. Despairing of reaching the Maumee River and opening the supply route, this force again strategically retreated to Detroit.

Hull was now despondent over his prospects of holding Detroit, although he possessed nearly a month's food rations, 5,000 pounds of gunpowder, 33 cannon (including some heavy 24-pounders), and 2,500 muskets. Listening to British propaganda about the atrocities their Native American allies might visit upon the Detroit garrison, Hull surrendered Detroit virtually without a fight on August 16th, 1812. At a stroke this victory (plus the surrender of Fort Dearborn [Chicago] on August 15th) gave the British and Indians the upper hand early in the War of 1812 in the Old Northwest.

Tecumseh immediately took advantage of this shift in the fortunes of war to launch an offensive along the western fringes of the Old Northwest. In lightning succession, battles between the Native Americans and the United States erupted in Indiana Territory at

Pigeon's Roost (September 3rd), Fort Harrison (September 4th), Fort Madison (further west, September 5th), and Fort Wayne (September 6th); all were the progeny of Tecumseh's planning and leadership.

The siege of Fort Wayne, located at the strategic portage between the Maumee and Wabash Rivers, was certainly the largest and most serious of these attacks. Five hundred Native Americans, under the Potawatomi chief Winnemac, invested the fort for seven days between September 5-12, 1812, and threatened the garrison with annihilation.

Between the fall of Detroit and the late summer Native American offensive, a most important event occurred. Kentucky Militia commander Major General William Henry Harrison, until lately the Territorial Governor of Indiana, was ordered by the military staff in Washington to gather a force of Kentucky militia and begin moving it north. Harrison quickly built a force of 2,200 soldiers and concentrated it at the headwaters of the St. Mary's River, christening it the Second North Western Army. At the same time, U.S. Regular Army Brigadier General James Winchester was also ordered to gather a mixed force of mostly Kentucky militia and a few Regulars, which he concentrated in the southern Ohio area. Upon receiving the first word of the attack on and seige of Fort Wayne, the active Harrison moved down the St Mary's to relieve the besieged installation. Concurrently, acting as head of the Kentucky Militia, Harrison ordered Winchester to move northwest to Fort Wayne to support the Second North Western Army.

A significant clash of ranks could have occurred at this point. Winchester, as a Regular Army brigadier general, nominally outranked Harrison, a major general of militia. However, the vast majority of the western army *was* militia. The federal military staff in Washington, bowing to the reality of the militia's support for the charismatic Harrison, quickly moved to head off controversy and named Harrison as a Brigadier (later Major) General in the Regular Army and commander of all forces in the Northwest, effective September 17th, 1812. With the naming of the brilliant and efficient Harrison as western commander, the first step on the road to victory in the West was taken.

At the approach of Harrison's army from the southeast on September 12th, 1812, the Native American forces lifted the seige of Fort Wayne and melted away to the north. Winchester's 1,200-man wing arrived on September 18th. Harrison now began to plan for the recapture of Detroit, a key to victory in the Northwest. While Harrison's command secured the Fort Wayne/Indiana Territory area, he ordered Winchester to march northeast down the Maumee toward Fort Defiance, with the ultimate goal of moving on to and attacking Detroit. Harrison realized that this force must be supported with supplies and ammunition, and that the roundabout route via the St. Mary's River and Fort Wayne was long, out of the way, and difficult to protect from attack. Studying the area which great commanders like Wayne and mediocre commanders like St. Clair and Hull had viewed in the past, Harrison came to the same conclusion as Wayne: the key to movement and supply in the Old Northwest was the Miami Valley / Great Black Swamp Corridor. To facilitate the movement of arms and supplies from his commissaries in Cincinnati, Dayton, and Piqua, Harrison proposed to build a chain of forts approximately one travel-day apart, using roughly the same route upon which Wayne advanced in 1794 - directly through the heart of the Great Black Swamp. Each of these fortresses north of old Fort Loramie was begun in the October-November, 1812 timeframe.

While this line of communication and supply was shorter and safer than the route through Fort Wayne, it certainly was not impervious to attack. The Native Americans had proven their willingness to attack fixed fortifications in their early September offensive. Harrison, recalling his 1811 campaign, must have brooded over the presence of Indian villages in west-central and northern Indiana Territory. A review of a topographical map would have also revealed a series of four rivers running from southeast to northwest along the western flank of his line of forts, providing easily traversed passages for attack on this supply line. Noting this danger, General Harrison moved to secure his western flank.

Harrison determined that the best way to protect the line of forts being constructed in western Ohio was to conduct a series of offensive raids in Indiana Territory during the fall of 1812. General Samuel

Hopkins, commanding yet another unit of approximately 1,250 Kentucky mounted militia and Indiana Rangers, left Fort Harrison (current Terra Haute, IN) on November 11, 1812, and moved up the Wabash River. Hopkin's unit destroyed deserted Prophet's Town and two other villages in the Tippecanoe River area a few days later. Retracing its steps back south, a wing of this army was attacked by Native Americans on November 22nd and suffered 18 killed and wounded in the ambush. Hopkin's army ultimately returned all the way to Vincennes, marching in bitterly cold weather.

At approximately the same time, Harrison dispatched Colonel Allen Trimble and 500 horsemen on a raid to the northwest of Fort Wayne. Although this detachment failed to reach its destination of White Pigeon's Town, which it intended to demolish, it did succeed in destroying several villages west of Fort Wayne, easing the pressure in this area.

Probably the most successful of the raids to secure the western flank of the army was Lt. Colonel John B. Campbell's attack on the Mississinewa River villages. In late November, Campbell gathered between 600 and 800 troops at Dayton and supplies at Eaton. Projecting from Fort Greeneville, Campbell rode hard to the west and destroyed two villages on the lower Mississinewa on December 17th. Campbell's force was counterattacked the next dawn by a substantial force of Miami and Delaware Indians. Campbell drove the attackers off, inflicting significant casualties on the Native Americans. Campbell lost many horses in the march and battle, and incurred a large number of wounded, many of whom suffered greatly in the bitterly cold weather. Campbell sized up the entire situation and immediately retreated to Greeneville, arriving there on Christmas Day. *(See Appendix C: The Battle of Mississinewa, for more details.)*

Although not extraordinarily successful in terms of overall destruction, these raids rocked the Native American forces in Indiana Territory back on their heels, and denied them food and shelter in a harsh winter environment. Harrison felt confident there would be no Native American offensive operations on his western flank in late 1812. He ordered General Winchester to again move forward to the northeast from the confluence of the Auglaize and Maumee

Rivers (where the brigadier had camped and erected the substantial Fort Winchester, close to decaying Fort Defiance) to the Maumee Rapids.

General Winchester gladly left the Auglaize River area, where the Kentucky detachment had spent an unhealthy and hungry fall. His army had battled many illnesses, including an outbreak of typhoid fever. As Harrison had accurately forecast, the extended supply lines via the St. Marys River to Fort Wayne and thence down the Maumee to Fort Defiance had not been able to keep pace with the needs of Winchester's army. Supplies had slowly dwindled, then virtually stopped. It was a weakened army of 1,200 militia that departed for Lake Erie on December 29, 1812.

Winchester arrived at the Maumee Rapids on January 8th, 1813, and immediately put his ill and demoralized men to work on a fortification. While at work on this defensive structure, Winchester received specific instructions from Major General Harrison not to advance too quickly against the British at Detroit. Harrison wished to build a more overwhelming force at the Rapids before turning north. Yet on January 13th, Winchester received a plea for assistance from the American village of Frenchtown (now Monroe, Michigan), on the River Raisin 30 miles to the north of the Rapids. Their village was in danger of imminent attack from allied British and Indian forces in the area (commanded by the British Colonel Henry Procter and the Wyandot war leader Roundhead). Winchester was aware that Harrison was not in possession of all information relating to the situation, and was certain Harrison would not wish for him to stand by in the immediate vicinity as an American village was destroyed. He made a field command decision to send 600 of the healthiest and best-equipped soldiers, under Colonel William Lewis, forward to Frenchtown to head off the impending invasion and determine the exact tactical situation.

Lewis left the Maumee Rapids on January 17th, 1813. Moving as quickly as conditions allowed, Lewis and his command arrived in Frenchtown on the afternoon of January 18th. There he found a small force of British and Indians on the north side of the Raisin, which he easily dispersed and pursued for several miles. During this pursuit, Lewis gathered intelligence which convinced him larger enemy forces were in the area, therefore he broke off the pursuit and returned to Frenchtown.

General Winchester arrived on January 19th, while the remainder of the force (approximately 334 soldiers) arrived on January 20th. Winchester sent army scouts fanning out from the village to determine the strength and position of the enemy, while the majority of the army camped and rested in the village. Strangely, since he was concerned about the close proximity of large enemy forces, Winchester was careless regarding the disposition of his encampment. His deployment of security pickets was lax, his men were bivouacked in dispersed locations throughout the village, and many of them were camped with their backs to the river in unfortified positions.

The scouts completely missed the advance of approximately 597 British and 800 Indians to the Frenchtown area on the night of January 21st, 1813. Between 4:00 and 5:00 on the morning of January 22nd, a thunderous artillery barrage, coupled with a howling Indian attack, jarred the slowing stirring American army awake. Efficiently dividing the scattered Americans, whose ability to rapidly concentrate their forces was hampered by the deep snow, the allied British and Indians quickly dismantled and forced the surrender of Winchester and the little American army. The Kentucky soldiers comprising the majority of the army suffered 100 killed, 500 captured, and approximately 60 severely wounded. Of the Americans engaged in the brief battle, only 33 escaped death or capture. On the 23rd, Colonel Procter withdrew to Brownstown, 25 miles to the north, leaving the wounded in the possession of Roundhead and the allied Indians. The Native Americans murdered between 30 and 60 wounded soldiers, in what would become known as the River Raisin Massacre.

Harrison's winter offensive was over, his hopes dashed in the deep snow and savagery of Frenchtown. He moved reinforcements to the Maumee Rapids, and began building the mighty bastion of the northern frontier, Fort Meigs. Unable to assume the offensive with the limited personnel and supplies at his disposal, Harrison now turned to his administrative talents. Harrison determined that he must complete and streamline his supply line from Piqua, and recruit replacements for those soldiers lost in the failed advance on Frenchtown. Far from executing a simple move to capture Upper Canada in a bloodless advance, the Americans now faced a desperate struggle for survival on their own soil.

The year 1813 loomed as an uncertain period of decision for the United States in the Old Northwest Territory.

CHAPTER 7

The Empire Contested:
The War of 1812 in the Old Northwest

1813: The Chain of Defense

There is a generally accepted theory for one reason the South was able to contest the North so strongly during the first years of the Civil War. This theory states that many of the United States Regular Army officers with combat experience gained from the Mexican-American War (1846-'48) chose to cast their lot with the southern states. Such Confederate generals as Robert E. Lee, Thomas J. "Stonewall" Jackson, A.P. Hill, Pierre G.T. Beauregard, Joseph E. Johnston, James Longstreet, George Pickett, and Richard Ewell all became battle-tested as junior officers in the successful campaigns of Zachary Taylor and Winfield Scott during the Mexican War.

If it is true that success breeds success, then the Confederate Army built upon an American tradition formed more than half a century earlier. In "Mad Anthony" Wayne's triumphant campaign into the heart of the Old Northwest in 1794, he was accompanied by junior officers Ensign Hugh Brady, Major Henry Burbeck, 1st Lieutenant Ferdinand L. Claiborne, Captain Leonard Covington, Captain Moses Porter, and Cornet Solomon Van Rensselear. All these officers, among others, gained positive combat experience under Wayne, and all rose to become generals in the United States Regular Army or state militias, either during the War of 1812 or sometime thereafter. No veteran of the 1793-'94 expedition ever conducted a more successful operation than the remarkable 1813 campaign directed by the Wayne-influenced commander of the Second North Western Army in the War of 1812, William Henry Harrison.

In January, 1813, the ultimate success of General Harrison's northwestern campaign was not apparent to the world. Harrison's first attempt to recapture Detroit from the British invaders and Native American defenders ended in the snows of Frenchtown, south of Detroit, when subordinate James Winchester's army moved north from the Maumee River without adequate support and was annihilated. Winchester's captured wounded were murdered by Native American warriors in the infamous "River Raisin Massacre."

Yet, in the ashes of this defeat, the seeds of final victory were planted. Two major factors arose from the depths of this reversal. The first was the powerful psychological factor of revenge. Most of the massacred soldiers were Kentucky militia, and most of the manpower subsequently utilized the northwestern campaign would also come from Kentucky. One cannot underestimate the strong impetus provided by the urge to avenge one's countrymen, as "Remember the Raisin" became an oft-repeated battle cry in the Old Northwest.

The second factor to arise from the defeat was the realization by William Henry Harrison that the recapture of Detroit required a combined political-administrative-military effort to succeed. Harrison must use his political ties with the War Department to acquire soldiers, supplies, and equipment to build a defense, while preparing to later launch an offensive in the Northwest, all the while battling with the needs of the commanders of other theaters of action for scarce military resources. He must use his administrative talents to husband these resources and find a way to move them to the lower reaches of the Maumee Valley, where very little physical infrastructure existed before 1812, to be applied against the British. Finally, when it was fully staffed and equipped, Harrison as commanding general in the Northwest must lead the army in battle against the seasoned British and their Indian allies, the latter fighting for their very existence in defense of their homeland. The pursuit of these three difficult keys to victory would bring out the very best attributes in the character of William Henry Harrison.

Harrison found a powerful ally in his quest for men and equipment in Governor Isaac Shelby of Kentucky. Kentucky had been ravaged by British-supported Native Americans many times in the years preceding 1812. Shelby realized the best defense for his state was an offense that pushed the Indians into Upper Canada

– far from the northern border of Kentucky, the Ohio River. As governor of Kentucky, the most populous territory or state in the West, and the head of its military forces, Shelby commanded the manpower and some of the supplies to help fuel Harrison's build-up. He proved unhesitant to call upon both.

Administratively, General Harrison had to manipulate his three keys to victory in the effort to conquer Detroit. First, Harrison had to organize and control a defensive perimeter that was strong enough to hold the British and Indians to the north and west as he brought manpower, weapons, and supplies from the south and east to contest the alliance. Second, he had to build a logistical structure that could both store and forward manpower, weapons, and supplies to the front lines. Third, the defensive perimeter and logistics supply line had to be flexible enough to enable Harrison to switch from defense to offense as the opportunity presented itself. All this must be done in a howling wilderness virtually devoid of roads, bridges, communications systems, and other support facilities.

Harrison responded brilliantly to the challenge. As a student of military history and geography, he studied the map of the Old Northwest Territory. He realized the main British strength was its sea power on Lake Erie, which allowed its armies to be easily supplied and reinforced, as well as providing rapid transportation for British troops in an invasion scenario. Thus, Harrison had to block all river passages into the interior. Using existing forts and building additional ones where needed, Harrison established vertical chains of fortifications that blocked all river entrances into the northwest Ohio area via the Sandusky, Portage, Maumee, and St. Joseph Rivers.

If the vertical chains of forts were the defensive bulwark of the Northwest, then there was one front-line cornerstone in the overall structure. Studying the maps further, Harrison confirmed that the Maumee Rapids area was the key to the defense of Ohio, as well as the prime launching point for any move against Detroit. In January, 1813, he began building the mighty bastion of the northern frontier on the south bank of the Maumee River rapids: Fort Meigs. This ten-acre timber-and-earth-palisaded fort, professionally designed by West Point-educated engineer Captain Eleazer Wood, included seven blockhouses and five artillery batteries among its defensive strong points. It would serve as the linchpin of U.S. military activity in the Northwest in 1813.

As strong as the chains of forts were defensively, Harrison ingeniously combined certain of them to form another needed attribute for success in the Northwest – an early version of an "all weather" supply route. Harrison studied Hull's trace and the chain of forts established on the early move to Detroit. The log/corduroy road connecting these forts (and the now-building Fort Meigs) left much to be desired. It was rough and bumpy in dry weather, impassible in the frequent deep snows of a Midwestern winter, and sank into a morass with the spring and fall rains. Harrison looked to the west – to the Miami Valley / Great Black Swamp Corridor. Here was a nearly full-water route between Cincinnati, Harrison's main commissary on the Ohio River, and the northern frontier. In winter, sleds could be drawn over the smooth, flat, snow-or-ice-covered surface of the rivers, steadily moving men and supplies north. In spring, summer, and fall, pirogues and canoes could move these same men and supplies north on the water.

Further, many of the links in the chain were already in place. Piqua, Fort Loramie, and St. Marys could quickly be made ready to anchor the chain. In the north, Fort Winchester, built to guard General Winchester's ill-fated wing of the 1812 offensive, served as a sentinel at the confluence of the Auglaize and Maumee Rivers. By completing just three more forts already being built in the Auglaize Valley and enhancing facilities at a couple more points, a protected, all-weather supply line from Cincinnati to Fort Meigs could be established. Further, the exposed outpost of Fort Wayne, guardian of the Second North Western Army's western flank, could be supplied and supported by the trunk line of this route and the St. Marys River. Harrison accelerated the improvement of the Miami Valley / Great Black Swamp Corridor and developed it into his main supply umbilical to the northern frontier.

All this activity was rapidly occurring in the winter and spring of 1813. The side that could build up supplies and soldiers the fastest would be the side that could first move to the offensive against the other. Harrison knew two factors worked against him. First, he could never capture and hold Detroit while the British fleet controlled his far northeastern flank - Lake Erie. Second, his long supply line between Cincinnati and Fort Meigs could once again become vulnerable to Native American attacks from the western areas of Indiana and Illinois Territories. The western command structure could do little about the former – the U.S. Navy must complete the fleet being built at Presque Isle, Pennsylvania, so the British fleet could be defeated and Harrison could have its support and transport in his attack on Detroit. The commanders could, however, do something about the latter. The Indiana and Illinois territorial governors attacked the problem of the Western Indians throughout the spring and early summer of 1813.

The raids of Hopkins, Trimble, and Campbell had done much to stabilize the western flank in the fall of 1812, while Winchester was moving northeast and the western forts were begun. However, the effect of these raids had worn off with the budding spring of 1813. The governors of Indiana and Illinois Territories had not wasted the lull provided by the sacrifice of the frozen mounted infantry raiders the previous winter. Throughout early 1813, Acting Governor John Gibson of Indiana and Governor Ninian Edwards of Illinois hastily erected an east-west cordon of citizen-built blockhouses stretching north of the settled areas of Indiana and Illinois. They commissioned companies of U.S. or territorial rangers and state militias to garrison these blockhouses. Commanders such as U.S. Ranger Colonel William Russell and Indiana Major John Tipton then responded with their units to distress calls from isolated frontier villages to chastise various marauding Indians for atrocities committed in their local areas.

Many typical western missions on the Indiana and Illinois frontier during the period of February to July, 1813, were similar to the following. On March 18th, 1813, Major Tipton and his Indiana Territorial Ranger unit received word that a group of settlers had been attacked outside one of the crude Indiana blockhouses called Fort Vallonia, approximately 90 miles east of Vincennes. Tipton and his rangers rode in hot pursuit. Catching the raiders on an island in a river in the Vallonia area, Tipton's men killed one Indian and scattered the raiding party.

Through the long distance raids of Russell and the multiple response actions of Tipton and other local commanders, Governor Edwards was able to report that in March, 1813, between 300 and 400 militia volunteers were on regular patrol in Illinois Territory, radiating from 17 small forts. Indiana was operating similar numbers of both men and installations. By the summer of 1813, due to the military operations of the rangers and militia, most of the hostile Native Americans had moved out of the Indiana/Illinois area. The left flank of the Second North Western Army and its supply route in the Miami Valley / Great Black Swamp Corridor was secure from attack from the west.

The focus of the war in the Old Northwest now shifted to the crucial Maumee Rapids area. Major General Henry Procter, commander of British forces in the Northwest Theater, was able by virtue of his then-superior line of supply and transportation on the Great Lakes to secure enough men and supplies to attack Fort Meigs in mid-spring, 1813. Procter assembled 1,200 British soldiers and around 1,200 Indian warriors under Tecumseh (now a brigadier general in the British army) at Fort Malden and moved them to the vicinity the Maumee Rapids.

Harrison was aware that Procter and his Indian allies were preparing to move on the Maumee Rapids, and ordered engineer Captain Eleazer Wood to hasten back to Fort Meigs and expedite its completion. Harrison himself would return to the interior and gather soldiers to garrison Meigs. The fort was completed in late April, its garrison swelling rapidly during this period. At this time, some 2,000 American soldiers occupied the stout and well-designed bastion.

The completion and garrisoning of the fort occurred none too soon, as on April 28th scouts to the northeast reported that enemy columns and gunboats were in sight. Shortly thereafter the British encamped at the site of the ruins of old Fort Miami. The British completed positioning their artillery by dawn, April 30th, and shelled Fort Meigs for two days, the heaviest bombardment occurring on May 1st.

Earlier, General Harrison sent a message to Fort Winchester for General Green Clay to quickly move about 1,200 Kentucky militia down the Maumee River to Fort Meigs. Further orders from Harrison on May 5th instructed Clay to split his force near Meigs, the left wing of 800 soldiers to attack British artillery batteries on the north bank of the Maumee, while the right wing of 400 forced an entry into the fort through the Native American lines. Both forces completed their mission to a degree, but Green's left eventually met disaster. After successfully landing on the north bank of the Maumee and spiking the enemy cannon located there, the force commander, Lt. Colonel William Dudley, with his left wing commander, Captain Leslie Combs, underestimated the size of the British and Indian counterattack, and led their men directly into an ambush. Approximately 600 of Dudley's 800-man wing were killed or captured.

Meanwhile, the smaller right (south) wing successfully fought its way through the siege and entered the fort. Harrison used the confusion sown by the two attacks to launch a 350-man raid, commanded by Colonel John Miller, to destroy a particularly troublesome British artillery battery east of the fort. Miller's sortie was successful, as he destroyed the battery, captured 40 prisoners, and retreated to the fort before the British could react.

The British tactically won the battle but lost the siege. They inflicted significant casualties on the relief force, but the Native Americans soon lost interest in the siege after the May 5th battle and drifted away to divide the spoils of war and parade their prisoners. Stripped of a substantial portion of his force, General Procter retreated back to Detroit on May 9th.

Procter had not been altogether displeased with the results of the May attack on Fort Meigs, and wished to carry the battle to the Americans once again. Procter wanted to probe east and strike either at Presque Isle, where the U.S. fleet was nearing completion, or at the Sandusky River line of forts. However, Fort Meigs was a particularly irksome symbol to Procter's Native American allies, and they pressed for a renewed attack upon it. Since Native American support was crucial to continuing the war in the west for Britain, Procter bowed to the inevitable and, as soon as supplies could be accumulated for a renewed offensive, struck once more against Fort Meigs.

Harrison had again moved to the interior to facilitate the movement of men and supplies to the northern battle area, and left General Green Clay in charge of Fort Meigs. The combined British and Indian force, estimated at 3,000 to 4,000 men, arrived at the Rapids on July 20th and began the second siege of Fort Meigs on July 21st.

After reconnoitering the area, Procter and Tecumseh realized the fort was too strong to be taken with the light weapons and manpower on hand. They therefore planned a cunning ruse to fool the fort's garrison. Out of sight but not out of hearing of the fort, Tecumseh and Procter staged a mock battle. They reasoned the garrison would figure an unsuspecting relief column was being attacked by the siege force, and would send a substantial unit out of the fort to rescue the column. Tecumseh and Procter could weaken the garrison by destroying this detachment. The mock attack occurred on July 26th. Clay, resisting the pleas of his subordinate officers to rescue their supposed comrades, refused to be drawn out - he was not expecting supplies any time soon and had been informed by courier that none was in route. Once again frustrated at their inability to invest Fort Meigs, the British and Indians slipped to the southeast to attack one of Procter's original targets, Fort Stephenson at the exposed northern end of the Sandusky River line of forts.

Fort Stephenson was located at the head of navigation of the Sandusky River, and as such was strategically important to the American defense of northern Ohio. The British and Native Americans were desperate to crack the northern chain of forts and establish a presence in Ohio south of the Lake Erie – Maumee River line. They chose Stephenson as a potentially less strongly held position than the western forts. The allies did not know that Fort Stephenson, like Fort Meigs, had also been professionally designed and built by the brilliant Captain Eleazer D. Wood. Though far from large, the fort was stout and defensible. The British and Indians moved to Fort Stephenson in the July 29th – 31st period, and by August 1st, were busily engaged in investing the fortification.

Harrison had grave doubts about the viability of the small fort, its one 6-pounder cannon, and its 160-man garrison to withstand an attack by British and Indians in numbers such as those which had recently laid siege to Fort Meigs. Harrison ordered the fort's commander, Major George Croghan, to abandon and destroy the fort and retreat toward his command post, ten miles south at Fort Seneca. Croghan received the message too late, as the allied force was nearly upon him at the receipt of the order. Croghan decided to defend the fort against awesome odds, rather than risk certain casualties and possible destruction in an attempt to break out to the south.

Croghan had several factors working for him, although not all were apparent to either side at the outset of the battle. The British assault force could not convince their Indian allies to accompany them and make a coordinated effort to storm the fort: the Indians would observe the British assault and then determine whether it was wise for them to join in the attack. Secondly, the British and Indians were not able to bring heavy assault cannon with them across the neck of the Great Black Swamp to Fort Stephenson: thus, they could not blow holes in the stout timbers through which to pass. Third, both the British officers and the American commander, Croghan, had correctly determined the weakest point of the fort. The British planned to attack this point, however, Croghan placed and concealed his lone cannon, *"Old Betsy,"* at this weak spot and double-shotted the gun with cannister, turning the weapon into a huge, deadly, short-ranged "shotgun." Finally, the British had neglected to transport proper equipment to breach the fort. They failed to bring ladders for use in scaling the walls, and the axes they did bring with them were too dull to cut the timbers of the fortification.

On August 1st, 1813, Generals Procter and Tecumseh demanded the surrender of the fort. Major Croghan refused to do so. The allies then began shelling the fort with their light cannons on August 2nd, hurling over 500 balls at the structure. The well-built fortress resisted damage from these small cannons, and Procter determined the fort must be taken by storm. At 4:00 in the afternoon of August 2nd, 115 officers and men of the 41st Regiment, led by Lt. Colonel William Short, attacked the apparent weakest point of Fort Stephenson. As they drew close, the U.S. gunners unveiled *Old Betsy* and loosed a tremendous volley. A huge crimson swath cut through the attacking force, and it staggered in confusion. Some of the more hardy attackers made it to the wall, but could not breach it with their dull axes and sabres, and suffered further grievous casualties in the lingering effort. The Indians, noting the heavy losses the British assault force accumulated, declined to attack with their huge numbers. The attack sputtered to a stop.

The Battle of Fort Stephenson was over by 4:30 PM. The British attackers had suffered very high losses in comparison to the numbers engaged: 26 officers and men died (including assault commander Lt. Colonel Short), 41 were wounded, and 29 officers and men were captured (including experienced Captains Dixon and Muir). The Americans lost 1 dead and 7 wounded.

Although neither side realized it at the time, a turning point of the war in the Northwest occurred with the double reverses at Forts Meigs and Stephenson. These would prove to be the last offensive operations the British and Native Americans would undertake in this theater. Stung by losses in men, supplies, and equipment which were difficult to replace at the end of an increasingly vulnerable and sporadic supply line, and opposed by an enemy who was steadily building substantial quantities of each at the end of an increasingly secure and efficient supply line, the allied army retreated toward its northern centers – Forts Detroit and Malden. The British high tide ebbed in the Northwest.

It remained for a tiny, makeshift fleet, commanded by a young but brilliant commander, to assist Harrison, his crudely efficient supply/defense chain, and his rough-hewn army in sealing the doom of the British and Indians in the Old Northwest Territory in the War of 1812.

CHAPTER 8

The Empire Contested:
The War of 1812 in the Old Northwest

1813: The Route to Victory

One realization to which a reader of history must certainly arrive at some point is that history *does* repeat itself. The First World War (1914-1918) is remembered as a terrible stalemate in which armies faced each other over a front of many miles, neither side able to accumulate enough strength to break through the other's lines and end the war. It took the combination of two extraordinary events (the exhaustion, and later utter defeat, of the massive German Spring 1918 offensive and the arrival of huge amounts of fresh troops and materiel from America) to break the stalemate and end the war.

Yet this was not the first time stalemates had occurred in war. America itself experienced this phenomenon in its wars, from the earliest history of its martial efforts. For example, in the early stages of the War of 1812 in the Old Northwest, the United States tried to capture British Upper Canada, failed, and lost Detroit as a result. In response, the British-allied Native Americans launched a ragged series of attacks against U.S settlements along the western fringes of the Northwest Territory in the fall of 1812 and were checked. The United States subsequently directed an aggressive movement toward Detroit and was crushed at Frenchtown in early winter, 1813. The British then launched two separate offensives against the United States' northern line of fortifications during 1813 and were unsuccessful each time. Thus, by mid-1813, both sides had come to an uneasy status quo along the Lake Erie-Maumee River line – neither strong enough to push the other from its positions. It remained for an extraordinary event to break the deadlock on the Northwestern Front.

During 1813, U.S. General William Henry Harrison's political and administrative efforts began to turn the tide of war in the Northwest Territory. His secure supply/communication routes (most notably the all-weather route along the Miami Valley / Great Black Swamp Corridor, supported by Hull's Trace plus lesser roads from Cleveland and Pittsburgh) allowed him build up sufficient men and supplies in the north for offensive operations. By August, 1813, he had accumulated approximately 3,000 Regular Army troops and 5,000 militia at various posts in the Old Northwest. This included approximately 5,000 soldiers at forward positions along the Sandusky River and another 1,000 in the Maumee River valley, all within 20 miles of Lake Erie. His logistical efforts had secured a relatively steady flow of supplies to the northern frontier, allowing him to hold these soldiers in place as he waited for Lake Erie, his northeastern flank, to be secured.

In contrast, his antagonists, British army Major General Henry Procter and naval Commander Robert Heriot Barclay, suffered at the very end of an increasingly tenuous supply umbilical. American naval activities on Lake Ontario, while not spectacular, had created enough problems to periodically disrupt supply traffic on this route. Meanwhile, the U.S. Army's very active efforts in the Niagara area served to constrict the flow of supplies through this bottleneck. Finally, there was the fact that the vast majority of British supplies must travel across the Atlantic Ocean, then filter through several theaters to eventually reach Procter and Barclay at the extreme western end of the supply chain. This meant that for all practical purposes, officers in the eastern theaters commandeered supplies intended for western use. All these factors had created a rapidly approaching supply crisis for the British war effort in the Northwest by August, 1813.

Commander Barclay's naval force maintained one huge advantage up to the period of mid-1813, but saw it slip away with the passage of time. This advantage was that Barclay actually had ships operating on Lake Erie. All but a few of the smallest gunboats of the American fleet, commanded by young Captain Oliver Hazard Perry, were still being built at Presque Isle on the southeastern shore of Lake Erie. Because his ships were operational, Barclay could use them to blockade the American shipyard, or use them as transports to move an invasion force to the Presque Isle area to raid and destroy the ships on their blocks. He proposed both these actions. Barclay's plan for an amphibious raid against the shipyard was rejected by his superior officers. However, he was allowed to use the fleet as a blockading squadron against the American ships being built on Lake Erie.

Perry continued to complete the American fleet at Presque Isle (current Erie, Pennsylvania), even though there were serious questions whether it could break out and be employed on the lake. The strength of the fleet was undoubted. It was led by the fine 260-ton brigs USS *Lawrence* (20 guns) and USS *Niagara* (20). These well-built warships were supported by the 85-ton *Caledonia* (3); the 65-ton schooner *Somers* (2); the 50-ton sloop *Trippe* (1); and the 50/60-ton gunboats *Tigress, Porcupine, Scorpion,* and *Ariel,* collectively carrying 8 cannon. The two large warships drew too much water to cross the sandbar at the mouth of the inlet. Perry would have to trust Providence to provide a multi-day window of opportunity for his men to laboriously haul the ships across the bar with the aid of flotation devices, unimpeded by the British.

Barclay operated under the knowledge that if the American fleet reached the open lake, the British fleet would be heavily outnumbered and outgunned. Barclay's five operational ships included the 200-ton corvette HMS *Queen Charlotte* (17 guns); the 96-ton schooner *Lady Prevost* (13); the 75-ton brig *General Hunter* (10); the 60-ton sloop *Little Belt* (3); and the 35-ton schooner *Chippeway* (1). Importantly, the 300-ton corvette HMS *Detroit* (19 guns) was nearing completion at Amherstburg/Fort Malden, near the mouth of the Detroit River. The *Detroit* could help ease the severe numerical inferiority the British would soon face.

But the gross numbers of "guns carried" hid even more significant facts. The British artillery was a motley collection of mixed-caliber, long-range cannon, which required differently prepared gunpowder charges and differently sized cannon balls. The American ships were armed with lesser numbers of 32-pounder *carronades*, which were short-range weapons but had tremendous "smashing effect" at this short range.

Statistics can be tedious, but this case, they readily serve to illustrate the advantage the Americans were building on Lake Erie:

	American Fleet	*British Fleet*
Number of Ships	9	6
Number of Men	553	440
Number of Artillery Weapons	54	63
Total Weight of Fire	1,536	887
Weight of Broadside Fire	936	496
Weight of Long-Range Cannon	304	208
Weight of Short-Range Carronades	632	288

Captain Perry got the break he was waiting for on Sunday, August 1, 1813. Lookouts reported the British fleet had left its blockading stations near Presque Isle. No adequate reason has ever been provided for Barclay's move. Conjecture runs the gamut from fear of incoming storms to the need to aid the completion of HMS *Detroit* to Barclay's desire to visit an attractive widow in Amherstberg. Whatever the reason, the British were gone, and Perry at once shifted his smaller ships to the open lake to provide a defensive shield as he nudged the lightened big ships (their cannons had been removed and defensively placed on the dunes surrounding the inlet) onto the bar. All worked frantically, knowing that for the British to return and catch the big ships unarmed or still on the bar would spell disaster.

For three strenuous days, the crews furiously worked the floatation "camels" non-stop to get the big ships across the sandbar. By first light, August 4th, the *Lawrence* was across but unarmed, while the *Niagara* still lay stranded on the bar. Then the sails of the British fleet appeared on the horizon. The feared moment of greatest danger was at hand. The decisive Captain Perry did not hesitate; he sent his small ships sailing directly at the British fleet, noisily banging away with as much fury as their 12 cannon could muster. The aggressive bluff worked - Barclay was convinced he faced the entire fully armed American fleet and quickly returned to his base at Amherstberg/Fort Malden.

August 4th, 1813 was a key to ultimate victory – with the retreat of the British, the Americans swiftly completed the movement of

Niagara across the bar, and both she and *Lawrence* were quickly rearmed. Perry immediately sailed to western Lake Erie, anchoring at the mouth of the Sandusky River on August 16th and conferring with General Harrison. The next steps were clear. Perry's squadron would establish its base at Put-in-Bay in the Bass Islands, only 30 miles from Canada, and patrol from that base. Now that all supplies were cut off to the western theater, Barclay must soon come out and attempt to destroy the American fleet, thus reestablishing his supply line across Lake Erie.

By early September, the British situation in the Detroit area was desperate. Only a few days' supply of flour remained, while supplies piled up at Long Point, 150 miles to the northeast. Barclay was forced to fight. On September 9th, he completed the arming of *Detroit* and the British fleet left its base at Amherstberg/Fort Malden. At dawn on September 10th, American lookouts spied British sails on the horizon to the west.

Barclay's strategy was to use his only possible advantage: to stay at a distance from the American ships and use what might be superior gunnery skills with long-range cannon to pick off the American ships one by one. Yet, even the weather conspired against him. The wind shifted to the southeast, giving the Americans the wind advantage in their quest to close quickly and attack with the superior weight of their short-range carronades. At 11:45 AM, USS *Lawrence* came within range of the British fleet. Perry had directed each ship captain to engage a like-sized opponent in the British fleet. However, Lt. Jesse Elliott, captain of *Niagara*, backed off his main topsail and declined to engage his designated opponent, *Queen Charlotte*. Thus, for two-and-a-half hours, *Lawrence* received all of the punishment *Detroit* and *Queen Charlotte* could deliver. By 2:30 PM, the last of her cannon was silenced and *Lawrence* lay disabled and dead in the water.

Then occurred one of the most dramatic acts in the history of the United States Navy. Boarding *Lawrence's* cutter, Captain Perry directed four sailors to row him the half mile to the undamaged *Niagara*, as British small arms fire chopped the water around him. Boarding *Niagara*, he assumed command and sailed her directly back into the teeth of the British attack.

The British had disabled *Lawrence,* but both *Detroit* and *Queen Charlotte* paid a tremendous cost in the effort. Both were heavily damaged, had lost cannon, and (reminiscent of St. Clair's Defeat 22 years before) had lost their senior officers to death or injury. As British junior officers struggled to maneuver their damaged ships to meet the new threat posed by the *Niagara,* the big British corvettes collided and their rigging became entangled. Perry saw their unfavorable situation, and quickly moved in for the kill. Maneuvering between two lines of British men-of-war, he unleashed several broadsides from each of the undamaged *Niagara's* fresh cannon. All guns fired double-shot rounds, and the effect was devastating. In fifteen minutes, the battle was over, as one by one the British ships struck their colors. Lake Erie was now an American pond.

It is rare that a sea battle has such a tremendous effect on a land war. British General Procter immediately knew his position at Detroit/Fort Malden was untenable, in that he now had no hope whatsoever for resupply. He had also lost his advantage of using the fleet as transports to quickly move his army for any invasion of the American defense's weak points. Conversely, this power of maneuver now accrued to the Americans. Moving back to his base at Put-in-Bay and then on to the mouth of the Sandusky, Perry prepared his ships to cooperate with Harrison's troops as transport vehicles for an invasion of Canada, even as the British under Procter prepared to retreat into the interior.

Harrison had anxiously awaited the outcome of the Battle of Lake Erie, but not while standing still. With great effort, he concentrated his expeditionary force in the narrow isthmus between the Portage and Sandusky Rivers in northwest Ohio, and collected 80 crude bateaux to help ferry his troops across Lake Erie. With the appearance of Perry's fleet, Harrison employed the navy ships and army bateaux to move the army in stages from the Portage/Sandusky isthmus to South Bass Island and thence to the invasion point, Fort Malden, Upper Canada.

British General Procter was having his own struggles. Out of supplies and with no hope of replenishment now that his line of communications was cut with the east, he was forced to abandon the Fort Malden/Amherstberg/Sandwich/Detroit area. Military logic clearly stated that Procter must move east toward his supplies if he was to have any chance of saving his army to fight another day. Yet, a substantial part of his army was composed of the Miami/ Shawnee *et. al.* alliance forces, led by Tecumseh. The concept of strategic withdrawal toward supplies and for defense was foreign to the Native American alliance forces. They had fought no enemy recently, their quivers were full of arrows, their bows and tomahawks were intact, and the woods were full of game. Why should they retreat? The British had many times stated they were fighting in the Northwest to maintain and restore native lands to the Indians, and had assured them they would never again voluntarily abandon Northwestern lands, as they had at Fallen Timbers/Fort Miamis in 1794. To the alliance warriors and its leadership, this retreat was just another example of British duplicity or worse, cowardice.

Eventually, Procter convinced Tecumseh that the strategic withdrawal was necessary. Tecumseh agreed to keep as much of the alliance together for as long as he could in the move to the east, upon receiving the promise that the British and Indians would make a stand at a defensible position somewhere along the Thames River, Upper Canada. Neither Procter nor Tecumseh was familiar enough with the region to designate a point for turning upon their enemy, but this counterattack was a key part of the withdrawal strategy, particularly for the Native American confederation.

Procter ordered Fort Malden razed, moved north to Sandwich and destroyed military stores there, then prepared to move east. Yet, even as the withdrawal up the Thames was ordered on September 26th, 1813, the Indian confederation began to unravel. Certain tribes drifted to the north and sent peace feelers to the invading Americans. Every day saw increased desertions of both Native American warriors and British Regulars.

Harrison had feared that the British would strenuously oppose his amphibious landing on the Canadian shore, but these fears proved unfounded. He landed a large portion of his army near the recently self-destroyed Fort Malden on September 27th, while another large Kentucky mounted militia force, under Colonel Richard Johnson, moved from Fort Meigs toward the now-abandoned Detroit. This force crossed the Detroit River and united with the northward-moving amphibious invasion force. Harrison's combined force had approximately 3,500 soldiers ready to pursue the deteriorating British/Native American alliance forces up the Thames River.

The alliance was unraveling more rapidly than the Americans could fathom. The Indians retreated up the Thames on the south side of the river, while the British moved up the north side – each barely in contact with the other. Each group lost substantial numbers of soldiers daily through sickness, exhaustion, or desertion. In addition, the Native American families of the warriors were stringing out far to the rear of the retreating armies, making a tactical destruction of the bridges behind the retreat impossible. Near Chatham was a rapid in the Thames suitable for fording the river. Tecumseh grew anxious at the length of the unimpeded advance of the Americans, and on October 4th decided to make a stand at the rapids. The American army brought up several pieces of artillery and shelled Native American positions. Native American forces typically were disconcerted by artillery fire, and Tecumseh's warriors quickly abandoned their positions – some fording the stream to unite with the British and some fading to the southeast and out of the war forever.

The British/Native American allied army continued its stumble to the northeast, demoralized and undisciplined – a ghost of the army that only three months before had efficiently conducted a seige of Fort Meigs. Signs of the army's implosion were everywhere. Three ships loaded with vital supplies and ammunition, which should have been carefully protected at the vanguard of the column, fell behind and were found burning in the river. Stands of small arms in buildings converted to armories were discovered only partially destroyed, exhibiting inept attempts at destruction. Dispirited British deserters drifted into the American camps, and spoke freely of the demise and positions of British and Indian forces. All signs pointed to an impending climatic battle.

General Procter moved ahead of his retreating army and surveyed Moraviantown, on the banks of the Thames River. Moraviantown was defensible, with suitable ground nearby and a ravine to the west of the town. However, Procter had purchased the village as his army's winter quarters and hoped to stall the American advance further west. By this time he was down to approximately 430 British Regulars and 600 allied Native Americans. Procter chose another defensible position approximately two miles west of Moraviantown. This position offered opportunities to maximize the few possible advantages he could utilize, given his dwindling force. To the south, the Thames River anchored Procter's left flank; a strip of beach trees growing along the banks provided additional defense and anchorage for the left. In the center, the clearing through which the main east-west road passed narrowed to a defensible width. It also limited the area into which Harrison could squeeze his deadly mounted infantry – a martial arm in which Harrison was vastly superior to Procter. Procter chose to divide his Regular infantry into two successive lines in this sector to thwart the American advance. On the right, the large Backmetack Marsh provided a tangled fastness suited to the fighting style of the Native American contingent of the army. Tecumseh's 600 remaining stalwarts secreted themselves in this bottomland. Between the road (on which the army's only artillery, a solitary 6-pounder cannon, was placed) and the marsh, a small swamp split the clearing.

As Harrison came upon and reconnoitered the enemy line, he drew his forces up for battle. On the American right, Colonel Paul's 120-man corps of Regulars drew the assignment of rushing and neutralizing the cannon. In the center, Colonel Richard Johnson's thousand-man regiment of mounted infantry faced the British regulars. This powerful mounted regiment was backed up by three brigades of Kentucky militia under Major General William Henry. Finally, on the American left (which was refused to the west-northwest at an acute angle to protect the open left flank), Major General Joseph Desha commanded two more Kentucky militia infantry brigades. All told, Major General William Henry Harrison, ably assisted by Governor/General Isaac Shelby (who had accompanied his militia into Canada), could muster nearly 3,000 soldiers bent on avenging the River Raisin massacre against Procter's 1,030 disgruntled survivors of the retreat. As if this numerical and moral superiority were not enough, Harrison noted that the British, expecting their Regulars to be opposed by infantry, had drawn their forces up in open formation. Like Anthony Wayne 19 years before,

Harrison made a field command decision; also like Wayne's, the move was novel given the tactics of the day. He would launch a mounted infantry charge against his enemy - this time, the British Regulars. Colonel Johnson, noting the narrow front facing his regiment, made a second crucial command decision: to split his regiment, sending half under Lt. Colonel James Johnson against the British Regulars while he personally commanded the other half to cross the small swamp and assault Tecumseh's allied warriors in the marsh.

The mounted assault succeeded beyond Harrison's wildest dreams. At the first crash of musketry, the horses drawing the cannon became frightened and dragged it into the woods out of the battle. The well-drilled mounted infantry of James Johnson absorbed a volley or two from the Regulars (about three minutes of battle time), at which point they ruptured both lines of infantry and completely routed the British. On the left, Richard Johnson's mounted infantry crashed into the tangled marsh, dismounted, and overwhelmed the outnumbered defenders in a half-hour pitched battle. At the height of the battle, Tecumseh, who had courageously held his line on the allied right while the British ran pell-mell toward Moraviantown in hasty retreat, was killed. Legend says that Colonel Richard Johnson, himself badly wounded, fired the lethal blast into Tecumseh. With their leader and their allies gone, the Indian resistance soon ended and those that could faded into the woods to the east. The British lost 18 killed and 22 wounded while the Indians lost at least 33 killed and an indeterminate number wounded. The Americans had 15 killed and 30 wounded, capturing 601 prisoners in the Thames campaign.

The battle was over, and for that matter, the war in the Old Northwest was essentially over as well. There would be other armed actions in the Northwest, and squabbles with officialdom in Washington would soon cause William Henry Harrison to resign as regular army major general and commander of the Second North Western Army. But the territory comprising America's first empire had been secured, as most empires normally are secured: by wresting it from its native inhabitants and direct foreign influences.

Indirect foreign influences would still be a matter of concern, however. Far to the south, another Indian nation and two old

European powers still vied to exert a kind of control over the Old Northwest. Another roughhewn frontier general, perhaps considered by posterity to be even greater than William Henry Harrison, arose to protect and conquer the West.

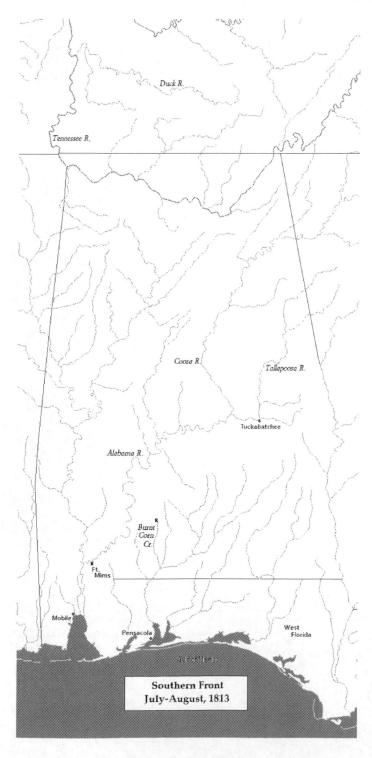

Southern Front
July-August, 1813

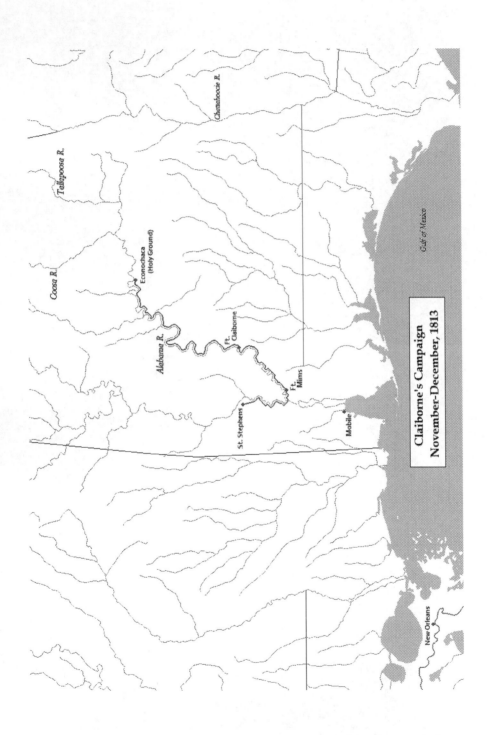

Claiborne's Campaign
November-December, 1813

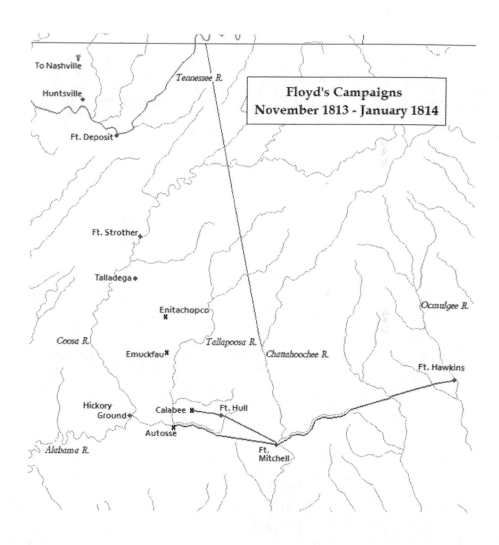

Floyd's Campaigns
November 1813 - January 1814

To Nashville

Huntsville

Ft. Deposit

Tennessee R.

Ft. Strother

Talladega

Enitachopco

Coosa R.

Emuckfau

Tallapoosa R.

Chattahoochee R.

Ocmulgee R.

Ft. Hawkins

Hickory
Ground

Calabee

Ft. Hull

Autosse

Ft.
Mitchell

Alabama R.

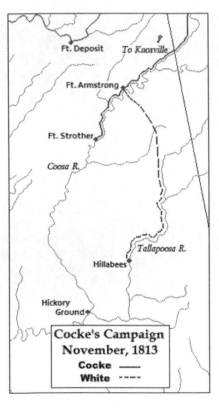

Cocke's Campaign
November, 1813
Cocke ———
White -·-·-·

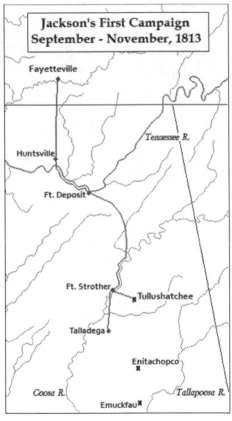

Jackson's First Campaign
September - November, 1813

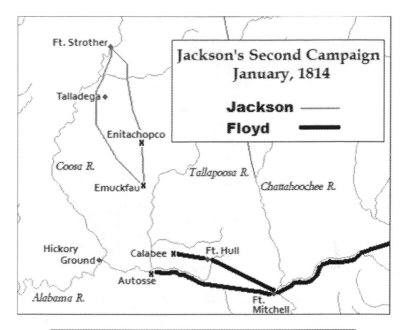

Jackson's Second Campaign
January, 1814

Jackson ....
Floyd ━━━━━

Ft. Strother

Talladega

Enitachopco

Coosa R.

Tallapoosa R.

Chattahoochee R.

Emuckfau

Hickory Ground

Calabee

Ft. Hull

Autosse

Alabama R.

Ft. Mitchell

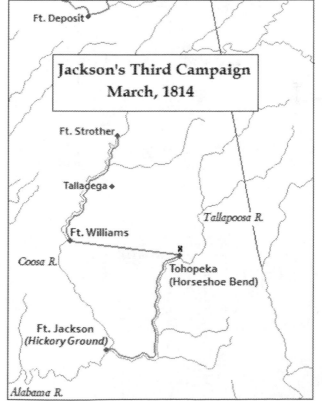

Ft. Deposit

Jackson's Third Campaign
March, 1814

Ft. Strother

Talladega

Tallapoosa R.

Ft. Williams

Coosa R.

Tohopeka
(Horseshoe Bend)

Ft. Jackson
(Hickory Ground)

Alabama R.

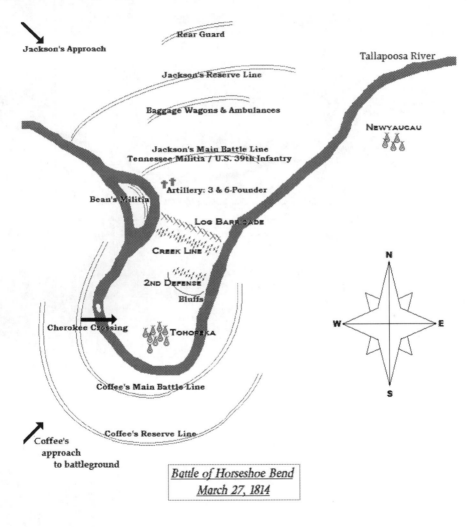

Jackson's Approach

Rear Guard

Jackson's Reserve Line

Tallapoosa River

Baggage Wagons & Ambulances

NEWYAUCAU

Jackson's Main Battle Line
Tennessee Militia / U.S. 39th Infantry

Artillery: 3 & 6-Pounder

Bean's Militia

LOG BARRICADE

CREEK LINE

2ND DEFENSE

Bluffs

Cherokee Crossing

TOHOPEKA

Coffee's Main Battle Line

N

W   E

S

Coffee's
approach
to battleground

Coffee's Reserve Line

Battle of Horseshoe Bend
March 27, 1814

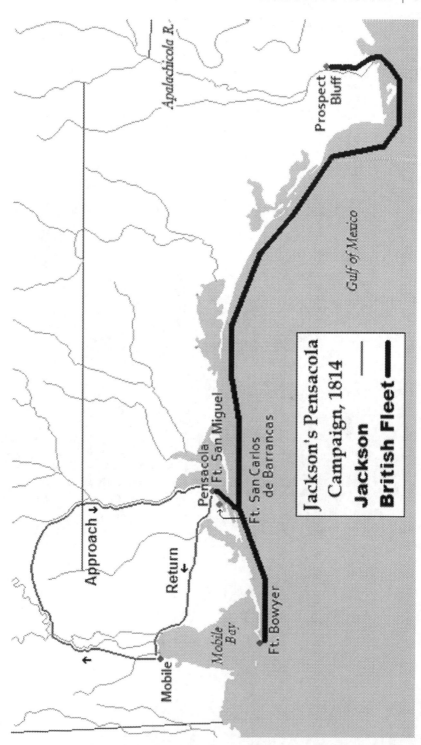

Jackson's Pensacola Campaign, 1814
Jackson
British Fleet

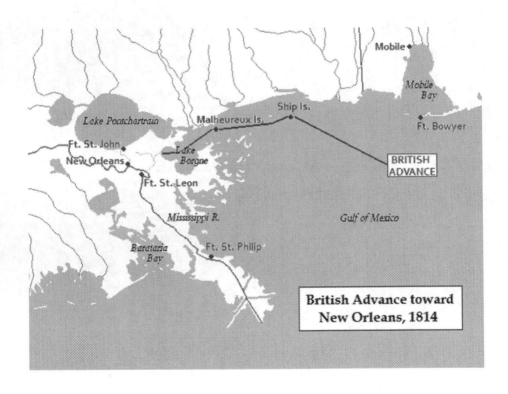

British Advance toward
New Orleans, 1814

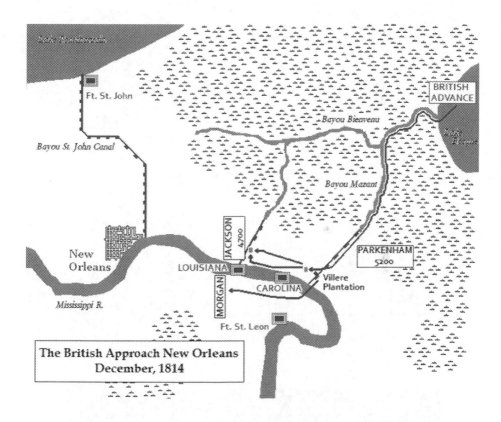

The British Approach New Orleans
December, 1814

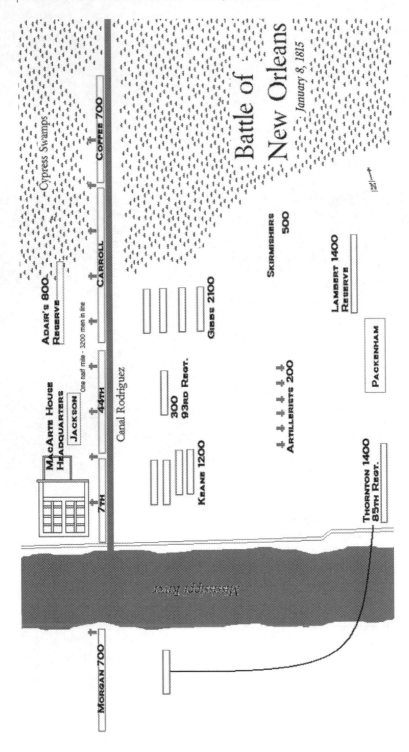

Battle of
New Orleans

January 8, 1815

THE SOUTHERN FRONT

CHAPTER 9

The Empire Shielded:
Background to the War in the South, 1811–1818

The portion of the War of 1812 that erupted in the Old South was very confusing, not only in the day in which it was fought, but to readers and historians today. The shear numbers of entities engaged in political combinations or adversarial relationships is confusing enough, but the complexity of these relationships only adds to the struggle to make sense of the war in this theater.

First, we had the young and exuberant United States, growing rapidly and bumping up against the incumbent Native Americans in the Old Southwest region. The Indians there were far from monolithic, even though they may have been lumped in American and European minds as the "The Five Civilized Tribes." To the east were the Cherokees - intelligent, somewhat trusting, and able to see the handwriting on the wall, given the arrival of vast hoards of white settlers to the east and among them. They chose to embrace the white man's way, adopting forms of government, laws, and even a written language (and a corresponding press) very similar in concept to the European model. To the west, along the Mississippi River and its shorter tributaries lived the Chickasaws and Choctaws. Because of their exposure to white commerce and civilization along the Mississippi, they too chose accommodation with the white man's culture, although not to the extent of the Cherokees. To the south, the war-like, fractious, and dissimilar Seminoles lived on the Florida Peninsula, resisting any kind of acculturation with European civilization. The Seminoles were so persistent and stubborn in their pursuit of freedom that as an entire people they never were completely subjugated by any foreign power. Indeed, some one hundred years later, when the United States entered World War II, descendents of the remnant of those Seminoles who retreated far into the Florida Everglades refused to register for the draft, claiming to be not Americans, but members of the unconquered Seminole nation.

In the middle of this diffuse Native American civilization stood the Creek nation. Possibly the most bipolar tribe of all, the Creeks were split into two factions that grew more dissimilar as the years passed. The Lower Creeks resided in the western Georgia border area. Like the Cherokees to their north, the Lower Creeks slowly embraced the white man's societal values, but also like the Cherokees would be cruelly repaid for their willing accommodation. To the west in the Coosa/Tallapoosa River valleys lived the Upper Creeks. The Upper Creeks were physically more remote from white civilization than several other tribes in the region, and thus were less acclimated to European/American society. As time went on, these two groups grew further apart, as the older, more powerful and entrenched leadership of the Lower Creeks became more assimilated to the white man's ways. At the same time, the Upper Creeks grew more reactive and fell back more and more on traditional Indian ways. The conflict of these two societies, which broke into open civil war in 1813, was the impetus for the beginning of war in the Old South.

Against the above backdrop, America engaged in the War of 1812 with Great Britain, supposedly over the impressment of American sailors on the open sea for British duty, but more realistically, as a continuation of the American Revolutionary War. Britain had never really given up hope of reconquering her North American empire, and maintained pressure on the United States both diplomatically and geographically. She applied pressure on the north from Canada, and on the east from her overwhelming navy. On the south, she engaged in an interesting diplomatic combination with an age-old imperial relative, Spain.

In Europe, French emperor Napoleon Bonaparte had risen to power and conquered most of continental Europe, while applying great pressure to Britain's holdings in the Middle East. Napoleon could not match Britain's sea power, which had rebuffed him at both the Battle of the Nile and Trafalgar. Checkmated at sea, Napoleon turned to land, hoping to capture or dominate all ports in Europe and thus economically squeeze Britain into submission. In the early 1800s, he moved against the decaying homeland of the Empire of

Spain, attempting to add more blocks to his continental European fortress. The fighting on the Iberian Peninsula was fierce, and Spain reached out to her ancient enemy, Britain, for assistance. Britain, happy to add any counter weight she could to the scale of war against Napoleon, came to Spain's assistance as a formal ally.

But for Spain, this assistance came as a double-edged sword. While the aid in the ground war in Europe was much needed and appreciated, it also meant that an allied Britain gained access to Spain's still vast colonial holdings. Two of these holdings were East and West Florida. Britain had ceded these colonies to Spain at the end of the American Revolutionary War, preferring them to be held by a weak, crumbling European power which she could easily dominate versus giving them up to a young, vibrant, expansive United States. (Even then, it was apparent Britain was looking forward to the day when she could reestablish her dominance in all of North America.)

The relationship between Great Britain and Spain in the New World during this period was extraordinarily complex. In general, it is sufficient to say that Britain's assistance to Spain in combatting Napoleon in Europe influenced Spain to be somewhat amenable to British intrigues in her North American possessions. Britain now used her access to Spanish East and West Florida to unofficially foment unrest among the Native American tribes of the southern United States via independent merchants and low-level quasi-agents. There was precious little Spain could do about this, given the weakness of her military resources overall and especially her military resources in North America. Spain had just as much about which to be concerned with the expansive and aggressive United States, and thus was little disposed to restrain her trouble-fomenting ally, Great Britain.

Further adding to the confusion was the French sale of the Louisiana Territory to the United States as the *Louisiana Purchase* of 1803. The border between French (and now American) Louisiana and Spanish West Florida was never clearly delineated. It was not clear whether important possessions such as the city of Mobile were a part of the *Purchase* or a part of Spanish West Florida, adding to tensions both in the immediate area and between the United States and Spanish central governments.

Thus as we look back from today's view at the then-contemporary United States standpoint, the entire American campaign in the Old Southwest in the period from 1811 to 1818 can be viewed as an elimination of threats:

1) Elimination of the immediate Native American threat: The Creek War: 1813-'14.
2) Elimination of the British threat: Pensacola, New Orleans, and Mobile: 1814-'15.
3) Elimination of the long-term European/Native American threat: The Patriot War: 1811-'14; Prospect Bluff: 1816; and the First Seminole War: 1817-'18.

Each of the segments of these conflicts in the Old Southwest was unique, yet interrelated. Each had an impact on the independence and viability not only of the Old South, where they were fought, but also of the Old Northwest Territory as well, and ultimately on the Miami Valley/Great Black Swamp Corridor. We will examine several phases in the American elimination of these threats in the next several chapters.

CHAPTER 10

The Empire Shielded: The Creek War Begins: 1813

Tecumseh was dead, but his influence lived on.

The great Shawnee warrior breathed his last in mortal combat with his implacable foes – William Henry Harrison and the United States Second North Western Army. Yet, Tecumseh's impact on the War of 1812, and the history of the Trans-Appalachian area, was not over. After a heated confrontation with William Henry Harrison in July, 1811, Tecumseh made good his threat to attempt to build a great Midwestern/Southern Native American confederacy, in an effort to block the flow of American setters rushing onto Indian lands. He traveled south to the lands of the "Five Civilized Tribes" – the Choctaws, Chickasaws, Cherokees, Creeks, and Seminoles. His words found unreceptive ears in the lands of the Choctaws, Chickasaws, and Cherokees; these tribes, due to the positions of their native lands, had many social, economic, and even blood ties to the Americans living among them. The Seminoles lived far to the south, in Spanish East and West Florida, and were similarly unreceptive to Tecumseh's approach.

The story was quite different with the Creeks; the Creek people were a nation divided. The so-called Lower Creeks lived to the east of and along the Chattahoochee River valley. With the Lower Creeks' close proximity to and association with the white settlers in their midst, this group had begun to assimilate white culture into their own. Many had blood ties to the settlers, particularly with Scottish traders from several generations previous to the 1800s. Due west of the Lower Creeks was the land of the Upper Creeks. Their more remote physical location, far inland from any trade routes, limited their contacts with European/American civilization; thus the Upper Creeks clung more intensely to the "old ways."

In early 1811, a religious revival swept the Upper Creek nation. This theme of this awakening was a call for closer observance of traditional values and religious beliefs, and further rejection of white society's culture. Hard on the heels of this revival came the visit of Shawnee leader Tecumseh to the united Creek capital of Tuckabatchee in late-October, 1811. Tecumseh's overtures carried special weight; his mother was a Creek, and in that matrilineal society, this made Tecumseh a Creek in the tribe's eyes – a brother from the north. His message of Native American unity, adherence to the old ways as a mental and social bulwark against white hegemony, and an independent confederated Native American state as a buffer between the Americans in Kentucky and the British in Canada found fertile, receptive minds within the younger, militant Upper Creeks. His words exacerbated an already radical trend. On the other hand, the older, more established leadership of the Lower Creeks (headed by Big Warrior) carefully listened to the great leader's message, deliberately rejected it, and politely asked Tecumseh to leave.

Some Upper Creeks (also known as the "Red Sticks" for their practice of sending a bundle of sticks to another group to denote a special occasion; if the sticks were red, the bundle indicated the number of days until a war began) embraced not only Tecumseh's *words*. A group of Red Sticks, led by Little Warrior, returned to the northwest with him and took part in the "Raisin River Massacre" of American troops on January 22, 1813. Their bloodlust thus whetted, this group engaged in a series of bloody massacres of settlers in the Duck River area of Tennessee on the way back south again. At nearly the same time, a series of murders within the Creek nation shocked the tribe. These massacres and murders raised the ire of both the Tennessee settlers and the conservatives among the Lower Creeks. Big Warrior, at the behest of both his leadership council and American Indian agents, sent committees called "law menders" to execute the perpetrators of these crimes - including Little Warrior. The executions were completed as directed. "Creeks killing Creeks" convinced the Red Stick leadership that the conservative power structure of the Lower Creek nation was bent on their destruction. The Red Sticks determined to strike back by attacking Big Warrior's village, the seat of Creek internal government, Tuckabatchee.

In the early summer of 1813, a substantial number of Red Sticks descended on Tuckabatchee and demanded the surrender of Big Warrior to them in retribution for the killing of Little Warrior. The village refused to give up its leader and fighting broke out. A call went out to surrounding villages for assistance. The timely arrival of 200 warriors from the neighboring Lower Creek village of Coweta allowed the Tuckabatchee defenders to escape that village before the Red Sticks overran and burned it. As the defenders retreated toward Coweta, the victorious Red Sticks rampaged throughout the surrounding countryside, killing virtually everything that moved – Lower Creeks, whites, and livestock.

The Red Sticks were bolstered by their victory, yet sobered by the knowledge that at most they could muster only 4,000 warriors to wage the civil war against their brethren. They reasoned that if they could acquire more supplies and ammunition, perhaps they could defeat the more numerous Lower Creeks through superior logistics.

In an ominous parallel to the Northwestern Theater, the British (through their Spanish patrons, who in Europe were allied with the British to oppose Napoleon) maintained a malignant presence in the Spanish colony of West Florida. The Spanish military presence was so weak in the Floridas that the British could basically move and do as they pleased in both colonies, and the Spanish leaders there essentially had to acquiesce to the arrangement. Anyway, a strong Native American presence to the north of the colony was good for both the British and the Spanish as a counterweight to the expanding United States.

Peter McQueen, a Red Stick leader of both Scottish and Creek descent, led a 350-man expedition to the West Florida capital of Pensacola to bargain with either (or both) the Spanish or the British for the purchase of arms and supplies in July, 1813. The Spanish were reluctant to provide the Red Sticks with weapons, because they were not officially involved in either the Creek civil war or the British-American War of 1812. Yet, under pressure from the dominant British, against whom he was powerless to resist, the Spanish governor of West Florida supplied McQueen with a half-ton of gunpowder and enough ammunition for five rounds per warrior.

McQueen and his party started back north with their supplies toward the Red Stick villages in Mississippi Territory. The leadership of the Mississippi Territorial Militia learned of the Red Stick expedition, and grew concerned at the prospect of militant Native Americans in possession of large quantities of gunpowder and ammunition. On July 27th, 1813, approximately 80 miles north of Pensacola, this expedition was intercepted and attacked by between 180 and 200 Mississippi militiamen under the command of Colonel James Caller, the senior militia officer in the area, at Burnt Corn Creek, Mississippi Territory. Caller's soldiers ambushed the warriors as they were crossing the creek, and the ferocity of their attack caused the Native Americans to scatter in confusion. However, the undisciplined militia failed to pursue the scattering Indians, choosing instead to examine and plunder the wagons full of supplies. McQueen was able to gather and regroup a contingent of approximately 100 warriors in a heavily wooded swamp nearby. From this redoubt, the Native Americans savagely counterattacked the unsuspecting soldiers and sent them into a headlong flight away from Burnt Corn Creek.

It was never established how many casualties were suffered on the American side at Burnt Corn Creek, but the Red Sticks lost about 20 men and most of their supplies. However, the Red Sticks were widely heralded to have routed an American military unit, and the opening white-Indian battle of the Creek War was rightly viewed as a Native American victory. As such, the battle had an ominous portent on the frontier for the immediate future.

As the situation between the settlers and Indians had become more and more tense in 1812 and 1813, the settlers built hastily erected wooden stockades across the Mississippi frontier. These forts were intended as local defense centers if hostilities suddenly broke into open conflict. After the militia's defeat at the Battle of Burnt Corn Creek, Mississippi settlers began congregating in these regional defense centers.

One of these rather poorly designed forts was Fort Mims, along the southern reaches of the Alabama River. After the nearby Battle of

Burnt Corn Creek, about 180 white, Lower Creek, and mixed blood men, women, and children crowded into the fort. In anticipation of coming hostilities, 120 Mississippi Territorial Militia soldiers under the command of Major Daniel Beasley were ordered to the fort to reinforce and garrison it.

Major Beasley led the defense forces in a rather cavalier manner, given the nature of the threat to his command. He sent out only a few undermanned scouting patrols, which were not very vigilant and made only cursory searches of the area surrounding Fort Mims. The main gate of the fort was propped open, and remained in this state for so long that sand drifted against it in sufficient quantity to render it immobile. The day before the attack, two local slave boys ran breathlessly into the fort, reporting to have seen large numbers of Native Americans bedecked in war paint, in close proximity to the area surrounding the fort. Another lackluster patrol found nothing in the area, and the two boys were whipped for giving a false alarm. Major Beasley was then alleged to have become drunk shortly thereafter.

Red Stick leader Peter McQueen, Paddy Welsh, and newly recruited military mastermind William Weatherford gathered 750 warriors from 13 towns to strike Fort Mims in retribution for the unprovoked militia attack on the Red Stick pack train at Burnt Corn Creek. At noon on August 30th, 1813, several Red Stick warriors ran headlong through the open gate of Fort Mims. The fort's sentries, to their credit, quickly determined what was happening and shot several of the attackers. However, the attack swelled into a torrent of onrushing Red Stick attackers. Major Beasley himself attempted to close the fort doors, and was still struggling to free them from the sand as he was killed.

Red Stick warriors, led by Welsh, crowded against the fort's walls and fired through portholes located four feet above the ground into the crowded, milling mass of soldiers and settlers inside the fort, sowing panic and confusion there within. As a portion of the Red Stick attack force gained control of the portholes, the remainder rushed into the fort. The terrified occupants of the fort scattered into hiding places within the fort, destroying efforts to develop a unified defense of the interior. Red Stick attackers set several of the interior buildings afire, forcing the inhabitants into tighter and tighter quarters in the remaining buildings. Finally crowded so tightly that they could no longer load their weapons, a few elected to cut their way through the outer walls and attempt an escape into the surrounding countryside, while others bolted into the fort's interior and were quickly cut down. Surrender was not an option, as the revenge-minded Red Sticks killed all they captured – men, women, and children.

Several weeks after the battle, relief parties arrived at the fort. To their horror, they found the corpses of 247 defenders inside. In an indication of the ferocity of the battle within the walls of Fort Mims, they also found the remains of about 100 Red Stick attackers. News of the massacre spread rapidly, and cries of fear mixed with outraged calls for the destruction of the Red Stick nation.

A civil war between internal factions of the fractured Creek tribe now exploded into another, more destructive phase of the frontier War of 1812 – a southwestern conflict between European-supplied Native Americans and a fledgling, struggling United States. A massive attempt to answer the call for war against the Native Americans, reminiscent of that which was just now reaching a decisive climax in the Northwest Territory, was beginning in the Old Southwest. It would rival and mirror its northern counterpart in many ways.

CHAPTER 11

The Empire Shielded: Marginally Effective Campaigns Against the Creeks – 1813-'14

The massacre at Fort Mims created much the same outrage among the settlers of the Southwest as the River Raisin Massacre generated in the Northwest. The cries for revenge were, if anything, more vociferous among Tennesseans, Georgians, and Mississippians than those cries raised in Kentucky, Ohio, and Indiana Territory after River Raisin. Yet, a set of problems and situations every bit as vexing as those encountered in the Old Northwest bedeviled the war effort in the Southwest, and kept the small Native American Red Stick nation viable as an enemy for much longer than the facts would indicate was possible.

The first problem for the United States was a lack of unified control among the state militias which made up the bulk of the southwestern fighting forces arrayed against the Red Sticks. Two states and one territory raised a total of four armies to wage war against the Red Stick nation, yet there was virtually no communication among them, and coordination in the armies' deployment and movement was almost non-existent. As a consequence, the Red Sticks were able to shift their meager forces and supplies to meet various crises at different times and places. Although they rarely won or even broke even in the battles after Fort Mims, the Red Sticks were repeatedly able to parry the uncoordinated thrusts of the Americans, and thus lived to fight another day.

The Red Sticks had several unconventional "allies" aiding them in their efforts to survive. A problem continually vexing the Americans was an on-going lack of supplies to the forward fighting troops. Time and again throughout the war, the victorious American armies were unable to press an advantage gained in battle because they did not have the supplies to range forward and totally vanquish a defeated foe. Many times, armies moved forward from military bases to attack the Red Sticks with only a few days' supplies in their supply trains because promised provisions had not arrived. The army commanders pressed forward in the hope that the capture of an enemy village would secure supplies contained in the village and thus enable the army to surge on and fully destroy a defeated foe. In those cases where the supplies were not secured, the armies were forced to make a retrograde movement toward their conventional sources of supply, in hopes that the rearward logistics officers had forwarded needed supplies and ammunition toward them.

A factor which worsened the already critical supply problem was a nemesis common to all military operations in frontier areas: lack of infrastructure – namely, inadequate roads. The roads in the southwestern wilderness were hardly better than those found in the Old Northwest: Indian paths, or the slightly better military corduroy roads. Even when supplies and ammunition existed for use by the advanced units of the armies, getting those supplies forward over the rough, crude roads, which were always subject to interdiction by hostile Red Stick raiding parties, was a chancy proposition.

Many times, the army commanders were forced to move against their foes for a reason much simpler than a lack of supplies: they had to move while they still had an army with which to fight. A characteristic of the militia raised in the southwestern states was *short terms of enlistment* - usually 60 to 90 days. With this very short time frame in which to work, several of the commanders were forced to march, with or without supplies, in order to at least do some damage to the enemy while they still had recruits on the armies' duty roster. More than once, an army was reduced to a short-term raid against a single relatively close target, although the commander would have preferred to properly train his troops and use them in a well-balanced, coordinated offensive against multiple objectives.

All of the above problems could have been eased were it not for one unfortunate geographical factor that created a deep division of authority. As the war progressed, Secretary of War John Armstrong found it necessary to divide the nation into "military districts" to raise and move critical men and supplies between the various active fronts. The Sixth Military District was comprised of the states of North Carolina, South Carolina, and Georgia. Command of this district was assigned to Major General Thomas Pinckney, with headquarters in Charleston, South Carolina. The Seventh Military District was made up of Louisiana, Tennessee, and Mississippi Territory. Command of this district was originally given to Major General James Wilkinson, but by the time the Creek War broke out in July, 1813, command of the Seventh District had been assigned to Major General J. Thomas Flournoy, headquartered at New Orleans in the state of Louisiana.

While the concept of military districts was sound, the composition of the Sixth and Seventh Military Districts created several problems in the prosecution of the war against the Red Stick Creeks. The first problem was that the central boundary between the Sixth and Seventh Districts was the Western Georgia state line: basically the Chattahoochie River valley. This was precisely the area where a large portion of the Creek Nation was centered and where in fact many of the battles of the Creek War subsequently occurred. Essentially, this meant that neither senior general had full command of the main physical theater of operations in the war.

Second, with Pinckney headquartered in Charleston and Flournoy in New Orleans, there was no way for the two commanders to communicate with each other. The Red Sticks were located almost exactly midway between the district headquarters, there were no alternate roads or other means of land communication between the Mississippi and the south Atlantic seaboard ports, and the British controlled the sea between New Orleans and Charleston. Coordination of troop movements and resources was impossible under the existing command structure.

Finally, the choice of J. Thomas Flournoy as commander of the Seventh District was unfortunate. Flournoy had almost no military experience prior to the opening of the War of 1812, but he had good political connections with the Madison Administration. Besides being virtually ignorant militarily, Flournoy had several character flaws which inhibited his effectiveness as an administrator. He got along with almost no one in the district, and especially angered the local political elite in the New Orleans area to the point where they would no longer cooperate with him on any issue. Flournoy had a personality weakness in that he was easily offended, and sought revenge for any slight, real or imagined. These weaknesses were almost disastrous to the coming American war effort.

Secretary of War Armstrong could see all the weaknesses of the command situation and structure in the Old South as the Creek War escalated from civil war to open warfare against the United States. He knew that one commander must be named to control overall administrative efforts in the war against the Creeks in the Southwest. He gave this command to Major General Thomas Pinckney of the Sixth Military District.

General Flournoy immediately took offense to this move. Betraying his lack of strategic vision, he could not see that the battles of Burnt Corn Creek and Fort Mims were leading to a general war in the Southwest with the Red Sticks, or even a possible combination of Red Sticks and British against the United States. He also could not appreciate the logistic and communication nightmare a split command of the operational theater would create. All he could envision was a conspicuous slight to his command authority, possibly initiated by internal political or military enemies in Washington. In his fury, he halted all military preparations and support for the Creek War being planned in the Seventh District and forbade subordinates from cooperating in the war effort. This included those plans and preparations for the army being developed by the operational commander of the Mississippi Territorial Militia, Brigadier General Ferdinand L. Claiborne.

General Claiborne, like General Harrison in the Northwest, was a holder of dual commissions at the outbreak of the Creek War. He was Brigadier General, Mississippi Territorial Militia, and also Brigadier General, Mississippi Volunteers, U.S. Army. As commanding general of the militia, he gathered state troops at St. Stephens in the second week of October, 1813. General Flournoy initially sent the Third and Seventh U.S. Regular Infantry and the Mississippi Volunteer Dragoons toward St. Stephens to reinforce Claiborne. However, after Armstrong's decision to give Pinckney command of the theater, Flournoy, in a fit of anger, recalled the Regulars to New Orleans and dismissed the Mississippi Dragoons from federal service.

Brig. General Claiborne vigorously objected to Maj. General Flournoy's withdrawal of a considerable number of his best troops. He barely had enough militia in southern Mississippi Territory to maintain a defensive posture, let alone mount an offense against the Red Sticks. Claiborne argued so strongly against his commander's orders that Flournoy reprimanded him for insubordination. Yet, Claiborne's well-reasoned arguments eventually won Flournoy over. The Seventh District's commander partially relented and authorized Claiborne to move ahead with the offensive against the Red Sticks, even sending the Third Infantry to rejoin the campaign.

By November 13th, 1813, Brig. General Claiborne had assembled 1,200 regulars and militia near the mouth of the Alabama River in southern Mississippi Territory. His plan was to work his way up the Alabama River valley, fortifying the valley with a series of small forts, killing Red Sticks, and destroying villages and supplies as he went. His ultimate goal was to drive to the confluence of the Coosa and Tallapoosa Rivers, where armies from Georgia, East Tennessee, and West Tennessee would converge as well. The four armies would crush the Red Sticks in the center of this unavoidable vice.

General Flournoy's resistance to the war effort had dealt a fatal blow to Claiborne's ultimate plan, however. Many of his militia soldiers were 90-day recruits. The delay in the arrival of the Third Infantry, coupled with the plan to build forts along the route of the march, meant that General Claiborne could not reach the confluence of the Coosa and Tallapoosa before the militia's terms of service ran out. Thus, Claiborne had to modify his plan. He now strove to move about 100 miles up the Alabama River to Econochaca (also known as *The Holy Ground*), the home village of William Weatherford, and there attempt to force a decisive battle with as many Red Stick warriors as he could engage.

Weatherford warily monitored the American army's progress up the Alabama River. He noted that as Claiborne advanced, he built forts and garrisoned them with soldiers from his army. The farther Claiborne moved north, the weaker his army became. Weatherford reckoned he could meet Claiborne's army at Econochaca with a fair chance for victory.

Weatherford was hampered by the holy men of Econochaca in his efforts to engage and defeat the American army, however. In particular, Josiah Francis (Hillis Hadjo), a leading Red Stick mystic, convinced many of the warriors that he had placed an invisible barrier around the village, and any white man that stepped inside the ring would instantly die. When the American army approached Econochaca in three columns on December 23rd, 1813 (Major Joseph Carson commanding the right, Colonel Gilbert Russell commanding the center, and Major Henry Cassells commanding the left), the right column attacked first and immediately entered the ring without falling dead. Many of the Red Stick warriors, fearing the strength of the Americans to overcome Indian magic, immediately fled the scene of battle. Weatherford and the contingent of warriors who remained with him fought fiercely against overwhelming odds in a doomed cause. Weatherford himself fought to the last, escaping the net closing around the village by leaping with his horse off a 30-foot cliff into the Alabama River. Horse and rider then swam across the river to safety.

The Battle of Econochaca was over. The Red Sticks lost 33 killed and two hundred houses destroyed. The Americans lost one killed and 20 wounded. On December 24th, Claiborne's army moved a few miles north and destroyed another village. Then, with his militia's terms of service almost expired, Claiborne retreated back down his line of communication bastions to Fort Claiborne, where he disbanded his militia and directed the Third Infantry to garrison the line of forts. Claiborne resigned his commissions on January 17th, 1814.

General Claiborne's offensive had been somewhat successful. Although he had not attained his goal of cornering a large segment of the Red Stick fighting force and destroying it, he had forced the Red Sticks to the north toward the other American armies. His army had destroyed a considerable amount of Red Stick lodging and supplies, and its fortification of the Alabama River valley meant that the Red Sticks could no longer escape south to avoid the other American armies closing in from the east, northeast, and northwest. However, Claiborne's forced disbanding of his southern army meant than one of the other American armies must strike the fatal blow in the war against the Red Sticks.

One of these other attacking columns was the army comprised of the Georgia State Militia, under the command of Brigadier (later Major) General John Floyd. In September, 1813, Floyd was authorized by then Georgia Governor David Mitchell to gather the state militia at Fort Hawkins in west-central Georgia for a campaign against the Red Stick Creeks. Floyd's overall plan was to march westward to the confluence of the Coosa and Tallapoosa Rivers in conjunction with three other American armies coming from other directions, as previously described. General Floyd, however, having once assembled approximately 2,000 soldiers at Fort Hawkins, was not supported by Governor Mitchell and his successor, Governor Peter Early. A shortage of food and ammunition, plus a miserable logistics system to distribute the supplies to the forward troops, meant that General Floyd was required to stay at Fort Hawkins for two months as he laboriously built up a minimum supply level. The delay in turn meant that, like General Claiborne's army far to the southwest, Floyd would be unable to rendezvous with the other armies at the confluence of the Coosa and Tallapoosa Rivers.

By mid-November, General Floyd had accumulated an approximate 20-day supply of rations, and determined that he must move quickly to engage the Red Sticks before his militia's terms of enlistment further expired (Floyd was already down to about 950 soldiers through enlistment term attrition by this time). Under orders from Major General Pinckney to march to the Chattahoochie River and build a forward base, Floyd marched there and quickly erected Fort Mitchell. William McIntosh and approximately 400 allied Lower Creek warriors joined Floyd's army at Fort Mitchell at this time for action against their common enemy.

Floyd set as his army's target the Red Stick village of Autosse, about 60 miles due west from Fort Mitchell. While Autosse was not a key in the Red Stick's defense scheme, it was at least an enemy target in close enough proximity to Fort Mitchell that Floyd could quickly reach it in the time his army's term had remaining to it. The Georgia Militia set a rapid pace, and reached Autosse, on the banks of the Tallapoosa about 20 miles north of its confluence with the Coosa, on the morning of November 29th, 1813.

Major General Floyd approached the village with his army in three columns, his artillery leading the right column. His plan was to envelop Autosse with the right and left columns, surrounding and crushing the Red Sticks. However, as the left flank advanced, it discovered another small village further downstream, forcing it to make a large detour further left to surround both towns. The large sweep to the left was too much for the small army, leaving gaps between the left flank and the remainder of the forces. The Red Sticks, upon discovery of the attack, capitalized on these gaps, and the battle devolved into brutal hand-to-hand combat. The fighting on the left flank was fierce. The Red Sticks at Autosse fought well, but ultimately, American numbers, artillery, and small arms fire proved too much to overcome. Eventually, Red Stick survivors faded away to the north, some of Floyd's troops in pursuit.

The battle ended by 9:00 AM. The Red Sticks lost approximately 200 dead and had 400 dwellings destroyed. They forced the Georgia Militia to pay a high price for its victory, though, as the militia lost 11 killed and 54 wounded in the assault (General Floyd was among those wounded).

His supplies now low, General Floyd, though preferring to press the fleeing foe, was forced to return to Fort Mitchell to the east. A group of Red Sticks reassembled and attempted to attack the rearguard of the retreating army, but were successfully repelled by militia troops.

Having attained Fort Mitchell safely and recuperating from his injuries, Floyd now had to cope with his recurring problems of supplies and recruits. For a full six weeks, he slowly gathered both at Fort Mitchell. Painfully ignored by the state authorities, Floyd once again developed the minimum amount of supplies necessary for an advance. He also had 1,300 Georgia and Carolina volunteers and McIntosh's 400 warriors as an assault force. Many of his Army's enlistment terms were due to expire on February 22, 1814, so in mid-January, General Floyd's Georgia Militia swung back to the offense once again.

Floyd's army advanced about 40 miles into Mississippi Territory, where the general paused to build Fort Hull as a small intermediate supply and defense bastion. Floyd now discovered that many Red Stick warriors were building fortifications in the area near Hoithlewallee, a village not far from Fort Hull. Floyd immediately moved toward the concentration of Red Sticks, reaching Calabee Swamp on January 26th, 1814. By chance, General Andrew Jackson, commander of the West Tennessee Militia, heard of Floyd's advance and moved south from his base at Fort Strother to support it. This was the only time in the Creek War that anything like a coordinated offensive between two advancing columns was attempted (we will discuss this operation more fully in the next chapter).

William Weatherford probably never heard of Napoleon Bonaparte, but as a natural military leader, he intuitively knew the value of Napoleon's strategy of maintaining a central position between two superior advancing forces. Weatherford kept his 1,800 warriors concentrated between both Floyd and Jackson. Noting Floyd's Georgia Militia was moving more lethargically than the energetic Jackson-led West Tennessee Militia, Weatherford decided to strike the more rapidly moving Jackson before he could unite with Floyd.

Once Weatherford had blunted Jackson's advance at Emuckfau and Enitachopco Creeks, he turned to deal with Floyd's Georgia Militia. At this time, Weatherford's ability to influence his peers waned slightly. Although Weatherford could not convince the other Red Stick military leaders to adopt his tactics for the prosecution of the actual ambush of Floyd's army, he had performed a substantial service by properly positioning his army to attack and repulse Jackson first. Approximately 30 minutes before sunrise on January 27th, 1814, the Red Sticks, following tactics developed by other war leaders, fiercely attacked and streamed into the Georgia Militia's encampment near Calabee Creek. Floyd's army was completely surprised and nearly routed, but Floyd quickly gained control of the army. Even though the battle had become a general hand-to-hand melee, Floyd utilized his cannon to begin breaking the back of the assault. The Red Sticks, realizing the threat the artillery represented to their assault, made several fanatical charges in an attempt to capture the cannon. The

Georgia artillerymen suffered a higher attrition rate than the rest of the army, but the cannon were successfully defended.

With the coming of daylight, Floyd organized a portion of his army for an advance and personally led a bayonet charge into the teeth of the Red Stick assault. The Red Sticks staggered under the ferocity of the counterattack, and were routed shortly thereafter. Units of cavalry slashed after the fleeing Red Stick warriors, inflicting further casualties on the decimated foe.

The bloody Battle of Calabee exacted a high price on both Red Stick and militia forces. The Red Stick Creeks suffered 70 dead and 132 wounded, while Floyd's combined Georgia, Carolina, and Lower Creek allies had 22 dead and 147 wounded.

With many wounded soldiers, and supplies again reaching dangerously low levels, Major General John Floyd and his army retreated eastward to Fort Mitchell on the Chattahoochie River. Red Stick Creeks returned to Hoithlewallee and the Calabee Swamp area unmolested. The damaged Georgia Militia spent the rest of the war guarding the Georgia frontier against incursions from marauding Red Stick raiders and the Atlantic coast from British sea-borne raids.

Like Claiborne's Mississippi Territorial Militia to the southwest, Floyd's Georgia Militia ultimately was not able to occupy and defend the areas it attacked. Yet the Georgians were successful in engaging and destroying large numbers of Red Stick warriors, though they failed to strike the knockout blow against the Red Sticks.

Even as marginally successful as both Claiborne and Floyd were, they still were more effective than the northeastern-most prong of the four advances into the Red Stick nation, represented by Major General John Cocke's East Tennessee Militia. This politically motivated and dominated campaign was characterized by the almost total mismanagement of strategy on the part of General Cocke.

Tennessee Governor Willie (pronounced *Wiley*) Blount took a proactive stance in the War of 1812 almost from the declaration of hostilities. In November, 1812, the federal government asked Governor Blount to raise 1,500 militia for the defense of New Orleans, which Blount forthrightly provided. Although these soldiers did not make it to New Orleans and were subsequently recalled to Tennessee before duty in the far southwest, Governor Blount maintained a rotating force of 1,500 Tennessee militia in a state of readiness thereafter. With the outbreak of the Creek War, Blount again acted decisively, raising an additional 3,500 militia, and working hard to raise money to support the state troops (even to the point of securing personally guaranteed loans for the militia's use in obtaining supplies and ammunition). Governor Blount was an astute politician, and realizing he governed a very long and diverse state, he decided to raise troops from both the eastern and western parts of the state. Those raised in the western portion were dubbed the West Tennessee Militia; command was given to Major General Andrew Jackson, and the army was based out of Nashville. The army raised in the east was named the East Tennessee Militia; command was assigned to Major General John Cocke, and the base of operations was Knoxville.

Governor Blount gave the eastern command to General Cocke with the express order that Cocke was to march his army into Creek territory, complete a rendezvous with General Jackson's army, and turn command of the East Tennessee Militia over to Jackson. Cocke was then to serve as a subordinate to Jackson as second-in-command of the combined army.

This is where the trouble began. Cocke, also an astute politician, realized that once the rendezvous was completed, all the glory and political value to be derived from the campaign would be Jackson's, a favorite of Blount. Cocke therefore decided to eschew compliance with his orders, make a slow march to the periphery of the battle zone, and conduct parallel and independent operations east of Jackson for as long as he could. While Jackson moved south from Nashville through Huntsville and established Fort Strother at the northern edge of the theater, Cocke moved in a southwesterly direction from Knoxville and established Fort Armstrong as *his* advanced base on the northeast periphery of the theater, about 70 miles east of Fort Strother.

Cocke was not immune from the lack of supplies and logistics that plagued the other three armies. When supplies dwindled at Fort Armstrong, Cocke decided to make one raid on enemy territory before his supplies gave out completely. The closest hostile targets of any consequence to Fort Armstrong were the Creek Hillabee Towns, in the southern foothills of the Appalachian Mountain chain. Cocke prepared to strike what were known to be the fierce and hostile inhabitants of the Hillabee villages.

What General Cocke did not know because of poor communications was that General Jackson had just completed a devastating attack on the Red Stick village of Talladega only a few days before. A large group of Hillabees had helped defend Talladega from Jackson's rampaging infantry, and had been so thoroughly beaten that they immediately sued for peace, which Jackson had granted on November 17th, 1813. Just one day later, the East Tennessee Militia's cavalry, commanded by Brigadier General James White, assisted by a small contingent of allied Cherokees under Colonel Gideon Morgan, and both under the direct orders of Major General John Cocke, descended on the Hillabee Towns of Little Oakfusky and Genalga. Just before daylight, the mounted command thoroughly destroyed both villages. White and Morgan then surrounded the principal village in the Hillabee complex. The Creeks in Hillabee, believing they were at peace with the Americans, were caught completely by surprise and offered little resistance as White and Morgan thundered in to attack at first light. A total of 64 Creek warriors were killed, 29 were wounded, and 237 captives were bound back to Fort Armstrong, where General Cocke awaited news of the attack.

With the cavalry's return, Cocke realized he was out of supplies and that the terms of enlistment for the majority of his militia would soon be up. He decided now was the time to move to Fort Strother and rendezvous with his nominal superior, General Jackson. Jackson was furious at Cocke's action in attacking the peaceful Hillabees – indeed, the Hillabees, feeling massively betrayed, now became implacable enemies of the Americans and vowed to fight to the death. They were in fact some of the last Red Sticks to cease combat against the Americans. Jackson held his tongue, knowing he needed Cocke's troops to move against the seat of Red Stick power deep in the Mississippi Territory. When he found that Cocke's men were near the end of their enlistments, his temper exploded. Now Cocke would need much of Jackson's meager hoard of supplies just to get his men back to Nashville! He angrily ordered Cocke and the soon-to-be discharged militia north to Tennessee: Cocke was to inform Governor Blount more recruits and supplies were needed to prosecute the war against the Red Stick Creeks.

Cocke's campaign was worse than useless. Not only had he failed to effectively engage legitimate Red Stick opponents, he had made further mortal enemies among the Creeks, and had used vital supplies and ammunition in doing so! It remained for the rough-hewn, tough-talking, temperamental volcano of a man who currently commanded the West Tennessee Militia to salvage the Creek War of 1813-'14 for the United States of America.

CHAPTER 12

The Empire Shielded:
The Creek War Molds a General, 1813–'14

Governor Willie Blount may not have been the greatest politician ever to come out of the state of Tennessee, but he certainly must be ranked among the shrewdest. In 1812, Blount was charged by the federal government with raising the state militia of Tennessee in defense of the country. This responsibility included appointing many of the higher officers of the militia, including the commanding generals. His main goal should have been to appoint officers that were capable of running the army. However, politician that he was, Blount realized this was an outstanding opportunity to reward political patrons as well. If these appointees were competent soldiers, so much the better!

Further, Governor Blount realized he governed a state with at least two distinct geographical/political sections. The inhabitants of the eastern highlands were distinctly different from the western plainsmen in personal viewpoints and political tastes. The federal officials didn't tell Blount *how* to develop the militia; they merely told him to *do* it. When the Creek War began in 1813, Blount decided to split the militia into two armies – one from the east and one from the west.

Blount surveyed the many political candidates and patrons who had helped him get in office, stay in office, and govern the state over the years. Of the candidates from the east, he chose John Cocke to lead the army dubbed the East Tennessee Militia. In Cocke, he chose a good politician, but a poor general.

In the west as well, there were many people that had helped Governor Blount over the years. One was a gaunt, fiery, 46-year-old lawyer from Nashville. The lawyer had long been involved in Tennessee politics, attending the Tennessee Territory Constitutional Convention in January and February, 1796. He became the first federal congressional representative from Tennessee in October, 1796, but he had not made a good impression in Philadelphia. Temperamental, moody, and angrily passionate, he had clashed with the Jeffersonians. When Willie Blount had been removed from his Senate seat for murky land grant deals, the lawyer from Nashville had assumed Blount's seat. Depressed, homesick, and plagued by business reverses, the Tennesseean had resigned the Senate seat before the term expired.

In 1802, the lawyer/politician won election to a position he had long dreamed of holding – a major generalship in the Tennessee Militia – but had seen very little military action. In business, his casual association with Aaron Burr's intrigues in the Southwest cost him more political capital in Washington. When the War of 1812 broke, the Madison Administration advised Governor Blount not to retain the stained politician in command of the militia. But Blount respected loyalty, and rewarded those who had stood by him during his own tough times. Blount decided to ignore the federal pressure and confirm the middle-aged politician as major general and commander, West Tennessee Militia. With this appointment, the real rise of the lawyer/soldier/politician who would become the 7th President of the United States began. The general's name was Andrew Jackson.

In March, 1813, Jackson had already been involved in a misadventure in leading Tennessee troops to New Orleans. His militia unit had gotten as far as Natchez before Jackson received an inexplicable order to disband the command and return to Tennessee. With characteristic fury, Jackson ignored the order and kept the army together. He bore the rigors of the return march to Nashville through harsh weather and a lack of supplies with such fortitude and stamina that his men nicknamed him *Old Hickory*. The legend had begun.

At the outbreak of the Creek War in August, 1813, Jackson received command of the western army of the Tennessee Militia, as previously noted. Jackson faced the same barriers to success that plagued the other military commands attempting to converge and crush the Red Stick Creeks – short enlistments, poor communications, scarce supplies, and bad or no roads. The difference was that Jackson refused to be deterred by these obstacles, and chose *action* over *excuses*. Not yet fully recovered from a personal pistol duel, Jackson nonetheless ordered his militia to concentrate at Fayetteville, Tennessee. Once the army had gathered and Jackson had taken stock of its meager supplies, he immediately planned a course of action to remedy the situation. Jackson left Fayetteville, Tennessee, on October 10th, leading the bulk of the army south toward Creek territory. He planned to link with his cavalry under Brigadier General John Coffee at Huntsville, then continue south, building forts on the way to protect his line of advance. The first of these would be Fort Deposit, on the Tennessee River 20 miles south of Huntsville. After the rendezvous at Huntsville, Jackson detached his talented second-in-command, Coffee, with 600 men to attack the Red Stick villages to the southwest of Huntsville on the Black Warrior River. Coffee was to destroy the villages and any Red Stick warriors found there, and capture the food in the villages for use by the West Tennessee Militia. Coffee was successful and bore his captured supplies to Fort Deposit, to be enthusiastically welcomed by a famished West Tennessee Militia.

Jackson was so pleased with the independent action of General Coffee that he once again detached him for offensive activities. This time, Jackson would drive a portion of the army to the Coosa River and there establish the army's long-term base of operations, Fort Strother. Meanwhile, Coffee was to take 900 to 1,000 soldiers and attack nearby Tullushatchee, the northernmost hostile Red Stick village. The village contained many militant warriors and was a strategic threat to Fort Strother.

On the morning of November 3rd, 1813, as he neared Tullushatchee, Brigadier General Coffee split his force into two columns and a small central command. The right column under Colonel John Allcorn quietly circled Tullushatchee to the south, while the left under Colonel Newton Cannon did the same to the north. The central force under Lieutenants E. Hammond and Andrew Patterson advanced boldly to the village, attempting to draw the Red Sticks to it. The plan worked to perfection, as the warriors reacted to the central attack, then were in turn crushed by the closing pincers of Allcorn and Cannon. The Indians must have been short of ammunition, because they fired only once, then reverted to bows and arrows. The combination of superior numbers, superior firepower, and superior tactics overwhelmed the Red Sticks. The battle soon ended, with at least 186 warriors killed (and probably more killed in the hasty flight of the initial survivors into the surrounding brushland). The Tennessee militia lost 5 killed and 40 wounded at Tullushatchee.

Brig. General John Coffee returned to Fort Strother to receive the congratulations of General Jackson, but there was little time to bask in the glory. On November 7th, Jackson received a message that the allied Lower Creek village of Talladega, only a day's march from the fort, was under attack by a Red Stick strike force. General Jackson, believing General John Cocke was soon to arrive with the reinforcements of the East Tennessee Militia, decided to march with 2,000 troops to Talladega, leaving only a skeleton force at Strother to hold on for the arriving Cocke. Jackson was only a short distance from Talladega when he received news that Cocke would not be arriving as scheduled. Jackson knew Fort Strother was very vulnerable, but he decided to continue his aggressive move toward Talladega, leaving Strother to fend for itself.

Major General Jackson, on November 9th, directed the attack formation against Talladega to be structured similarly to that employed by General Coffee at Tullushatchee. Jackson positioned his main force of infantry in the middle, facing the village: militia on the left and volunteers on the right, backed by a small reserve of dismounted cavalry. Units of cavalry and mounted infantry in two columns swept left and right of the village. However, the Red Sticks discovered the enveloping movement before it was completed, and attacked a gap the frightened militia left in the line. The reserve cavalry plugged the gap as best it could, but as usual in battles where a sweeping pincers movement is not completely clasped, the battle was fierce, confused, and bloody. Jackson's army inflicted 299 deaths on the warriors, but William Weatherford and nearly 700 Red Stick combatants escaped. Jackson suffered a steep cost in losses as well, suffering 95 casualties in the bloodbath.

Like a ferocious hunting dog on a short leash, Jackson snapped at the heels of the retreating Native Americans. However, supply limitations and the unilateral action of General Cocke in allowing Fort Strother to remain nearly undefended meant that Jackson must retreat to that base to defend it and resupply his army.

General Cocke did eventually arrive at Fort Strother on December 12th, 1813, but any hopes General Jackson had of utilizing Cocke's men and supplies to continue attacks on the weakened Red Stick Creeks were soon dashed. Cocke's army was as short of supplies as Jackson's, and many of his men's terms of enlistment were soon to be up. Further, Cocke's attacks on the newly peaceful Hillabee Creeks meant that General Jackson's West Tennessee Militia now had even more enemies to combat. Jackson disgustedly ordered Cocke back to Tennessee with his nearly termed-out East Tennessee Militia army, sending with Cocke his own West Tennessee short-termers as well. By late December, Jackson was down to only 150 soldiers and had very little food and ammunition with which to feed and arm them.

The last few days of December, 1813 and the first few of January, 1814 showed Major General Andrew Jackson at his best as a gritty army commander. The few remaining militia and volunteer troops were tired, hungry, sick, and scared. Most wanted to abandon Fort Strother and abort the campaign altogether. The iron constitution of their steely-eyed commander saw them through these dark days. Virtually by the force of his fiery personality and will to succeed alone, Jackson kept the command at Fort Strother together. After several personal confrontations with mutinous soldiers, Jackson's perseverance was rewarded on January 14th, 1814, when Governor Willie Blount forwarded approximately 650 new 60-day recruits under the command of Colonel William Carroll, together with a proportional amount of supplies, to Fort Strother. Also entering the fort at this time were about 200 allied Lower Creeks. Having gotten wind of Major General John Floyd's Georgia Militia initiating an offensive movement by marching west toward the Tallapoosa River valley, Jackson decided to assume the offensive as well, moving south with 1,000 men and one cannon in support of Floyd's strike. He knew his militia was raw and undisciplined, but with only 60 days in which to work, Jackson still felt this was the (so far) uncoordinated campaign's best chance for overall success.

By the evening of January 21st, 1814, Jackson was nearing Emuckfau Creek, and formed his army into a hollow square for the evening bivouac. Red Stick leader William Weatherford had cunningly monitored the progress of both Floyd and Jackson from a central position between their two armies, and decided to strike Jackson first. At 6:00 AM on January 22nd, about 900 Red Stick warriors struck the left forward angle of Jackson's hollow square like a bolt of jagged lightning. The Tennesseans held their own until first light. With the arrival of fresh allied Creek and Cherokee warriors on the American side, General Coffee charged the Red Stick positions, forcing the Native Americans to a standstill. It was the break Major General Jackson needed, and having suffered significant casualties in the deadly contest, Jackson wisely decided to retreat toward Fort Strother.

The masterful Weatherford gave the West Tennesseans little rest. Two days later, on January 24, 1814, Jackson's retreat had carried his army to the banks of Enitachopco Creek. General Jackson had been alert for a Red Stick attack on his rear guard as he returned north. He gave explicit orders that if such an attack occurred, the left and right flanks were to pivot 180 degrees and rush to form a pincers about the attacking warriors. The wily Red Sticks waited until the precise moment the dreaded cannon was in the creek before attacking. To Jackson's dismay, the rear guard gave way before the flanks could complete their pivot. Jackson changed orders on the spot: the erstwhile pincers now became twin assault columns charging directly into the attacking Red Sticks. The sudden, unexpected twin hammer blows bought time for Jackson to set up his cannon, which he ordered to be filled with grapeshot. This huge, death-dealing "shotgun" broke the back of the Red Stick attack, and the Battle of Enitachopco Creek was over. Jackson's West Tennessee army continued on and reached Fort Strother safely. Twenty Americans were killed and 75 wounded in the two battles of the campaign, but about two hundred Red Sticks paid the ultimate price for their attacks in still more bloody repulses for the Native Americans.

The three battles of Emuckfau Creek (1/22/1814), Enitachopco Creek (1/24/1814), and Floyd's Calabee Creek action (1/27/1814) cost the Red Sticks hundreds of casualties, but the battles were not decisive enough to cause the Creeks to sue for peace. Both Jackson and Floyd were in retreat after their offensives, and the heart of the Creek territory remained unviolated.

This was to change shortly. Governor Willie Blount of Tennessee was forwarding men and supplies just as fast as he possibly could do so, General Coffee arriving with a contingent soon after the battle at Enitachopco Creek. More Cherokee warriors and Lower Creeks allied with the United States came to Fort Strother as well. Major General Thomas Pinckney, the theater commander, also stepped in at this time with crucial assistance. Having monitored the war from far-away Charleston, Pinckney became convinced that Andrew Jackson was the only commander in the theater that could achieve results – any results. He therefore began sending all the men and supplies he could muster to Jackson. These included the 600-man 39th U.S. Infantry Regiment and units of volunteers from Georgia. The addition of the Regular Infantry did more than just swell Jackson's numbers. The well-drilled infantry assisted Jackson by training the West Tennessee Militia's raw recruits. General Jackson instilled rigid discipline in the entire army – indeed, one teen-aged private who disobeyed orders was quickly tried and summarily executed during this February – early March period. Jackson learned bitter lessons at Emuckfau and Enitachopco about fighting with raw soldiers. He would not make the same mistake again.

By March 14th, 1814, Major General Jackson had between 4,000 and 5,000 well supplied, trained, and disciplined soldiers filling the ranks of his army at Fort Strother. He decided the time was right to strike at the unconquered heart of the Red Stick resistance – Tohopeka (popularly known as *Horseshoe Bend*). This village stronghold was situated in a bend in the Tallapoosa River near the very center of the Red Stick nation. It was a naturally strong position rendered much stronger by human improvement. The loop of the river nearly enclosed the peninsula on which Tohopeka was built. The 350-yard neck of the loop was closed by a log-and-tree-trunk, horizontal breastwork from five to eight feet tall. The zig-zagging fortress wall was complimented by cleverly placed loopholes which provided cross-covering fire against any attackers. A few hundred yards behind the defensive breastwork, a steep cliff protected against any attempt at approach from behind. Within the walls, a gathering of approximately 1,000 warriors from various hostile villages (including a sizeable contingent of the fierce Hillabees) prepared to defend the fortress to the death.

Jackson swung out of Fort Strother on March 14th with about 2,000 infantry, 700 cavalry and mounted infantry, 500 allied Cherokees and 100 allied Creeks, leaving his remaining soldiers to garrison Fort Strother. He moved down the Coosa River, stopping only to build Fort Williams on the Coosa as an intermediate defense and supply base before driving steadily forward. Jackson's army arrived at the fortified wall of Horseshoe Bend on the Tallapoosa River at 10:00 AM on March 27th, 1814. What he saw there gave the normally steely-nerved general pause:

> "It is impossible to conceive a situation more eligible for defense than the one they have chosen, and the skill which they manifested in their breast work, was really astonishing."

After a further review of the fortress, General Jackson regained his composure and reevaluated the position before him:

> They have "penned themselves up for slaughter."

The general quickly aligned his soldiers for the coming assault. He sent Brigadier General John Coffee, 700 soldiers, and 600 allied Indians across the Tallapoosa River opposite Tohopeka. This effectively cut off any escape for the Red Sticks. Jackson then set up his small battery of one 6-pounder cannon and one 3-pounder cannon across from the breastwork, and at 10:30 AM began a two-hour shelling of the fortification.

There now occurred one of those unusual events in the heat of battle upon which conflicts sometimes turn. The allied Native Americans on the far side of the river decided to cross it and destroy a line of canoes set up for the Red Stick's escape should this avenue be needed. The allies achieved their goal, but not content with this, without orders they advanced into Tohopeka, burned several buildings there, scaled cliffs in the rear of the village, and engaged the Red Sticks in battle in the rear of the breastwork defense. The

Red Sticks manning the fortifications were distracted by this attack, and Jackson seized the moment to charge the breastwork.

The pent-up emotion of the Tennessee army, built during the rigid two-month training period and charged to a fever pitch by the immediately preceding two-hour bombardment, now manifested itself in a fanatical assault on the Horseshoe Bend fortification. Jackson's army rushed the bastion and closed all the way to the wall, then engaged in firing through the loopholes at the now-frantic Red Stick defenders inside. Suddenly, after several minutes of this tough, close-range fighting, the determined soldiers were up and over the wall and invading the compound, led by the men of the stalwart 39th Infantry. With the tidal wave of violent soldiers now pouring over the wall, the end was near. Bayonet-wielding infantry swarmed among the dazed Red Sticks, while Coffee's command surged forward from behind. The killing went on all day, as frightened warriors were sought out and cut down in the compound, while the more desperate tried to leap into the Tallapoosa and swim the river. Most drowned or became easy targets for the long rifles of Coffee's mounted infantry. When it was all over, approximately 850 Red Stick warriors lay dead in the Tohopeka complex or drowned along the banks of the Tallapoosa River. Jackson's allied army suffered 49 dead and 154 wounded. The heart of the Red Stick resistance had been pierced, and the end of the Creek War was at hand.

After some false starts with different negotiators, including Major General Thomas Pinckney and Creek Agent Benjamin Hawkins, Andrew Jackson assumed direction of the treaty process to formally end the Creek War. During these false starts, Jackson continued his rampage through the now nearly defenseless Upper Creek nation, destroying and burning village after village. He arrived at the original ultimate destination of the combined armies, the confluence of the Coosa and Tallapoosa Rivers and, wielding a psychological stroke of which Anthony Wayne would have been proud, erected Fort Jackson directly on this holiest of Red Stick Creek grounds. From Fort Jackson, the general proclaimed that no negotiations could begin until arch rival Creek war leader William Weatherford had been captured. In possibly the most dramatic moment of the war, Weatherford walked boldly into Fort Jackson of his own volition to surrender, knowing his cause was lost. Jackson, impressed with the courage of his most worthy opponent, released Weatherford to return to his people and work for their surrender. Weatherford strode from the fort a free man, fading away into history.

Jackson, as head negotiator for the United States, was interested in only one thing: the security of the United States against European intervention or invasion. Jackson felt that any Native Americans left in close proximity to the Spanish and British along the Gulf Coast would be subject to the negative influences of these imperial rivals, and instability in the Old Southwest would be the continuing result. He therefore proposed bold and astonishing terms of capitulation: ALL Native Americans must be removed to an area above a line slightly north of Fort Williams, the territory south of this to be sold to and occupied by white settlers. The few Red Sticks left in Mississippi Territory (the most recalcitrant had already moved to Pensacola in Spanish West Florida) accepted their fate as the fortunes of a lost war. The astonished allied Lower Creeks and Cherokees read the terms of the Treaty of Fort Jackson in stunned disbelief. Surely this could not be true! But it was. General Jackson stated the only options available to the allies were to accept the terms of the treaty, which ceded nearly 22 million acres of combined Creek land to the United States (including 2.2 million acres of the allied Cherokees' lands – a people who had fought only as loyal allies of the United States in the war!), or suffer the fate of the hostile Red Sticks in a war against the now powerful West Tennessee Army. After a couple days of deliberation, on August 9th, 1814, the combined tribes signed the grossly unjust Treaty of Fort Jackson. In a final irony and humiliation, only three Red Stick leaders were left in the territory to sign the documents. So the vast majority of signees to the land-grabbing Treaty of Fort Jackson, the supposed instrument of capitulation and punishment for the Red Sticks, were allied Lower Creek leaders!

The Creek War of 1813-'14 was over. But Great Britain was still at war with the United States, and it would soon try its hand at dislodging the Americans from the Old Southwest. The effusion of blood in the South was far from stanched by the conclusion of the Creek War.

CHAPTER 13

The Empire Shielded: The British Threat is Eliminated in the Old Southwest; 1814-'15

For many years, as a casual reader of War of 1812 history, I wondered how the United States developed an army in the southwestern area of the frontier strong enough to contest and defeat the British at the Battle of New Orleans. I suspect that, like me before a couple of years ago, many readers of the history of this period fail to make the connection between the Creek War of 1813-'14 and Andrew Jackson's devastating repulse of the British on January 8th, 1815. It is clear that the confused cauldron of the war against the Creeks not only honed the skills of Jackson into those of a great commander, but also developed an experienced corps of senior commanders such as John Coffee and William Carroll in the Old Southwest. Most importantly, the Creek War created a battle-hardened core of frontier militia and volunteers on which to draw to contest the British in this theater.

Andrew Jackson was promoted from Major General, Tennessee Militia to first Brigadier, then Major General of Volunteers, United States Army; the major generalship being effective June 18th, 1814. Jackson negotiated with the Creeks and Cherokees to end the Creek War from this position of power, but it was unnecessary: his conduct of the war as leader of the West Tennessee Militia earned him the appellation *Sharp Knife* from his Native American friends and enemies alike. The Treaty of Fort Jackson was imposed on all the southern tribes based on his crushing of the Red Stick nation before the promotion, to the massive benefit of both the United States and General Jackson's reputation with the American people.

Command of the Seventh Military District was given to Jackson along with the commission as regular army major general. Because his relations with virtually everybody in the District were in a shambles, the irascible and inefficient General J. Thomas Flournoy had been replaced in favor of the victorious Andrew Jackson. With this new honor to Jackson came a tremendous responsibility: defending the Gulf Coast from a rumored imminent invasion by the British.

One of Jackson's first moves was to convert the existing structure of reliance on militia as the basis of the army in the southwest to reliance on volunteers. Many of the militia enlistees grumbled at the conversion from state control to federal control, but experienced subordinates like Generals Coffee and Carroll helped ease the transition into a manageable exercise.

Jackson then analyzed the possible avenues of attack. With Britain's preponderant strength on the sea, encompassing both the ability to transport soldiers/marines in an invasion and then supply them once ashore, Jackson envisioned attacks involving the three major harbors on the Gulf Coast: Pensacola, Mobile, and New Orleans. Jackson initially believed that Mobile was the target of at least a British raid from Pensacola, and ordered Major William Lawrence and 160 men to Fort Bowyer, at the mouth of Mobile Bay, to strengthen the little fort there. Lawrence arrived in early September, and immediately began strengthening the fort's defensive and offensive power. On September 12th, 1814, British ships from Pensacola appeared off the harbor, loaded with 130 marines and 180 Indians, and prepared for an amphibious assault. Fort Bowyer survived both a land assault (September 14th) that got within 800 yards of the rear of the fort and a naval bombardment (September 15th), the prosecuting of which cost the British the mid-sized warship *Hermes*, destroyed by cannon fire from the fort. The remaining British forces retreated to Pensacola, having suffered 27 killed and 45 wounded. The Americans lost 4 killed and 5 wounded, and Jackson moved his army to Mobile shortly thereafter.

Pensacola again! It was bad enough that a European power, even one as weak as imperial Spain, controlled the Floridas. But West Florida's Spanish governor had welcomed (or at least tolerated the presence of) approximately 900 Creek refugees into Pensacola's environs after Horseshoe Bend, to be followed by British Major (later Lt. Colonel) Edward Nicholls and 100 to 200 Royal Marines on August 14th, 1814. The British under Captain George Woodbine had also established a satellite base on West Florida's Apalachicola

River, variously called Prospect Bluff, and later British Post or Fort Apalachicola when fortified, in May, 1814. The British did not come empty-handed. Jackson's spies in West Florida reported that British Captain Hugh Pigot stocked Prospect Bluff with two thousand stands of arms and 300,000 ball cartridges, while Nicholls had one thousand pistols, one thousand carbines, five hundred rifles, and greater than one million rounds of ammunition at Pensacola. All these weapons and ammunition were earmarked for use by Indians. By summer, Jackson knew more than 4,000 Seminoles and refugee Creeks had answered British calls for raids on the Americans to the north. The situation was intolerable to General Jackson. During the summer of 1814, Jackson asked permission to invade West Florida and neutralize Pensacola. Official Washington refused: America was not at war with Spain.

Jackson watched the growing strength of the British augmenting Spanish forces in Pensacola, and decided that the overall situation in the city was a threat to United States security. In October 1814, without waiting for a reply to his latest request for official sanction to take action against Pensacola, General Jackson and 4,000 soldiers moved out of Mobile and marched toward Pensacola.

General Jackson was correct in his evaluation of overall British designs on the Southwest. Records subsequently showed that as early as November, 1812, Britain was interested in using the Floridas as a base for the conquest of the Gulf Coast area. The British were primarily interested in New Orleans, because control of the Mississippi River at New Orleans could stifle trade in the Trans-Appalachian West, and perhaps politically, economically, and militarily destabilize the area to the extent that it could be detached from the United States. Both Pensacola and Mobile had a place in this British strategy. Pensacola figured in because its naturally outstanding harbor was politically shielded by the facade of Spanish neutrality in the North American conflicts, and as such it could provide a jumping-off base for an attack on either Mobile or New Orleans. Mobile was important because 1) once forced, its long and wide bay was difficult for America to defend against a British attack, 2) it was relatively close to the ultimate prize - New Orleans, and 3) an overland route in attacking New Orleans from Mobile was much easier to utilize than a sea-borne amphibious attack directly against New Orleans from the Gulf.

Major General Andrew Jackson and his battle-toughened army arrived at the western approaches to Pensacola, Spanish West Florida, on November 6th, 1814. The British, noting their recent loss to the Americans at Mobile and being relatively assured this failed assault would bring a reprisal from the fiery Jackson, had moved their entire garrison to the fort at the entrance of the harbor, Fort San Carlos de Barrancas. There they anchored their small fleet of seven ships under the protection of the fort's guns. The Spanish garrison of approximately 500 men occupied the other military installation in the area, Fort San Miguel, located directly inside the city. Jackson studied the deployments, then devised tactics to capture Pensacola.

In tandem with his trusted subordinate, Brigadier General John Coffee, Jackson left 500 men on the west side of Pensacola. This unit was to stage a noisy demonstration attack as a feint. Meanwhile, Jackson with 3,500 men swung completely around the north side of Pensacola to the eastern approaches, eluding pickets from Fort San Miguel, Fort San Carlos, and the lookouts of the British fleet. On the morning of November 7th, the Spanish in San Miguel were completely surprised by the bold tactics of the Americans, who seemed to be attacking from both sides of the city at once. After a short battle, the Spanish in Fort San Miguel, and therefore the city of Pensacola as well, surrendered to Jackson and his brash army.

The British in Fort San Carlos were disgusted by the quick capitulation of the Spanish in Pensacola. They determined to destroy the town with cannon fire from the fort, but thought better of creating a large number of civilian casualties among their European ally, Spain. As a token display of their belligerence at the American takeover of Pensacola, the British loosed a few rounds of cannon fire into the dock area of the city. They then spiked the cannon of Fort San Carlos, blew up the fort's ammunition magazine, boarded their ships and sailed to the safety of Prospect Bluff to the east, where they continued with the construction of Fort Apalachicola.

The almost bloodless Battle of Pensacola had much greater ramifications than its small size would suggest. The British were denied the use of Pensacola as a base of operations for their planned attack on New Orleans. Having failed in their attempt to force an entrance to Mobile Bay and seeing that Mobile now seemed to be the base of operations for Jackson's army, the British were forced to try a much more difficult sea-based amphibious assault on New Orleans, with (as we soon will see) unfortunate results.

His work done at Pensacola, General Jackson marched his army back to Mobile to await word on British movements. He was still convinced that Mobile was the ultimate British target in the Gulf. It was not until he received unofficial intelligence from merchant captains plying the Caribbean who told him the British intended to attack New Orleans that Jackson finally believed the Crescent City was in danger, and he immediately headed toward it. He took many of his soldiers from Mobile with him, including Coffee's Tennessee Mounted Infantry, Hind's Mississippi Dragoons, and most of the 44th U.S. Infantry Regiment, all to assemble in New Orleans to compliment the 7th U.S. Infantry already stationed in the southern Louisiana area. Jackson arrived at New Orleans on December 1st, 1814.

The southern states rallied to the needs of the Gulf Coast as well. To cover Mobile in Jackson's absence, Tennessee sent the 2,000-man *1st Division, Tennessee Militia* (the previously-named "East Tennessee Militia") under the command of General Taylor. Georgia summoned the 2,500-strong Georgia Militia under Major General John McIntosh (second-in-command being Brigadier General Blackshear) and sent it to Mobile as well. The overall commander of the Mobile defenses was the recently exchanged General James Winchester.

Troops from all over the south converged on New Orleans. Kentucky sent a 2,500-man militia army under the command of Major General John Thomas, seconded by Brevet Brigadier General John Adair, a highly regarded officer possessing previous combat experience with General Harrison at the Thames. The brilliant Major General William Carroll, promoted to command of the *2nd Division, Tennessee Militia* (the formidable previously-named "West Tennessee Militia") with the ascension of Jackson to federal duty, brought his 3,000 stalwart Tennesseans to New Orleans, second-in-command being Brigadier General Byrd Smith. Louisiana rose to its own defense, raising several local militia units and placing them under General Jackson. One of these units was led by Major General Jacques Villere, who commanded the militia between the Mississippi River and Lake Borgne. Major General D.B. Morgan would command a significant body of the Louisiana Militia on the United States' far right during the climatic January 8th battle. The Mississippi Territory and the Choctaw Nation sent units of soldiers, and the U.S. Navy contributed several ships and gunboats to the defense.

Significantly, Jackson would enlist the aid of the Baratarian pirates under the command of Jacques Laffite. The pirates brought not only an intimate knowledge of the vast and tangled waterways of the southern Louisiana area to Jackson's aid, but they also brought *cannon*. Cannon would be one of the major keys to the ultimate defense of New Orleans.

Thus, Major General Andrew Jackson would have a large army with which to contest the British invasion of Louisiana, but he had large needs as well. The British could attack from any of five avenues: from the southwest via Barataria Bay; directly up the Mississippi River Delta; from the east via Lake Borgne and the Bayou Bienvenu; from the north via Lake Pontchartrain; or overland should they capture Mobile and utilize it, as Jackson still feared. Jackson had several advantages, but he needed men and time to bring these advantages into play. The area between Barataria Bay and New Orleans was swampy and unsuitable for troop and artillery movement, and the pirates helped block this route as well. The route up the river was 80 torturous, twisting miles from the Gulf to the city, was held by two relatively powerful U.S. Navy warships (*Carolina*[15 guns] and *Louisiana* [16]), and was guarded by two (2) American-manned old French and Spanish forts: St. Philip and St. Leon. The latter commanded *"English Turn,"* an S-shaped twist in the river where sailing vessels must wait for a favorable shift of the wind before moving on upstream. Both the routes via the Bayou Bienvenu and Lake Pontchartrain depended on being able to secure Lake Borgne, which the United States guarded with five gunboats (*Nos. 5, 12, 156, 162,* and *163*) and two small schooners (*Sea Horse* and *Alligator*). Further, the approaches from both Lakes Borgne and Pontchartrain were commanded by forts; Fort St. John between Lake Pontchartrain and New Orleans was considered particularly strong by the British. Finally, with Mobile firmly held by about 4,500 militia and a strong Fort Bowyer (containing a garrison of about 350 men and several large cannon) guarding the entrance to the bay, an attack via the overland route from the east did not look probable.

Jackson covered all his bases, which took a lot of men and artillery to do, but in conjunction with his subordinates, he correctly determined that the route via Lake Borgne and Bayou Bienvenu was the approach the British would use. As time went on, Jackson placed more and more of his men and other martial resources to block this approach.

The struggle at New Orleans was not a single battle, but a campaign of five battles; the four preliminary contests leading up to the fifth, climatic Battle of New Orleans on January 8th, 1815. The four early battles were not particularly important as to who won or lost, but were most important because they bought General Jackson *time*. Time was the one commodity Jackson needed most – time for more men, ammunition, cannons, and supplies to stream into the area just south of New Orleans. Time for these men to build and improve the earthworks and cannon emplacements that would need to become impregnable if Jackson was to stop the British.

The British arrived at Ship Island just to the east of Lake Borgne on December 12th, 1814, and concentrated their fleet there. Lake Borgne was too shallow for the British deep-draft men-of-war to traverse, so they transferred their 7,000-man assault force to shallow-draft vessels for the movement toward New Orleans. Master Commandant Daniel Todd Patterson was in charge of all U.S. Navy vessels in the New Orleans area, and his subordinate commander in the sector east of Lake Borgne was Lt. Thomas ap Catesby Jones. Jones slowly but progressively retreated toward Lake Borgne before the superior British escort squadron (a 1,200 to 183 advantage in men; a 42 to 23 advantage in cannon). He was finally forced by calm winds to make a stand west of the Malheureux Island passage into Lake Borgne. On December 14th, 1814, the two sides met, and given the inequality in the sizes of the squadrons, the outcome was predictable. The British succeeded in capturing or forcing the United States Navy to scuttle all seven of its ships. Yet, the battle was important because 1) Patterson did not commit his two larger warships to this battle, keeping them intact on the Mississippi River for critical use at later dates, and 2) Jones' spirited defense of the Lake Borgne approaches had bought a valuable delay in British assault plans. This gave General Jackson additional time to strengthen his defenses.

With the defeat of the U.S. Navy on Lake Borgne, the British moved ahead toward New Orleans utilizing Bayou Bienvenu. This bayou did not go completely to the Mississippi, but via Bayou Mazant and the Villere Canal, the combined channel gave close access to the river about 9 miles south-southeast of the city, at the plantation of Louisiana militia General Jacques Villere. General Robert Ross was to have commanded the British expedition against New Orleans, but his death in the Baltimore area meant that command of the land invasion force passed to Major General John Keane. Keane was to command until the new theater commander, Lieutenant General Edward Pakenham, a veteran of the Spanish Iberian Peninsula Wars, could arrive from Europe at the head of British veterans of the wars against Napoleon.

The British army spilled from the Bayou Bienvenu/Bayou Mazant/Villere Canal waterway on December 22nd and quickly overran the Villere Plantation. General Jackson knew his defenses further upriver at Canal Rodriguez were not ready, and a rapid assault on these defenses by the British would carry the American position and the city of New Orleans. He determined to attack the British at Villere Plantation the next day. All day on December 23rd, 1814, Jackson's army moved south. He massed about 2,000 troops, including Coffee's Tennessee Mounted Infantry, Hind's Mississippi Dragoons, a couple of units of local militia, and parts of the 7th and 44th U.S. Infantry Regiments, against 1,680 British advanced assault troops. Commodore Patterson also brought the *Carolina* down river to shell the British positions. Jackson was not able to get all his units into position until about 8:30 in the evening, hence the battle has sometimes been called the "Night Battle of New Orleans." With the dependable Coffee assaulting the British right and Jackson at the head of the Regulars attacking the left, the British were dealt a stinging blow. The tactical result was ultimately indecisive, as a thick fog around 10:00 PM caused the Americans to cease the attack in confusion. Although the American army under Jackson lost 215 men and later the *Carolina*, the British lost 275 men, and more importantly, were made cautious by the unexpected fury of the hammer-like U.S. attack. British General Keane decided to wait until General Pakenham arrived with more veteran troops and artillery before advancing. This, once again, bought General Jackson time to continue building defenses behind Canal Rodriguez on the route to New Orleans.

These defenses did increase in strength, as Jackson planned. General Carroll's 2nd Tennessee Militia arrived at New Orleans on the 22nd and shortly thereafter assumed the center of the growing line established behind the Canal Rodriguez on the east bank of the Mississippi River. The 7th and 44th Infantries occupied the right along the river, and Patterson's warship *Louisiana* added its heavy armament to the defense of the U.S. right. Coffee's steady Tennessee Mounted Militia occupied the left, with impenetrable swamps protecting its left. Most importantly, by this time, Jackson had erected four artillery batteries along his defense line, and these cannon would play a decisive role in the remaining three battles of the campaign.

Lieutenant General Pakenham arrived on December 25th and assumed command of the British assault force. He determined to attack the Canal Rodriguez line on the morning of December 28th. His attack was preceded by a tremendous barrage from the British artillery, which was answered by the United States' batteries and the *Louisiana*. Although one of his columns came close to turning the Regulars on the American right, powerful broadsides from the *Louisiana* and blasts from land batteries held the British, and they retreated with 120 casualties - the American defenses were growing firmer. Importantly, the British gunners used so many scarce cannonballs and so much powder that they had to wait three days to secure enough for another attack.

The resolute British tried again on January 1st, 1815, but the three days since the 28th had been important for the Americans – they increased their land batteries from four to eight in these intervening days. The result on January 1st was the same: although the British attacked with even more cannon than on the 28th, they still could not match the increased power and accuracy of the American artillery. The British were once more repulsed with heavy casualties.

On January 4th, the Kentucky Militia arrived at New Orleans, with between 2,250 and 2,500 effectives. Those sharpshooting backwoods militiamen who brought their own weapons arrived carrying long rifles, but many of the militia were unarmed, their federally-issued muskets still upriver on barges. New Orleans was scoured for weapons, and enough ancient firearms were gathered and repaired to equip (in total) around 800 to 1,000 Kentuckians. Major General Thomas, the Kentucky Militia commander, had taken ill, so command of this unit was assumed by the brilliant Brigadier General Adair. He led his musket-and-rifle-armed troops into position as a reserve directly behind General Carroll, where a prescient General Jackson envisioned the heaviest British blow would fall.

The attacks of December 28th and January 1st had revealed a British tactic: the Britons obviously felt the U.S right flank along the river was weak, and had made attempts to turn it. Jackson countered with moves of his own. First, he moved a unit of Choctaw sharpshooters under Captain Pierre Jugeat to the key swampy ground immediately along the river bank, which the Choctaws would valiantly defend in the upcoming battle. Second, he directed Commodore Patterson to land several of his largest naval cannon on the *west* side of the river, and there construct a battery that could sweep that area directly across the river which the British had twice previously contested. For protection of this battery, Jackson moved a 500-man unit of the Louisiana Militia under Major General D.B. Morgan to the west bank position. Weapons repair was completed for about 200 additional Kentucky militia, and they too were moved to the far west flank, under the command of Colonel Davis.

The stage was set for the climatic British assault on the United States lines on January 8th, 1815, forever after known as the Battle of New Orleans. Major General Sir Samuel Gibbs commanded the stronger British right flank column for the assault. It was surmised that having previously attacked the American right, that flank had been reinforced from the center and the center was now weakened: the central sector of the American line was Gibbs' target. In fact, the center was arguably the strongest part of the line. Approximately 2,000 Tennessee riflemen, backed by 800 to 1,000 Kentucky militia, a significant portion of whom were also rifle-armed, were packed into an 800 yard front up to six-men deep behind a breastwork 4 to 5 feet high fronted by a wet ditch 4 feet deep and 8 feet wide. In addition, several of the experienced, zeroed-in artillery batteries were in this sector. On the British "river" left, a smaller British column led by Major General Keane attacked the U.S. 7th and 44th Regulars and Choctaw sharpshooters. Colonel William Thornton led the veteran 85th Regiment across the Mississippi River to create a British "far left" front against the American battery placed there. The plan was for Thornton to capture this battery and turn it to sweep the American line from the flank, thus aiding Gibbs' and Keane's assaults. British timing was bad: Thornton indeed captured the cross-river battery, but not until both Gibbs and Keane had come to grief against the strong American Canal Rodriguez line. Advancing across a long open field directly into the teeth of American defensive fire, the British had first come into range of the accurate and deadly American artillery. Red swaths appeared in the British lines, but still they came, now advancing into the range of the sharpshooting long-rifle-armed backwoods Tennessee and Kentucky militia. Red-coated soldiers fell in droves, yet the resolute veterans of Napoleon and Wellington's campaigns pushed on, into range of the heavily gunpowder-charged, large caliber muskets of the Regulars and other American troops. Twice the British rallied; three times they braved the hellish inferno of American fire from behind Rodriguez Canal to continue the charge. The most valiant reached the edge of the water-filled ditch before falling, but fall they did. Lieutenant General Edward Pakenham and 300 of his brave European veterans died on the plain before the Canal; 1,262 lay wounded, including mortally wounded General Gibbs and severely injured General Keane; 484 were captured. Of the approximately 5,500 British soldiers who faced Jackson at the Rodriguez Canal that morning (only 3,600 of whom were actually engaged), 2,046 never returned to British lines whole later that day. American losses were 6 killed and 7 wounded. The British campaign to capture New Orleans was over.

Much has been made of statements that the Battle of New Orleans was fought after the War of 1812 had ended, and it was the last battle of the War. Neither statement is completely true. While it is true that American and British negotiators finalized the Treaty of Ghent on December 24, 1814, news of the treaty did not reach the Gulf Coast until February 13th, 1815. The Treaty of Ghent was not ratified by the United States Congress until February 15th, 1815, and by the terms of the treaty, the War of 1812 was not officially ended until 11:00 AM on February 17th, 1815. The United States was still technically at war with Great Britain at the time of the Battle of New Orleans. And the United States and Britain fought still one more significant battle after New Orleans.

With death or serious injury incapacitating the three senior officers, Major General John Lambert, until then in charge of British reserves, assumed command of the entire army at New Orleans. Lambert, stunned by the carnage on the plain before Rodriguez Canal, called off the offensive and loaded the surviving soldiers onto British ships. The ships and their compliment of soldiers headed east to Dauphine Island off the coast of Mobile Bay, and there prepared to assault Fort Bowyer at the mouth of the bay.

General James Winchester, of River Raisin infamy, had recently been formally exchanged as a British prisoner of war and was assigned to command the American defense of Mobile. As noted earlier, he had at least 4,500 troops in the vicinity of Mobile. Fort Bowyer itself, under the command of Lieutenant Colonel William Lawrence, had by order of General Jackson increased its garrison to approximately 400 soldiers. British General Lambert gathered nearly 5,000 soldiers scattered throughout Louisiana and landed 1,400 of them on the landward side of Fort Bowyer, thereby bypassing the fort's formidable seaward-facing big guns. Lambert brought large caliber cannon with him and his men stoically weathered American fire as these were placed in forward positions. By February 11th, Lambert was ready to begin the siege of Fort Bowyer.

General Winchester was fully apprised of the increasing danger to Fort Bowyer, and it is clear he had quite sufficient forces to aid in the fort's defense. Yet Winchester delayed sending reinforcements to Fort Bowyer until the siege began. It was too late. General Lambert opened up with his big guns on February 11th, 1815. After only a few rounds, Lt. Colonel Lawrence, succumbing to the hopelessness of his situation, surrendered the fort and its garrison of 360 men. Winchester's reinforcements arrived 24 hours after Fort Bowyer fell. The British lost 30 to 40 men in the preparation for the siege of the fort.

On February 13th, before British Major General Lambert could launch an attack on the city of Mobile, word reached the Gulf Coast of the signing of the Treaty of Ghent. The fighting in the War of 1812 was over.

The war in the Southwest was important for several reasons. It opened vast new southern areas rich in resources to United States' settlement. The western portion of the Gulf Coast was secured from foreign invasion once and for all. Most importantly for the Northwest Territory, the great watercourse known as the Mississippi River was protected from the threat of foreign and Native American interdiction of trade. Well, almost...

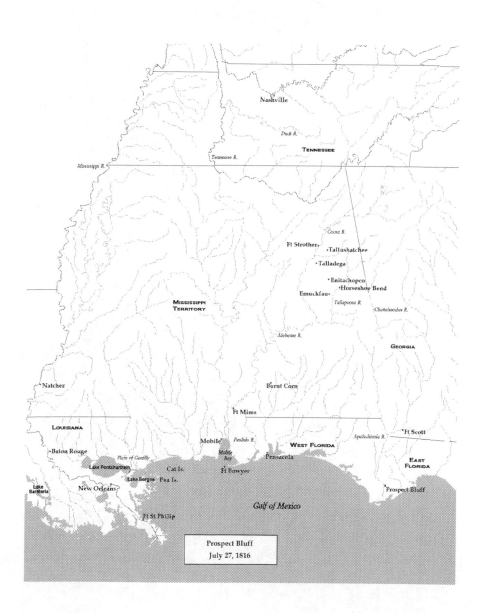

Nashville

Duck R.

TENNESSEE

Tennessee R.

Mississippi R.

Coosa R.

Ft Strother

Tallushatchee

Talladega

Enitachopco

Horseshoe Bend

Emuckfau

Tallapoosa R.

Chattahoochee R.

MISSISSIPPI
TERRITORY

Alabama R.

GEORGIA

Natchez

Burnt Corn

Ft Mims

LOUISIANA

Baton Rouge

Plain of Gentilly

Lake Pontchartrain

Lake Borgne   Pea Is.

Lake
Barataria

New Orleans

Ft St Philip

Cat Is.

Mobile   Perdido R.

Mobile
Bay

Ft Bowyer

WEST FLORIDA   Apalachicola R.

Pensacola

Ft Scott

EAST
FLORIDA

Prospect Bluff

Gulf of Mexico

Prospect Bluff
July 27, 1816

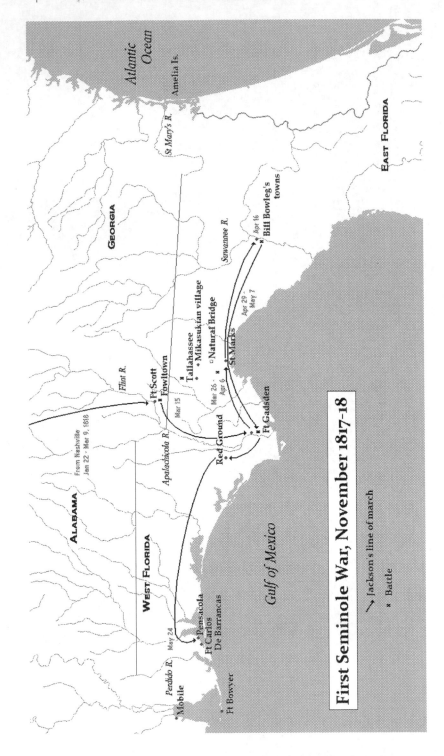

First Seminole War, November 1817-18

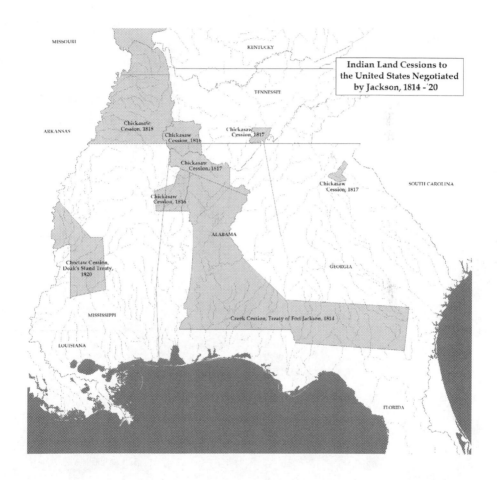

Indian Land Cessions to the United States Negotiated by Jackson, 1814 - '20

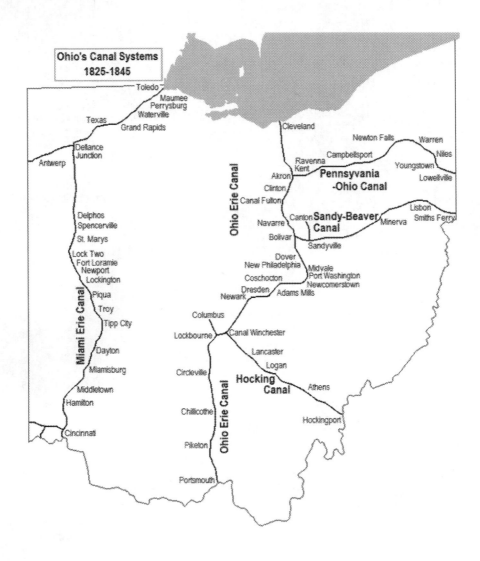

Ohio's Canal Systems
1825-1845

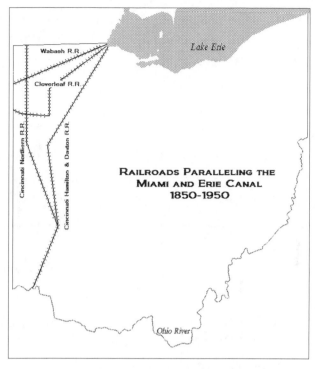

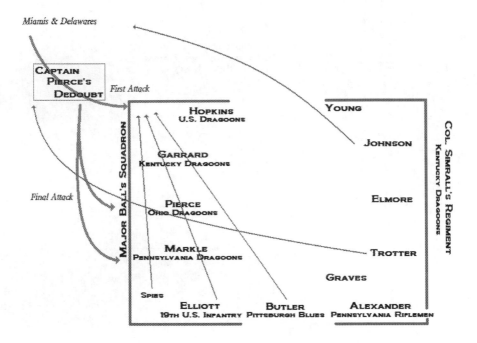

Miamis & Delawares

CAPTAIN
PIERCE'S
DEDOUBT

First Attack

HOPKINS
U.S. DRAGOONS

YOUNG

COL. SIMRALL'S REGIMENT
KENTUCKY DRAGOONS

JOHNSON

MAJOR BALL'S SQUADRON

GARRARD
KENTUCKY DRAGOONS

Final Attack

PIERCE
OHIO DRAGOONS

ELMORE

MARKLE
PENNSYLVANIA DRAGOONS

TROTTER

GRAVES

SPIES

ELLIOTT
19TH U.S. INFANTRY

BUTLER
PITTSBURGH BLUES

ALEXANDER
PENNSYLVANIA RIFLEMEN

The Battle of Mississinewa

December 18, 1812

↑
N

*Mississinewa
River*

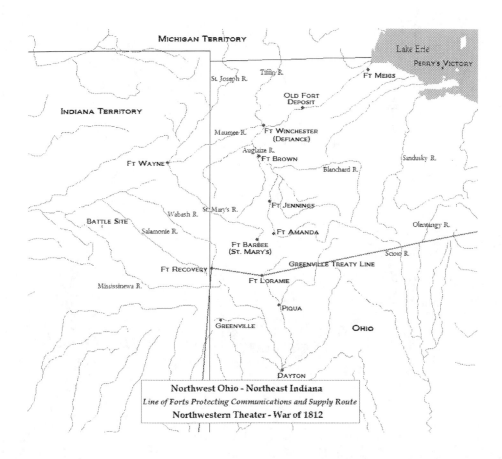

Northwest Ohio - Northeast Indiana
Line of Forts Protecting Communications and Supply Route
Northwestern Theater - War of 1812

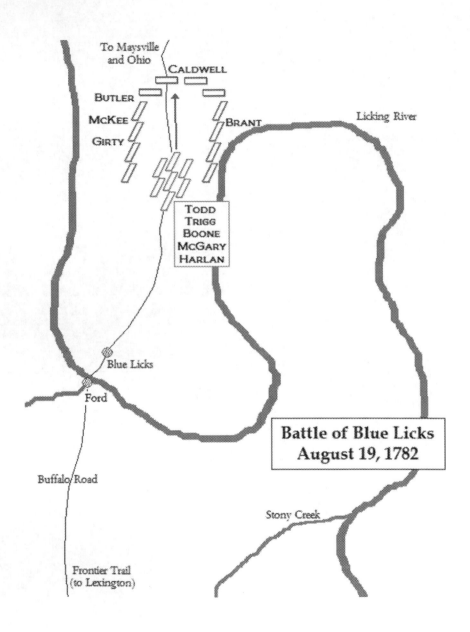

To Maysville
and Ohio

CALDWELL

BUTLER

McKEE

GIRTY

BRANT

Licking River

TODD
TRIGG
BOONE
McGARY
HARLAN

Blue Licks

Ford

**Battle of Blue Licks
August 19, 1782**

Buffalo Road

Stony Creek

Frontier Trail
(to Lexington)

CHAPTER 14

The Empire Shielded: Trans-Appalachia is Secured for America: 1811-'18

The War of 1812 went a long way toward securing the Northwest Territory and the southwestern area of Trans-Appalachia for the United States of America. Yet, certain destabilizing threats still remained in what would become the Deep South, and these threats had the potential to be detrimental to the security of the Mississippi Valley. Several actions, some of which had been in progress even before the War of 1812, were to be undertaken in the Deep South during the period from 1811 to 1818 before stability was finally achieved for the Old Northwest and Southwest areas.

The main problem in the far south was Spanish control of East and West Florida, in conjunction with the residence of Native Americans in those colonies. A weakening Spain maintained a tenuous hold on the Floridas even before her struggles with Napoleon in Europe. The pressures this war placed on Spain meant that even the small numbers of soldiers and supplies she had been sending to her overseas colonies were reduced to virtually nothing. The governmental structures of the colonies were basically on their own to meet their needs and police their territories as best they could with the resources they could hoard or develop. This may have not been too much of a problem in some Spanish colonies with more docile neighbors or constituents. For East and West Florida, to say it was a problem is an understatement.

To the north lay a young and robust United States, yearning to expand south and west to accommodate her exuberant and exploding population. America had cast longing eyes at the Floridas since the time these colonies had been ceded to Spain by Great Britain at the end of the American Revolution. The United States could see through Britain's sham of trying to put the Floridas on the shelf with Spain until that time when the British could reclaim them.

Spain's ally in the European struggle, Great Britain, used her relationship with Spain as a lever in Britain's war with the United States. Britain found Spain's Floridian harbors, particularly that of Pensacola, convenient bases from which to project power toward the southern United States and to shelter her navy. Britain also kept the Floridas' refugee Creeks and resident Seminoles in constant turmoil by arming them from British bases on Spanish soil. She then encouraged the Indians to use these weapons and ammunition for raids on American territory – Georgia and the southern Mississippi Territory being frequent destinations for these attacks. Spain, as owner of the territory, was expected to enforce the sovereignty of her possessions from misuse even by her allies, and to police the actions of the territory's inhabitants. However, the Spanish in Florida had only two bases of any consequence and very few soldiers to meet all of these responsibilities.

The capital of East Florida was St. Augustine, which contained the only fortification worthy of the name in the east: the Castillo de San Marcos. The few troops comprising the garrison of San Marcos were the only resources the governor of East Florida, Juan de Estrada, had to maintain order in the huge province. In the truncated colony of West Florida, the capital city of Pensacola had two forts for use in protecting the colony and projecting power – Fort San Miguel in the city and Fort San Carlos de Barrancas protecting the bay. With a total garrison of between 400 and 500 soldiers, the governor of the colony, Don Mateo Gonzalez Manrique (later replaced by Governor Jose Masot), could do neither. The Floridas were ripe for the picking, and the United States knew it.

The Patriot War, 1811-1814

By 1814, the War of 1812 had essentially emasculated West Florida. The machinations of the British, the tide of Creek refugees, and Jackson's incursion had proven that West Florida's government could neither police nor defend the colony. However, in comparison, East Florida at that time remained relatively unviolated, even though efforts had been underway since 1811 to do so.

There is little doubt that President Madison coveted the Floridas, and was initially willing to liberally interpret international agreements and laws to acquire part or all of them. He interpreted the *Louisiana Purchase* to include Natchez and eventually Mobile as parts of the territory purchased, even though it was not particularly clear to the French and Spanish that the agreement was written to mean this. Between January and June, 1811, Madison slid through Congress a secret resolution stating the United States was willing to assume control of the Floridas if some responsible authority willingly and without duress transferred the territories to America. The obvious plan was for an entity friendly to the United States to incite a small, relatively bloodless revolution in the Floridas, assume control, then offer the "new" country to America. Madison even went so far as to contact retired General George Matthews, a respected veteran of the American Revolutionary War. In concert with Secretary of State James Monroe, Madison strongly hinted at the plan and Matthews' role in it, although specific instructions or assurances were never uttered. Matthews left the conference fully convinced he would be backed by the U.S. Government in the hinted-at enterprise.

Matthews industriously gathered a group of people with vested interests in the Floridas, Georgia and/or the Mississippi Territory. This group organized as the "Patriots." In March, 1812, an "army" of approximately 79 Patriots entered the St. Augustine, Spanish East Florida area and captured Fernandia on Amelia Island, without the help or hindrance of two American gunboats, one brig, and 150 U.S. soldiers stationed in the harbor. From Fernandia, the Patriots laid siege to the Castillo de San Marcos, for practical purposes the military and political center of Spanish East Florida. They could not hope to take it without help from the American soldiers and sailors in the harbor, of which none was forthcoming.

There now emerged a curious equilibrium at St. Augustine: the tiny Patriot army camped just outside cannon range of the Castillo and called on the Spanish governor to surrender East Florida, which he refused to do. The Patriots then pursued the only course of action that might secure their goal. They declared the independence of East Florida, named Fernandia as their capital, drew up a constitution, and elected wealthy John Huston McIntosh as the director. McIntosh next offered the area between the St. Marys and St. Johns Rivers to General Matthews, in his capacity as "representative" of the United

States government. Matthews accepted it in the name of the United States. Both sides uneasily sat back to await the next move – whatever that might be.

Timing was against Matthews, McIntosh, and the remainder of the Patriots. In late March, 1812, the Federalists in the Senate noisily deplored the action in East Florida, and the British exerted diplomatic pressure, using this rather tawdry exercise as one of the final nails in the coffin of peace. On April 4th, President Madison, beginning to fear the action he had quietly initiated with war looming so closely, repudiated Matthews' intrigue, calling the entire program an error in judgment prosecuted with "commendable zeal." General Matthews began the journey to Washington to clear his name, but died en route on August 30, 1812. The Patriots withdrew from Fernadia but stayed on Spanish soil near the St. Marys River.

One day after war was declared between Britain and the United States, the House of Representatives considered the occupation of all Florida, Spain being an ally of America's now formal enemy, Great Britain. The Senate disagreed, and Madison was forced to tell Georgia Governor David B. Mitchell, successor to Matthews as quasi-agent, to remove the 150 U.S. troops from Florida. He did so with wording that implied Mitchell might be wise to ignore the U.S. Government's wishes. To the delight of the Patriots, Mitchell got the drift and the troops stayed in East Florida.

In early 1813, a dogged President Madison made another attempt at getting Congress to authorize the annexation or acquisition of the Floridas. Congress once again refused. This time, Madison told the third agent, General Thomas Pinckney, in plain terms that the troops must go. From this time on the Patriots were on their own for good.

The persistent Patriots were not finished. In the fall of 1813, this pseudo-political/ military group was under the direction of Buckner Harris. Harris had an aggressive plan to force the U.S. to take action in East Florida. He led a Patriot colony deep into Seminole country and erected a blockhouse, to be the center of an independent political entity called the District of Elotchaway of the Republic of East Florida. From this stronghold, Harris sent raiding parties into Seminole territory to loot and steal, knowing it would draw reprisals from the indignant Native Americans. Harris gambled that word of Seminoles attacking what were still American settlers in an independent district would lead to calls from the United States populace for intervention by the United States government on the Patriots' behalf.

The gamble failed. The United States officially refused to recognize the District of Elotchaway as a political entity, the 150 settlers at Elotchaway were defeated in battle by a group of escaped slaves and Seminole warriors, and Harris was killed by a war party of Indians on May 5th, 1814. Leaderless, with no hope of support from the American government, the colonists rapidly and carefully made their way back to the United States. The long, twilight intrigue known as the Patriot War ended not with a bang, but with a whimper.

Prospect Bluff, 1816

The War of 1812 ended on February 17th, 1815, but the trouble the British created in the Floridas went on long after the British left the south. Fort Apalachicola at Prospect Bluff was physically located on the east bank of the Apalachicola River, so technically it was a part of East Florida. Yet during the war it was a prime instrument of British war activity in West Florida and indeed along the entire Gulf Coast. British Lieutenant Colonel Edward Nicholls remained at Prospect Bluff after the war, working on behalf of his former Creeks allies for a repudiation of the Treaty of Fort Jackson and enforcement of more liberal terms regarding Creek territory contained in the war-ending Treaty of Ghent. Nicholls was ultimately unsuccessful, and in June, 1815, he and the army garrison left Fort Apalachicola for Britain, never to return. Before he left, however, Nicholls made sure the fort was well stocked with cannon, firearms, ammunition, and gunpowder. Fort Apalachicola had been a haven for runaway slaves as well as Indians during the war. With Nicholls' failure in treaty negotiations, the Native Americans drifted away from the fort, but the blacks remained. In the racial parlance of the day, the fort became known as the Negro Fort.**

Early in 1816, Jackson's commander in the southern Georgia area, General Edmund Pendleton Gaines, forwarded to General Jackson disturbing reports gleaned from spies in the Prospect Bluff area. Gaines reported a fort located on a cliff commanding the Apalachicola River, with an earthen parapet 120 feet in circumference, 18 feet thick, and 15 feet high. A mote around the fort was 14 feet wide and 4 feet deep. Directly in the middle of the compound was a large, octagonal-shaped powder magazine constructed of earth and wood. The fort was heavily armed with cannon of the following sizes: one 32-pounder, three 24-pounders, two 9-pounders, two 6-pounders, and a howitzer. The spies estimated the fort and its immediate environs contained at least 6,000 stands of rifles, carbines, and pistols, and vast quantities of ammunition. Gaines' reports stated three hundred "negroes" lived in the fort and wore red coats. Many blacks settled in the vicinity of the fort, and the agricultural community serving the area supposedly extended for 50 miles along the river north and south of the fort. Some disaffected refugee Red Stick Creeks also called Prospect Bluff home.

British Lt. Colonel Nicholls had outfitted 400 to 500 former slaves residing at Fort Apalachicola into three companies known as the "Negro Colonial Marines" during the War of 1812. It was not too much of a stretch for General Jackson to envision these "three hundred negros wearing red coats" at the fort might be those troops. When word came to Jackson that the inhabitants of Prospect Bluff had organized a government and appointed a military leader, he had heard enough. In Jackson's mind, the presence of the fort represented an obstacle to the peace and security of the planters in the Mississippi Territory and Georgia, so he swung into action. Jackson ordered Gaines to construct a fort just north of the Georgia-Florida border, and without full approval of the federal government, he gave express authority for General Gaines to use this new fort as a base to attack and destroy the Negro Fort.

Gaines followed his instructions to the letter. He constructed Fort Scott on the northwest bank of the Flint River, and ordered a detachment under Colonel Duncan Clinch, along with 200 Lower Creeks under William McIntosh, to move toward the Negro Fort and destroy it. At the same time, Gaines requested (through Jackson) that a squadron of gunboats be dispatched from New Orleans to aid in the reduction of the fort.

In early July, 1816, Clinch and McIntosh began working their way down the Apalachicola River valley, laying waste to the agricultural gardens and structures they found in their path. On July 10th, the Navy gunboats arrived at the mouth of the Apalachicola River and began their ascent toward Prospect Bluff. By July 27th, both the land and naval contingents were ready to begin their assault on the fort. The sailors heated their cannonballs to create "hot shot," which was particularly useful for setting fire to wooden structures within a fortification's walls. On the very first volley, a salvo of hot shot hit the large powder magazine in the middle of the fort. A tremendous explosion destroyed much of the interior of the fort, immediately killing 270 people and wounding 61 more within the bastion. The fort surrendered shortly thereafter, and another perceived "negative influence" on the peace and safety of the southern United States was eliminated. Jackson and the United States military establishment barely paid lip service to the issue of Spanish sovereignty over the Apalachicola River valley during the execution of the entire operation.

The First Seminole War, 1817-1818

The Patriot War of 1811-1814 was in itself a rather inept and inconclusive attempt to wrest East Florida from the Spanish, but it did lay the groundwork for an escalating conflict that eventually would have decisive results. When the Patriots began their effort to detach East Florida from Spanish control, the local Spanish government, in desperate need for manpower, asked the Seminoles for help in combatting them. The Seminoles declared themselves neutral in what they saw as a conflict between different groups of whites. However, the Patriots, sensing Seminole sympathy for their Spanish hosts, threatened the Seminoles with war if they sided with the government of East Florida. The Seminoles, finding it difficult to distinguish between white Patriots and white U.S. nationals, began raiding American settlements in Georgia in the summer of 1812.

These raids brought escalated responses from the states of Georgia and Tennessee. In the fall of 1812, a raid by Georgia militia struck north Florida Seminole towns. This early raid was followed by a more powerful one by Tennessee militia under the command of

Colonel John Williams in the winter of 1812-'13. The Tennessee militia penetrated as far as the Alachua prairie, where many of the East Florida Seminoles resided. This devastating raid destroyed much of the food supply of the Seminoles of north-central Florida, and caused extreme hardship during that winter.

This was the beginning of a relatively low level, but inexorably increasing, pendulum of violence that swung back and forth between the north Florida Seminoles and the south Georgia white settlers throughout and shortly after the War of 1812. By 1817, the Seminoles at the mouth of the Apalachicola River had joined their brethren in north Florida in conducting raids into Georgia, destroying property and killing white settlers as retribution for white raids and murders in the Floridas. They also welcomed Red Stick refugees from Mississippi Territory into their tribes as co-warriors in the increasingly destructive conflict.

In late 1817, Neamathla, Native American leader of Fowltown, a Seminole settlement north of the border of East Florida on land claimed by the United States, informed Major David E. Twiggs, commander of Fort Scott, that the Flint River was the dividing line between the Seminoles and the United States. This was communicated through General Gaines to General Jackson, overall commander in the South. Jackson's famous temper snapped yet again. He had fought two major wars and directed endless negotiations to establish that border, and he would not have his authority contested by the renegade chief of an out-of-bounds village. Gaines was fully in tune with his commander's attitudes, and informed Jackson he intended to destroy Fowltown and thus remove the source of the controversy. Gaines ordered Major Twiggs and 250 men of the 1st Brigade to move from Fort Scott to Fowltown and execute his orders. Twiggs and the 1st came upon Fowltown on the morning of November 21st, 1817, and were immediately fired upon by the inhabitants of the village. The American troops counterattacked, killing five Seminoles and wounding several more. They then burned the village of Fowltown. The initial battle of the First Seminole War had taken place. The second would not be long in following.

On November 30th, 1817, a large number of Seminole warriors attacked a boat on the Apalachiacola River about a mile below the junction of the Chattahoochee and the Flint Rivers. The boat was carrying supplies, 40 soldiers, seven women (wives of the soldiers), and four children upriver. Most of the party was killed except for six soldiers who escaped (four of them wounded in the effort) and a couple of the women who were carried off.

News of the disaster reached Secretary of War John C. Calhoun, who wasted no time. If the Spanish were unable to restrain the native inhabitants of the Floridas, then the United States would. On December 26th, 1817, Calhoun ordered Andrew Jackson to take command of American troops in the south Georgia/southern Mississippi Territory area and chastise the Seminoles. However, it is clear that Calhoun and Jackson meant to challenge Spanish control of the Floridas at the same time. A reported 2,700 Seminoles in the region stood ready to repel the invaders and protect the land.

Jackson clearly felt the only way to secure peace in the Floridas was to both 1) force U.S. acquisition of the Floridas by moving freely through the colonies regardless of Spanish intent, and 2) break the power and spirit of the Seminoles as a result of this movement. He began with his plan even before formally being ordered to south Georgia. On December 23rd, 1817, General Gaines captured Amelia Island outside the port of St. Augustine from pirates who had occupied it earlier in the year. This effectively closed St. Augustine, the Spanish capital of East Florida, to traffic unfriendly to the United States.

Shortly after General Jackson assumed command of forces in south Georgia, there arose a confusing set of contradictory orders about whether Jackson was to directly confront Spanish authorities in military fortresses if the situation arose. The details made little difference. Jackson had definite ideas on how he would handle any Spanish situations if they arose (and he intended to see that they *did* arise). No matter that he planned illegal actions with international repercussions!

Jackson began moving from Nashville to Fort Scott on January 22nd, 1818, and as he did so, he put out a call for volunteers to staff his army. He called on eight officers of his old West Tennessee Militia to raise 1,000 mounted Tennessee riflemen for service in Florida. A small contingent of Kentucky militia moved south. The Georgia

Militia contributed 1,000 militiamen, and 800 regular army soldiers of the 4th and 7th Regiments awaited his arrival at Fort Scott. Lower Creek leader and staunch friend William McIntosh also answered the call, at the head of 2,000 allied Indians. In all, Jackson had approximately 5,000 soldiers to begin his operations in Florida.

It took General Jackson 46 days to travel the 450 miles from Nashville to Fort Scott through horrendous weather and across even more horrendous roads. He arrived on March 9th, 1818. Upon reaching his destination, Jackson found the same bad weather had halted the transport of food to Fort Scott, and his army was in danger of starvation. Jackson knew supply ships had left New Orleans bound for the mouth of the Apalachicola River. Without hesitation, on March 10th, Jackson distributed the three-day supply of food on hand at Fort Scott and began his march to the Gulf along the Flint and Apalachicola Rivers. On March 15th, two days after supplies had run out, Jackson reached the site of the destroyed Fort Apalachicola ("Negro Fort") and found there a large boatload of food sent from the ships anchored at the mouth of the river. The expedition was saved!

His army fortified with nourishment, Jackson ordered the rebuilding of Fort Apalachicola. He assigned the task to engineer Lieutenant Gadsden. The lieutenant did such a fine job that Jackson named the reconstituted bastion Fort Gadsden. On March 26th, using the newly rebuilt fort as a base of operations, Jackson began his march on the town of St. Marks, which contained a small Spanish fortification and garrison. General Jackson believed it to be a haven for refugee Creeks and rebellious Seminoles, both groups armed by the Spanish.

Jackson's march to the northeast from Fort Gadsden meant he would encounter the Mikasukian towns, thought to contain hostile Seminoles. As he approached these villages around the end of March, Jackson's advanced companies ran into hostile Indians, and a small but heated battle occurred. Jackson rushed up outreaching columns from his main army to encircle the Native Americans, but the Indians saw the movement developing and precipitously retreated. Jackson investigated all the Native American towns in the area, noting the presence of Red Stick accoutrements in several. It was clear from this evidence that to these Red Sticks, the current struggle was a continuation of the Creek War. To Jackson, it mattered little what the Creeks, Seminoles, or Spanish thought. His army gathered Indian corn and cattle to supply its march, then burned nearly 300 Native American houses, leveling several villages.

General Jackson's powerful army arrived at St. Marks late in the day on April 6th. He made it clear that because the Spanish garrison stood accused of arming hostile Creeks and Seminoles in the area, Jackson meant to occupy St. Marks and the Spanish fortification there, whether or not the Spanish agreed. They certainly did not agree. After a few hours of perfunctory negotiations, companies of Jackson's 4th and 7th Regular Army regiments occupied both the town and the fort without a fight on April 7th, 1818.

Jackson's army did not stay in St. Marks long. Garrisoning the town to prevent the now scattered Indians from reoccupying it when he advanced, Jackson pointed his army toward Bowlegs Town, around 100 miles to the east. He had only 8 days worth of rations at the start of the march, but Jackson trusted his army's ability to march quickly and capture provisions on the way.

The route to the east was marshy and not conducive to rapid marching. On the morning of April 12th, the army approached Natural Bridge on the Ecofina River, and there encountered a large party of Seminoles massed on the edge of a nearby swamp. McIntosh's allied Native Americans, plus a corps of approximately 50 Tennesseans, struck and routed the Indians. The Seminoles suffered 37 warriors killed, six warriors and 97 women and children captured. Almost as importantly, the allied Creeks captured about 500 cattle. Jackson's army would have sufficient provisions to reach Bowlegs Town.

The army moved on eastward toward its destination, Bowlegs Town, which was reputed to be inhabited by Seminoles and runaway slaves. On the morning of April 15th, 1818, at what Jackson thought was approximately twelve miles from the town, the army skirmished with a small band of Seminoles, killing one warrior, and capturing 4 Seminoles. Jackson decided this was a good place to make camp – with a hard march the next morning the army could reach Bowlegs Town by 1:00 PM. However, Jackson had misjudged the distance. On April 16th, after a hard march of sixteen miles and reaching a large pond at 3:00 PM, his advance forces sent back word that the main body of the army was still six miles from the Town. Jackson intended to camp at the pond for the night. However, a Seminole scouting party discovered the Americans, escaped capture, and was reported to have rushed east to warn the village. Jackson rapidly formed his army and pushed on, reaching the outskirts of the village at sunset. His left flank advanced under the command of Colonel Thomas Williamson, leading the 2nd Regiment, Tennessee volunteers and a contingent of allied Creeks under Colonel Noble Kinnard. Jackson himself commanded the center, comprised of the U.S. Regulars, the Georgia Militia, and a unit of Kentucky and Tennessee guards. The right was made up of the 1st Regiment, Tennessee volunteers under Colonel Robert H. Dyer and another contingent of allied Creeks under Brig. General William McIntosh. The right flank was expected to project over the river and cut off the escape of the combined Seminole/black force should they attempt a retreat.

In a vicious twilight attack, the combined Seminole force was completely defeated. Although fighting furiously, the Seminole/black army was heavily outnumbered and outgunned. In the end they abandoned the town and retreated to the river. The fleeing inhabitants of Bowlegs ran straight into the Dyer/McIntosh wing, compounding their losses and turning the retreat into a rout. In the end, Jackson's troops recovered 11 bodies, but speculated the Seminoles carried more dead off with them.

The surprised Seminoles abandoned a large quantity of corn, about 30 cattle, and a large number of horses in their haste to vacate Bowlegs Town; all these were badly needed resources for Jackson's army. These supplies assured a hunger-free and mounted passage back to the west. Taking their time, the American army spent several days completely destroying the three hundred houses of the village.

Jackson considered his campaign in East Florida at an end. He had destroyed many north Florida Seminole villages, captured or destroyed most of the Indians' food supply, blockaded St. Augustine, and humbled St. Marks. At the completion of his destruction of Bowlegs Town, Jackson led his army the 107 miles back to St. Marks in 5 days. Jackson wanted to take his victorious army back to

American soil, and there disband it. The army had suffered almost no casualties during the war in the Floridas to date. However, Jackson knew the Spanish governor in Pensacola, the capital of West Florida, awaited the evacuation of the American army to the north to reassert what control he could establish after that movement. Perhaps he would even try to govern East Florida from Pensacola. There was talk that hostile Indians moved into and out of Pensacola at will, freely supplied with Spanish weapons and regularly using them to strike Alabama in bloody raids.

Jackson mulled these thoughts as he headed west toward St. Marks. By the time he reached the town, his mind was made up. Jackson would take his army west to Pensacola and prove once and for all that an American army could move throughout the Floridas, wherever it wanted and whenever it wanted. This move would also disrupt the Indians' use of Pensacola as a sanctuary.

Early in the morning of April 29th, Jackson and an army of 1,200 soldiers departed St. Marks westward for Fort Gadsden, where they would reprovision and continue on. Following the plan, Jackson marched steadily to the west and on May 24th his army arrived at the edge of Pensacola. The Spanish garrison guarding Pensacola had already retreated to Fort San Carlos de Barrancas at the entrance to the bay, so Jackson swept into the city, virtually ignoring the weak effort the locals put up to resist the occupation. Jackson called on the commander of Fort San Carlos, Jose Masot, to surrender, but the Spaniard refused, possibly thinking Jackson was bluffing with his threat to take the bastion by storm. He certainly misread General Jackson. Throughout the morning of May 27th, Jackson's artillery of one 9-pounder cannon and one 8-inch howitzer blasted Fort San Carlos, and Jackson's men, with ladders in hand and in full view of the fortress, massed for the assault. A white flag appeared over the fort, and the 300-man garrison surrendered.

Jackson determined the war was over. He installed a provisional government over the Floridas, with Colonel William King as governor, then issued a pledge that Spanish laws would remain in effect and Spanish personal property would be respected. He said nothing of Creek and Seminole laws and rights.

Jackson's campaigns in East and West Florida certainly made an impression on the Spanish colonial officials in Madrid. They knew Spain was weakened by the war against Napoleon, and America had proven it could take the Floridas any time it wished. Better to negotiate the cession of the Floridas to the United States now as nominal owner and possessor, rather than have America simply annex them, as it certainly would in the near future. The Adams-Onis Treaty between Spain and the United States was signed on February 22, 1819. By the terms of the treaty, Florida officially became U.S. territory in July, 1821.

Jackson rewarded his "friends" the Choctaw, Chickasaw, and Cherokee Nations, loyal allies in the wars against the Creeks, British, Seminoles, and Spanish, with a series of land-grabbing treaties between 1816 and 1820. The cumulative result of this series of treaties was the virtual extinguishment of Chickasaw and Choctaw land rights east of the Mississippi, and a significant reduction of Cherokee land in the East. Jackson would go on to orchestrate an especially cruel and duplicitous set of negotiations with the Cherokees in the 1830s, sentencing his "allies" to tread the *Trail of Tears* into the west.

The Mississippi Valley was secured for the United States. America was now free to enjoy the fruits of her newly confirmed empire. One of the first places she would do so was through the economic development of the Miami Valley / Great Black Swamp Corridor.

** The contemporary term *Negro* was used in direct quotations from the era being studied, as well as becoming the historical name for the fort that succeeded British Fort Apalachicola. No disrespect is intended to African-Americans through the use of this term.

AFTERMATH OF CONFLICT:
The Fruits of Empire

CHAPTER 15

Economic Exploitation of the New Empire: The Development of the Miami Valley/Great Black Swamp Corridor: 1825-'45

Want to get an idea of the American Westerner's mindset toward westward expansion in the late 1800s? I don't think anyone will disagree that the railroads were the principal means of population growth and economic expansion in the Old West (the area west of the Mississippi River) during the period from 1870 to 1910. Of the four great transcontinental railroads, the Great Northern, spanning the continent from Minneapolis to Seattle, was the last to be completed, in 1893. James J. Hill was the mastermind and driving force behind the building of the Great Northern Railroad. He not only built the road, but he sent agents into Scandinavia to recruit settlers as farmers for the northern plains. Hill assisted them in establishing free homesteads along the tracks, or sold them land he owned along the railroad right-of-way for $2.50 an acre. He also established feeder lines and grain elevators along the route of the transcontinental road. As he established the growing of wheat in the northern plains, Jim Hill grew more aggressive in recruiting peasants from Europe to the lands along the Great Northern Railroad. Hill instituted a program to transport farm peasants from Europe to the northern plains for $25 per person. He was extraordinarily successful. By 1922, 42% of Montana's area was settled by homesteaders – most drawn to the state by Hill's agents and his efforts in publicizing the virtues of the north.

Did the people of the time know what they were building? A published Great Northern transportation advertisement from 1904 touted "Greatly Reduced One-Way **Colonist** Rates to all points in Montana, Idaho, and Washington." (Author's bold and italics). The Great Northern Railroad's number one passenger train was named the

"The Empire Builder." Indeed, Hill himself was popularly nicknamed the Empire Builder. One writer stated, "Jim Hill hitched…places and things together. They comprised the Hill Lines. The Hill lines comprised an empire." There is little doubt the American people of the Nineteenth Century knew that economic development of their newly acquired lands was a stage in the building of an empire. They might have thought it metaphorical, but they were closer to the truth than they knew. They wrested the west from the Indians, protected it from any dangers foreign interests (such as Mexico, Russia, or France) might present, and developed it by building the great infrastructure of the transcontinental railroads.

If the *railroad* was the principal infrastructure for building the great American empire in the Old West from 1870 to 1900, then its predecessor for the building of the first American empire of the Old Northwest Territory from 1825 to 1845 was the *canal*. Specifically, one of the first great agricultural empires of the United States was the flat prairie and rolling hills of west central and northwest Ohio, populated and developed by the improvement of the Miami Valley / Great Black Swamp Corridor known as the Miami-Erie Canal.

In 1818, almost concurrently with the elimination of the Spanish threat to the Mississippi Valley, Ethan Allen Brown proposed a canal system in Ohio which would tie Lake Erie to the Ohio River. He felt a canal system would develop trade in Ohio's budding agricultural community. With the Mississippi River politically secured all the way to the Gulf of Mexico, and a rapidly progressing Erie Canal in New York promising a route east toward the Hudson River and the Atlantic Ocean, Brown felt the time was ripe for the agricultural development and exploitation of Ohio's rich interior. Two canal systems were proposed and eventually built: the Ohio and Erie Canal in eastern Ohio, and the Miami and Erie Canal in western Ohio. In 1822, a canal act was passed by the Ohio General Assembly. By early 1823, preliminary surveys and reports were completed, stating canal navigation was the safest, easiest, and cheapest mode of transportation. On February 4th, 1825, a bill approving and authorizing both the Ohio and Erie Canal and the Miami and Erie Canal was passed by the Assembly.

Ground was broken for the Miami and Erie Canal on July 21st, 1825, at Middletown, Ohio. The legislature approved the building of the first stretch of the canal, 67 miles from Cincinnati to Dayton, and boats began reaching Middletown on November 28th, 1827. By 1828-'29, boats could make the entire trip from Cincinnati to Dayton, although work to completely finish the ten locks in this stretch continued until 1834. The so-called Miami Extension between Dayton and Toledo (utilizing a stretch of the Wabash and Erie Canal currently being built between Defiance and Toledo) was begun in 1833, and the first boat to make the trip from Cincinnati to Toledo completed the journey on June 27th, 1845.

The specifications for the canal were simple and easy for the relatively uneducated construction workers (many recent Irish immigrants or frontier farmers) of the day to follow: 1) 4 foot water depth, 2) 40 feet wide at water level, 3) 26 feet wide at the bottom, 4) towpath 10 feet wide, 5) all slopes 4.5 feet horizontal to 4 feet perpendicular, and 6) locks (of stone or timber construction) 90 feet long by 15 feet wide, with a 6 to 12 foot rise per lock (eventually there were 103 locks on the Miami and Erie Canal).

Dimensions of the Miami and Erie dictated the size of the boats that plied the Canal. Most canal boats were approximately 78 feet long (to give room for the gates to operate at the ends of the 90-foot locks) by 13 to 14 feet wide, drawing 3 feet of water, and able to handle 50 to 80 tons of cargo and/or passengers. The 3-to-6-horse team was capable of pulling the cargo at a sustained speed of 4 miles per hour: this was basically the limit for the canal because faster speeds created wakes which damaged the canal walls.

Fares for the use of the canal reflected the economics of the day. Passenger fees for the packets were 2 to 3 cents per mile, while some packets eventually charged 4 to 5 cents per mile. Freight rates on the Miami and Erie were 2 cents per mile, per ton, with rates going down to 1.5 cents per ton/mile for cartage over 100 miles. With the entire distance of the Miami and Erie Canal from Cincinnati to Toledo being 249 miles, a ton of freight could be moved this distance in 64 hours for $4.24. A passenger could make the same trip in the same time for $7.47.

The track of the Miami and Eric Canal followed the path of explorers and armies from Celeron de Bienville to Harmar to Wayne to Harrison: The Miami Valley / Great Black Swamp Corridor. Proceeding from Mill Creek at Cincinnati across to the Great Miami River, all the way to Piqua, up Loramie Creek and on to the St. Marys River, thence across the portage to the Auglaize and Maumee Rivers, the route of the canal is almost an exact combined track of Harmar's Trace from Cincinnati to the great northwestern bend in the St. Mary's River, then Wayne's march from the St. Marys turn to the Rapids of the Maumee at Toledo.

The preceding facts present a lot of numbers, but we *are* investigating the economic exploitation of the new empire: numbers form the basis of all economic evaluations. Beneath all the hard facts lie one contemporary observation: never before in the history of the United States had a public infrastructure of such magnitude been put into place for the economic exploitation of such a vast area.

The question upon the completion of such a prodigious effort by our forefathers must be: *Did the Miami and Erie Canal perform the service for which it was intended* (the reasons new empire infrastructures are created): *To foster both the population and the economic development of West-Central/Northwest Ohio ?*

The answer must be given by citing more facts:

1) For 25 years, from approximately 1828 to 1853, the Miami and Erie Canal (along with the Ohio and Erie Canal) was the principal means of transportation in Ohio. Ohio's population grew from 581,295 in 1820 to 1,980,329 in 1850, including a 68% increase in population between 1830 and 1840 - certainly at least in part due to the cheapness of canal transportation. In 1832, 1,000 travelers used the canal between Cincinnati and Dayton each week. In 1842, 52,922 passengers used the expanded canal. The great Eastern Europe mass immigration of the 1840s to the United States was greatly absorbed by using the Miami and Erie Canal to populate the eastern portion of the Old Northwest Territory (ie: West-Central / Northwestern Ohio and Northeastern Indiana).

2) Before the advent of the canals, the cost to move a ton of freight overland between the Ohio frontier and the east coast was $125. After the advent of the canal, that same cost was $25. Once the canal began operation, the price of a bushel of wheat grown in Central Ohio jumped from $.50 per bushel to $.75 per bushel. Between 1833 and 1850, Cincinnati received between 18,000 and 35,000 bushels of pork products from the interior each year. Cincinnati in turned shipped sugar and molasses from southern markets to Toledo up the Miami and Erie Canal and into Indiana via the Wabash and Ohio Canal connection at Junction, Ohio. Along with raw agricultural commodities as wheat, corn, and livestock, the canal handled more refined commodities such as pork, flour, and whiskey.

3) The development of the Miami Valley / Great Black Swamp Corridor known as the Miami and Erie Canal fulfilled its old purpose of military transport as well as its primary purposes. Shortly after its opening of the entire 249-mile route, the canal served as a transportation conduit for soldiers from Toledo, Michigan, and the entire Northwestern Ohio area to be carried to the southwest for service in the Mexican War (1846-1848). The officers traveled by packet, while the enlisted soldiers traveled on freight barges. Indeed, the federal military establishment considered the Miami and Erie Canal an important military conduit for the transport of military goods and personnel between New York and New Orleans until 1856.

The facts are impressive, but once again the big picture drawn from the hard facts tells the story. We must remember that in 1818, when the Mississippi Valley was secured and the first thought was given to building infrastructures to develop the interior of Ohio, the woods, rolling hills, and swamplands of West Central/Northwestern Ohio were barely disturbed. By the time the canals reached full maturity, they had been used to promote immigration to the extent that Ohio was the third most populous state in the Union. Industries using the transportation and waterpower generated by the canals and their feeders included flour mills, machine shops, foundries, distilleries, wool factories, and cotton factories. Basic resources such as iron ore and coal were stimulated. Management skills from the operation of the canals and the industries fostered by them flourished. The cash paid for the construction and operation of the canals and their attendant industries meant that Ohio changed from a barter economy to a cash economy, and the cash was used to purchase the manufactured goods fostered by the canals.

Ohio became a significant contributor to the overall economy of the United States, and with this came increased political power in Washington. Federal politicians had to be careful to court the votes of the new economic powerhouse.

It is safe to say the improvement to the Miami Valley / Great Black Swamp Corridor – the Miami and Erie Canal - was more than successful in fulfilling its primary purpose: the initial economic exploitation of the first United States imperial conquest.

Yet, the reign of the Miami and Erie Canal as the engine of economic exploitation was relatively short-lived. As the 1840s turned to the 1850s, the freighters on the Miami and Erie Canal were hired to carry rails and ties to build a new technology invading in the area – the railroad. This new competitor hastened the time when the canals would become economically less viable and technically obsolete. It is to that era that we now turn.

CHAPTER 16

Epilogue –

Economic Exploitation of the Empire: The Miami Valley / Great Black Swamp Corridor in Maturity: From 1850 to the 2000s

The Miami and Erie Canal reveled in the robust strength of its youthful maturity. Toll revenues for Ohio canals in 1840 were $532,688 and climbing. By 1851, revenues hit an all time high at $799,024. The future appeared healthy for the leading transportation technology of the day, the canal system.

But ominous clouds appeared on the industry horizon at the height of its growth and usefulness. Competition for the canals arose in the form of the increasingly efficient and cost-effective railroads. In 1848, just three years after the completion of the Miami and Erie Canal, the first railroad spanning the distance between the Ohio River and Lake Erie went into operation. In 1851, the same year in which operating profits reached their pinnacle for the Ohio canal system, the first railroad between Cincinnati, Columbus, and Cleveland went into operation.

The railroads had several advantages over canals. Steam-powered train systems operated more economically than canal systems; thus lower rates per unit of cartage could be charged to the customer. The physical rail beds could be constructed more cheaply than canals could be dug; therefore more mileage of tracks, and these to more diverse locations, could be built. This gave the railroads the advantage of more direct routes between destinations. Railroads were "all-weather, year-round" transportation systems: there was no 7 to 10 week disruption in service due to frozen canals.

The advantages were obvious, and railroad construction exploded. During the period of 1850 to 1860, railway miles in Ohio went from 375 miles to 2,946 miles of track in service. Canals attempted to compete with the railroad by adopting its method of locomotion, the steam engine. The first steam-powered canal boat, the *Niagara*, was built in 1845, but in general the technology was not successful on the canals. The extra power and potential speed of the steam engine could not be utilized on the Miami and Erie Canal - any speed over 5 miles per hour created wakes too large for the safety of other craft on the water and eroded the side banks of the canal. With canals failing to adapt new technology to their operations, it became clear that the transportation of passengers must be discontinued once the railroads became established. The competition between canals and railroads would be won or lost in the arena of cartage of freight.

Canals could not win: they had too many disadvantages compared to the new railroads. By 1856, overall expenditures on canal operations exceeded incoming revenues, and the canal's overall importance as a transportation system declined sharply after 1860. Although canals still had utility in the business of transportation of freight (as late as 1903 canal revenues still were greater than $70,000), the end was near. In 1906, only the mainline Miami and Erie and Ohio and Erie Canals were still operational, and even so, only parts of the main lines operated at that time. The last revenue-generating cargo boat to pass through Fort Loramie and Ottoville on the Miami and Erie Canal did so in 1912. Although from 1904 to 1909 the state spent money to revitalize the canals, the disastrous 1913 floods in Ohio did immense damage to the system, washing out large sections and destroying the aqueduct over Loramie Creek. The canals were finished as an engine of economic growth in Ohio. The Miami and Erie Canal officially closed in 1929.

Still, the history of the Miami Valley / Great Black Swamp Corridor as a thoroughfare of economic commerce was far from over. Railroads crisscrossed west-central and northwestern Ohio, including all four of the eastern "trunk" rail lines (the Baltimore and Ohio, Pennsylvania, New York Central, and Erie Railroads), these mostly bearing transcontinental cargo. However, at least four "local" lines combined to virtually parallel the route of the Miami and Erie

Canal and assume its role as carrier of bulk commodities from the heartland of the Corridor. The railroad line most closely following the path of the canal was the Cincinnati, Hamilton, and Dayton Railroad. Originating in Cincinnati, the railroad was virtually built on the towpath of the Miami and Erie Canal as far as Piqua, and for good reason. The brilliant original canal surveyors had ingeniously followed the path of least resistance in laying out the canal between Cincinnati and Piqua in the tricky Great Miami River valley. The railroad surveyors and engineers found it difficult to improve on the route. The C. H. & D. eventually deviated from the Miami and Erie Canal after paralleling it about 10 miles to the east from Piqua to Wapakoneta, Ohio. From there it made its own way northeast to Toledo.

Taking up the task of common carrier in the area north of Grand Lake St. Marys (a feeder lake for the Miami and Erie Canal) was the Cincinnati Northern Railroad. This steel ribbon paralleled the route of the canal, approximately 10 to 15 miles to the west, the entire distance from Delphos to Defiance, and served the same purpose: the freighting of bulk commodities produced in Ohio's agricultural heartland.

Another railroad tied route of the new technology to that of the old: the original mainline of the Wabash Railroad. The Wabash emerged from Indiana east of the village of Woodburn and struck northeast toward Toledo. It intersected the Cincinnati Northern at Cecil, Ohio, and took up the torch of paralleling the Miami and Erie Canal from Defiance to Toledo: the Canal on the north bank of the Maumee River and the Wabash "Cannonball" on the prairie only slightly further north. Although the Wabash was a larger railroad than the others, and was involved in carrying a much more diverse freight roster, it still found the commercial route of the Miami and Erie Canal useful as a template for its Ohio operations.

Still one more local railroad must be mentioned as an integral part of the Black Swamp portion of the Corridor: The Clover Leaf Railroad. Inelegantly nicknamed "The Railroad to Nowhere," these rails paralleled the Piqua Road portion of Harmar's/Wayne's/Harrison's path to and from Fort Wayne, from Decatur, Indiana to Willshire, Ohio. Striking eastward, the railroad intersected the

Miami and Erie Canal at Delphos, Ohio. It then ran in an errant course toward Toledo, attempting to weave its way between every small town grain elevator anywhere close to its northeastward gyration. It thus "cut the angle" between Delphos and Toledo, eliminating the northwestward track of the Canal into Defiance. This railroad is important not only because it helped assume the bulk commodity transportation task the old Miami and Erie Canal once held, but because (with the Cincinnati, Hamilton, and Dayton Railroad) it forged the directional trail between the path of the old technology (the canal) and the path of the upcoming technology, the superhighway.

Railroads reigned supreme as the prime transportation system for the United States for nearly 100 years, from about 1855 to 1955. Yet, this state of affairs changed so rapidly that the railroads were toppled without much of a chance to adapt. As Yogi Berra said, "It's *déjà vu* all over again." A concurrent maturation of technologies occurred so rapidly that the dominant transportation system of the day could not adapt. (Does this sound like the canals in the 1850s?)

In the midst of the Cold War in the 1950s, President Dwight Eisenhower pushed into law a system of four-lane highways, ostensibly to facilitate the movement of military supplies and men to danger spots in the continental United States. The Interstate Highway System had the happy side effect of tying together major metropolitan manufacturing centers with a technologically advanced roadway which made travel at 55 to 65 miles per hour for long distances very feasible. At the same time, the automotive industry refined the diesel-powered semi-truck tractor to the degree of operational ease and safety that long distance hauls were also very feasible. The same factors that worked to make canals obsolete now came into effect against railroads. An almost infinite road net made direct point-to-point deliveries possible. The flexibility of a single relatively small load (40 tons), able to be rapidly moved to a point where it was immediately needed, by a vehicle operator basically only concerned with this particular delivery, enhanced the appeal of this mode of transportation.

In the 1960s, the superhighway system was extended into the Miami Valley / Great Black Swamp Corridor with the building of

Interstate Highway 75. This highway mirrored the Miami and Erie Canal from Cincinnati to Piqua, then followed a route paralleling the Cincinnati, Hamilton, & Dayton and Cloverleaf Railroads to Toledo. In the 1990's, Interstate 75 in Ohio was reputed to have the highest rate of semi-tractor/trailer traffic per mile of any highway in the United States. The Miami Valley / Great Black Swamp Corridor, through the infrastructure of Interstate Highway 75, remained alive and well as a transportation system for the economic growth of western Ohio, as well as for the entire eastern half of the United States.

The progression of transportation systems in the Miami Valley / Great Black Swamp Corridor is evident. In 1812, an army pirogue on the Auglaize River could handle possibly one ton of freight at about 4 miles per hour. A freight barge on the Miami and Erie Canal in the 1840s could transport 50 to 80 tons of cargo at this same 4 miles per hour. In 1933, a typical local freight train could handle perhaps seven times the weight of a canal freighter at 40 miles per hour, but had to deliver this freight to fixed locations along the rails, from which it must be distributed. By the 1970s and '80s, a semi-trailer on Interstate 75 could haul 40 tons of freight at speeds of 55 to 60 miles per hour, to precise locations at the precise time the cargo was needed.

As the 1900s turn to the 2000s, interstate highway engineers are attempting to determine alternatives to relieve the overall traffic pressure on the six-to-eight lane trunk of the Miami Valley / Great Black Swamp Corridor: Interstate 75 between Cincinnati and Piqua, Ohio. This modern leviathan, whose course would be virtually unrecognizable to the earliest travelers along its vistas, and which has been given various names and modes of infrastructure through the years, is still one of the main (if not the *premier*) transportation arteries of the eastern Midwest. The Miami Valley / Great Black Swamp Corridor remains what it has been from the beginning of United States' history: the path to America's first empire.

CLOSE-UP:
Details Relating to the Trans-Appalachian Wars

APPENDIX A

The Revolutionary War in the Old Northwest

War without end in the eastern Northwest Territory – A time-bridge between initial settlement and the Woodland Wars of 1790-1795

If military actions in the Woodland Wars of 1790-'95 and the subsequent Northwest Theater of the War of 1812 (1811-'13) are considered relatively under-documented and almost forgotten, the record of the Revolutionary War in what was to become the eastern portion of the Old Northwest Territory is really obscure. Most histories of the Western Theater of the Revolution are limited to recounting the exploits of American Colonel George Rogers Clark in capturing Kaskaskia and Vincennes from the British. There is no doubt that Clark's strenuous activities in capturing these villages are the stuff of legends, and were significant contributions to the ultimate colonial victory in the Revolution. Yet the period of 1774 to 1789 saw much more military activity than this in the region bounded by Lake Erie and the Maumee River on the north, the Wabash River on the northwest and west, the Ohio River Valley on the south and southeast, and the boundless forests between Presque Isle and Pittsburgh on the east – the area that would basically become the American states of Indiana, Ohio, and northern Kentucky. Not surprisingly, the ubiquitous George Rogers Clark emerged as the central military figure in the area during this entire fifteen-year period of warfare. The signing of the Treaty of Paris, "ending" the Revolutionary War between Great Britain and the new United States, did little to curb the fighting in what would become the Old Northwest Territory. At least two major military expeditions pitting the United States militia against Great Britain via its surrogate Native American allies occurred after the signing of the this treaty.

Perhaps the reason for the relative obscurity of these military operations was the small numbers of men involved in the various actions. "Armies" of less than 100 "soldiers" (in reality, usually little more than untrained militia) were not uncommon, and armies of more than 1,000 men were considered serious forces to be dealt with. Even by Revolutionary War and War of 1812 standards, these were very small numbers of soldiers and warriors. Yet even this factor is important, as one man or one small group of men could make a serious difference in the fate of an entire campaign or region.

The War Begins, 1774

An eerily similar presage to the War of 1812 in the Trans-Appalachian West is associated with the Revolutionary War. Just as some historians consider the 1811 "Battle of Tippecanoe" to be the first battle of the War of 1812, some historians consider the 1774 "Battle of Point Pleasant" (also known as "Lord Dunmore's War") to be the initial battle of the Revolutionary War (1775-'83). Both battles pitted essentially frontier militia armies against hostile Native American confederations in the contest to determine supremacy in the eastern portion of what would become the Old Northwest Territory. Likewise, both battles occurred before the generally accepted starting date of the wars with which they are considered to be associated.

Events leading to the Battle of Point Pleasant began many years before the first shots were fired. The 1768 Treaty of Fort Stanwix, NY established the boundary between European settlers and Native Americans at the Ohio River. However, increasing encroachment by the ever-expanding white colonists led to increasing animosity on the part of the incumbent Indians. Animosity grew to violent atrocities committed by both whites and Indians west of the Ohio. As Native American raids spread east of the river, Virginia's Governor John Murray, Lord Dunmore, received authority from the Virginia colonial government to pursue armed redress against the Native American alliance, composed of the Shawnee, Miami, Ottawa, Delaware, Wyandot, and Mingo nations. Dunmore conceived a campaign to break armed Indian resistance along the Ohio River – a war of land acquisition versus a war of Indian annihilation. Therefore, in the tradition of the day (and setting a precedent for similar campaigns in the future), Dunmore's goal was to advance on the Native American villages situated on the Scioto River (near present-day Chillicothe, OH), destroy them, and thus compel the allied nations to sue for peace and acquiesce to colonial settlement of the Ohio area.

To accomplish this, Dunmore assembled an army composed of two divisions. The northern 1,500-man force, commanded by Dunmore himself, would march from Fort Cumberland to Fort Pitt, descend the Ohio River, and unite with the second, southern division. This 1,100-man southern force, commanded by militia General Andrew Lewis, would march overland from west-central Virginia, descend the Kanawha River, and reach the confluence of the Kanawha and Ohio Rivers, combining with Dunmore's division at the river junction known as Point Pleasant.

As with all best-laid plans, the timing of this one ran amuck. Lewis's southern division reached Point Pleasant ahead of Dunmore's northern division. Shawnee chief Cornstalk, war leader of the Indian confederacy, monitored both the advances closely and duly noted the wide separation of the two armies. He decided to attack Lewis's stationary southern division at Point Pleasant before the divisions united. With between 800 and 1,100 warriors, Cornstalk crossed the Ohio River in the early morning hours of October 10, 1774, and attacked before dawn. In a violent, bloody battle lasting from an hour before dawn to an hour before dusk, Lewis's division succeeded in maintaining possession of the battlefield, but at the cost of 75 dead and 140 wounded. The Native American confederacy forces withdrew across the Ohio, also suffering grievously in the battle with the loss of between 35 and 75 warriors killed. The stage was set for continually increasing violence on both sides of the Ohio Valley.

British Strategy for the Old Northwest, 1777-'78

The notorious British territorial governor of the area just to the northeast of what would become the Old Northwest Territory, Lieutenant Colonel Henry Hamilton, fomented violence throughout the eastern half of Old Northwest Territory early in the Revolutionary War. Paying bounties for white settlers' scalps from his base at Fort Detroit, Hamilton soon became known as "Hair Buyer" to his

Native American war allies. To Indian nations already frantically alarmed by American intrusions into the Ohio River Valley area, this provided added impetus to an already strong tendency to violently oppose any further incursions by whites. Hamilton's bounties insured continuing bloody conflicts from Lake Erie to northern Kentucky and western Virginia.

There was a method to Hamilton's tactics, however. If Hamilton through his Native American surrogates could succeed in destroying the white settlements in northern-eastern Kentucky/western Virginia, and thus throw the Americans back across the Ohio, he could apply pressure to the patriots' westernmost military outpost, Fort Pitt, located in western Pennsylvania. Free of the American colonists' presence on his southern flank, and his northern flank secured by Lake Erie, he could mount a military campaign east from Detroit, capture Fort Pitt, and repel American influence back east across the Appalachian Mountains. Then he could reestablish Native American control to the area between Fort Detroit and the Ohio River, under the benevolence of the British Empire. The British would be assured of an uncontested monopoly of the lucrative fur trade with the Native Americans in the Old Northwest.

Hamilton's activities to establish and execute this strategy began to bear fruit in 1777. Depredations against colonist settlements on either side of the upper reaches of the Ohio River touched an early peak of violence in that year, homesteaders giving 1777 the eerie nickname of "The Year of the Bloody Sevens." There were numerous unnamed and forgotten skirmishes in the area during this period; the most notable were the two sieges of Fort Henry (present Wheeling, West Virginia) in September, 1777. These sieges cost the lives of approximately 41 settlers, making these the most costly of the early battles.

The famous explorer Daniel Boone was captured by Shawnees at Blue Licks near the Ohio River in what is now north-central Kentucky in January, 1778. He was taken north to the Pickawillany/ Old Chillicothe area north of the Ohio River and forced to run the gauntlet as punishment for his transgressions against the Shawnees. Boone's courage in facing the gauntlet, and his strength and fortitude in withstanding this fearsome treatment so impressed Shawnee Chief Blackfish that Blackfish adopted Boone into the tribe.

Boone accepted initiation into the tribe then bided his time through the first half of 1778, waiting for an opportunity to escape. This opportunity presented itself in the mid-June. Overhearing plans for a Shawnee attack on his own northern Kentucky fort, Boonsborough, Boone waited until his captors were distracted hunting wild turkeys and made his escape. Boone outdistanced his pursuers, traveling 160 miles in 4 days and 4 nights on almost no sustenance, and reached Boonsborough. Blackfish in turn arrived at Boonsborough in early-September with an approximate 450-man attack force of Shawnees and French-Canadian militia. With only 30 grown men and 20 older boys inside the fort, its defense seemed impossible. However, with the aid of the women, who loaded spare guns and provided food to the men at the gunports, plus a fortuitous rainstorm that extinguished fires ignited by flaming arrows, Boonsborough survived a seven-day siege. The defense of Boonsborough became a famous early symbol of settler resistance to the British and Indian offensive in the Kentucky country.

Alarmed by the attacks south and east of the Ohio, General George Washington took the offensive threat embodied by the British and Native Americans at Detroit seriously. In November, 1778, he ordered General Lachlan McIntosh and 1,200 troops to advance west from Fort Pitt into the Ohio territory and establish Fort Laurens (near present Bolivar, OH) on the Tuscarawas River. The fort was to serve as a western sentinel for Fort Pitt. It could be used either as a springboard for a 1779 American campaign against Fort Detroit, or a tripwire, warning of an approaching British campaign from Detroit against Fort Pitt. It was the only Continental Army fort built in Ohio during the Revolutionary War.

Clark in the West, 1777-'79

Clark's noteworthy 1778 campaign to capture the British-held old French villages of Kaskaskia, Cahokia, and Vincennes was perhaps the most significant activity in the relatively "under-documented" period of military activity in the northwestern area. In late-1777, Clark, already well known for his efforts in protecting Kentucky from rampaging Native American incursions, went to Virginia Governor Patrick Henry with an intriguing plan. With Henry's permission and financial backing, Clark would recruit Virginians (Kentucky was a district of Virginia until its 1792 statehood), purchase supplies and boats, descend the Ohio River to the Mississippi Valley, and capture lightly-held Kaskaskia in the "Illinois country." He would then send detachments both north (to occupy Cahokia, located higher on the Mississippi) and east (to capture Vincennes, on the banks of the Wabash River). Henry was enthusiastic; he readily consented and commissioned Clark a colonel. Although the turnout to Clark's call for volunteers was less than expected, 175 hard-bitten stalwart backwoodsmen were recruited for the venture, which began May 12, 1778.

The results were spectacular. Boats carrying the tiny army traveled down the Ohio River to its confluence with the Tennessee River. Clark and his company landed on the north bank of the Ohio at this point and headed northwest, crossing swamps, meadows, fields, and streams. On July 5th, Kaskaskia was caught unawares, as was Cahokia when Captain Joseph Bowman approached it a few days later, and both villages fell without bloodshed. A small detachment under Captain Leonard Helm then trekked the 180 miles east from Kaskaskia to Vincennes and captured both the town and its military installation, Fort Sackville, without a fight in late-July, 1778.

The British could not let this invasion of their territory go uncontested. Lieutenant Colonel Henry Hamilton gathered a force at Detroit (171 regulars and militia, and 60 allied Native Americans) on October 7th, 1778. His intent was to recapture the still relatively undefended town of Vincennes, on the lower reaches of the Wabash River. Hamilton's force moved south along the west coast of Lake Erie, ascended the Maumee River to Kekionga (present Ft. Wayne, IN), crossed the portage from the Maumee to the *Petite Riviere* ("Little River") and thence navigated to the "Forks of the Wabash" (current Huntington, IN), the confluence of the *Petite Riviere* and the Wabash River. The British army swelled to about 585 soldiers and warriors as it further descended the Wabash; Hamilton and his army captured Vincennes in December 1778 (he was further reinforced by 200 additional Native Americans at Vincennes).

This was a relatively epic march for a force of this size for the time period, through an area utterly devoid of any kind of assisting infrastructures. Hamilton's expedition succeeded in re-projecting a substantial military presence once again close to the southern and western limits of British influence.

At Kaskaskia, Col. George Rogers Clark learned of the fall of Vincennes on January 29th, 1779. Reasoning that the British would never suspect a winter invasion of Vincennes/Fort Sackville across 180 miles of flooded wasteland, Clark began to build a force to do exactly that. His army at Kaskaskia had dwindled due to sickness, desertion, and garrison duty, but he was able to recruit two small companies of former French/British citizens to rebuild his force. Having 180 militia soldiers (one for each mile of flooded swamp he would have to cross), Clark moved east on February 5th, 1779. Mile after torturous mile was crossed, the soldiers sometimes having to march in water up to mid-chest level.

Clark was absolutely correct in his projections. Hamilton, snugly ensconced in Fort Sackville on the edge of Vincennes, thought no force could cross the flooded swamps in February, and his garrison was not prepared to fight. Clark added a bit of cunning in his approach to the fort. He created many unit flags, then marched his soldiers again and again through the streets of Vincennes, regimental drums beating; sometimes within sight of the fort and sometimes not. Hamilton was convinced that he was facing a force which heavily outnumbered his garrison in the fortress, and for the second time Fort Sackville surrendered without a fight, on February 25th, 1779. The audacity of George Rogers Clark had once again been responsible for the capture of Vincennes, this time for good.

The Battles Shift Eastward, 1779-'80

As the "Illinois country" stabilized, the scenes of confrontation between the American revolutionaries and the British shifted to the east – basically to the Indian paths and rivers that coursed through the country between Cincinnati (Fort Washington) on a huge north bend in Ohio River, and Detroit, located between Lakes Erie and Huron. The main riverine passages tracing this course were the Greater Miami River north from Cincinnati to Pickawillany, then north again on Loramie Creek (past Loramie's Store) to the portage between Loramie Creek and the St. Marys River. Following the St. Mary's north to Girty's Town, the traveler could make a choice. Descending the St. Marys to the northwest would lead to Kekionga, the capital of the Miami Nation. Crossing a short portage to the northeast would gain the Auglaize River, which wound its way north through the heart of the Great Black Swamp to a confluence with the Maumee River; here stood the Grand Glaize (the AuGlaize Villages). Continuing to the northeast on the Maumee would give access to Lake Erie. Cruising north on Lake Erie (or walking on an ancient path along Erie's western shore), one soon came to the historic French (later, British) fort at *de troit*, or *the strait*, i.e.: The river system connecting Lake Erie and Lake Huron. This entire area (which could be considered the "Miami Valley/Great Black Swamp Corridor") would remain an axis of attack between the expanding Americans and the colonizing British (greatly assisted by their variously allied Indian nations) more or less continuously from 1779 to 1813.

In mid-1779, in retribution for continued Native American depredations south of the Ohio River into Kentucky, militia Colonel John Bowman led a group of mounted Kentucky troopers north from present Cincinnati toward the Native American stronghold at Pickawillany (current Piqua, OH). Bowman and his command were met at Old Chillicothe (near present Oldtown, OH) by a Shawnee war party under Chief Blackfish, defeated, and sent reeling back to Fort Washington. A direct result of this defeat was that Colonel George Rogers Clark was summoned from the west to assume command of the 100 Regular and additional irregular troops (currently under Colonel George Slaughter) manning the Ohio River line at the Falls of the Ohio.

The British in Detroit monitored activities to the south. Noting the impending arrival of Clark in the eastern sector, Captain Henry Bird received permission from his superior, Major Arent S. DePeyster, for a raid into Kentucky before Clark's presence could be felt. Bird assembled an army of 850 soldiers (which eventually swelled to between 1,000 and 1,200 men on the march). He traced the Miami Valley / Great Black Swamp Corridor from north to south, using the

Maumee/Auglaize/St. Marys River-Loramie Creek line to advance during May and June, 1780. Sliding past Fort Washington further to the east, Bird crossed the Ohio River and advanced into Kentucky via the Licking River. Bird moved fairly deeply into Kentucky, utilizing the Licking River to capture Ruddle's Station on June 24th. Bird then moved up Stoner Creek to nearby Martin's Station, capturing it on June 28th. Bird destroyed both settlements, took 470 prisoners, and made good his escape by a wretched march back to Detroit, arriving on August 4th.

Stung by Bowman's defeat and Bird's well-organized foray into Kentucky, newly-promoted Brigadier General George Rogers Clark built a stronger Kentucky militia army in 1780. In mid-summer, Clark moved north along essentially the same track Bowman took earlier. With 100 Regulars and 1,000 Kentucky volunteers, he advanced up the Great Miami River all the way to Pickawillany and on August 8th defeated the British and Shawnees in battle. He suffered 19 dead in the battle, but succeeded in burning both the village and the fort at this location. Clark's victory was important because it forced the Shawnees to base their raiding operations further north, at the village of Wapagoneda (present Wapakoneta, OH), for a period of time.

At nearly the same time (Autumn, 1780), Colonel Auguste LaBalme devised a scheme to advance from Vincennes up the Wabash River and capture the British fort at Kekionga, on the upper Maumee River. His ambitious plans encompassed the eventual taking of Detroit. The reckless LaBalme was able to convince only 100 militiamen to accompany him on the bold venture, but this did not deter him. LaBalme made it all the way to just west of Kekionga, where he captured stores and revitalized his campaign. LaBalme heard of more stores and supplies a few miles to the north on the Eel River. He left about 20 men in the vicinity of Kekionga and moved toward this additional bounty. However, LaBalme rapidly approached the home villages of the great Miami leader Little Turtle, and the war chief moved to stop the incursion. Near the Eel River on November 5th, 1780, LaBalme was surprised by superior numbers of Native Americans and overwhelmed. LeBalme and both of his separated commands were annihilated.

Yorktown ends the War? Not in the Northwest: The Year 1782

One might be excused for thinking the American victory in the Battle of Yorktown, October 19th, 1781, ended the Revolution, and that the time spent between that date and the signing of the 1783 Treaty of Paris was composed of peaceful negotiations. This might have been true in the eastern theater, but west of the Appalachian Mountains, raids, counter-raids, and battles raged across the Ohio wilderness, as British, Native Americans, and settlers battled for survival. Indeed, during 1781, American frontier militia forces under Colonel Daniel Broadhead met and defeated the Delawares north and west of the Ohio River at the pitched Battle of Goschochgung (present Coshocton, OH).

The year 1782 was an especially violent one north of and in the Ohio River Valley; a massacre and several raiding campaigns drenched the Ohio territory in blood. As if to make up for the disaster at Yorktown, the British started campaigning early that spring. In March, Captain William Caldwell moved south from Detroit, essentially following what would in 1812 become parts of Generals Hull and Harrison's supply lines through the swamps and plains of north-central Ohio. With "several hundred" soldiers and warriors, Caldwell penetrated the Mac-o-chee (Shawnee for "whispering streams") highlands of west-central Ohio (near present Bellefontaine) and continued further south to raid Springfield. As had Captain Bird two years earlier, Caldwell made an unscathed return to Detroit.

Unrelenting Native American atrocities continued unabated in Ohio. The scourge was so great that many Americans assumed the horrendously unchivalrous attitude that "the only good Indian is a dead Indian." This assumption eventually led to two of the most horrible events in the history of westward expansion – one perpetrated by white militiamen and one by Native American tribesmen.

The Delaware Nation's territory had originally stretched from mid-Ohio into western Pennsylvania. In the Pennsylvania wilderness, the Delawares came into contact with proselytizing German/Christian missionaries known as *Moravians*. The missionaries succeed in converting a substantial number of Delawares into "Moravian Indians," then induced them to move to the eastern

Ohio area to develop a separatist Christian settlement. The Indians did in fact move to an area having such Germanic village names as Gnadenhutten and Schoenbrunn. There they peacefully settled into tending gardens and raising livestock, their young attending organized churches and schools. It could be argued the Moravian Indians were the most "Christian" of all the varied settlers on the Ohio frontier.

However, this idyllic setting was not to last for long. Hostile Native American raids by Indians other than the Moravians along the Pennsylvania/Ohio frontier inflamed white hatred for all things Indian. In March 1782, an irregular regiment commanded by militia Colonel David Williamson moved from the east into the eastern Ohio area and rounded up about 90 Moravian Delawares, locking them in their church. Williamson then announced that all were to be killed shortly in retribution for Indian atrocities. The Moravians asked only for a few moments to pray and say goodbye to each other; this they were granted. Then, true to their word, the militiamen mercilessly slaughtered the entire congregation – men, women, and children alike.

The "Moravian Massacre" shocked and outraged both white settlers and Native Americans. Continental Army Commanding General George Washington sent his trusted subordinate, Colonel William Crawford, to the Pennsylvania frontier to subdue hostile Native American elements before they could visit retribution upon white settlers. Crawford promptly complied, arrived at Fort Pitt in the spring of 1782 and assembled a militia regiment of about 480 soldiers. Unfortunately (for Crawford), many of these militiamen were the same soldiers that had recently participated in the Moravian Massacre. Crawford gathered his scattered command near current Steubenville, OH on May 25th and drove steadily westward toward the upper reaches of the Sandusky River, the home territory of the Delaware, Wyandot, and Seneca Nations. Upon reaching the area near present Upper Sandusky, Ohio, Crawford and his command were defeated in a bloody engagement at Battle Island, June 5th, 1782. The running battle continued into the next day, and it finally resulted in a rout of Crawford's regiment. When Crawford stealthily attempted to escape through the underbrush, he was captured by

Native American warriors. Because of his association with members of the militia who had participated in the Moravian Massacre (and notwithstanding the fact that Crawford himself had nothing to do with the massacre), Crawford was gruesomely burned at the stake on June 11th, enduring hideous tortures for two hours as he slowly burned to death.

As previously noted, British Governor Henry Hamilton's strategic plans for the Old Northwest fell apart due to George Rogers Clark's activities, outlined earlier. Hamilton was captured at Vincennes when it fell to Clark in February, 1779, and his activities as governor and "hair buyer" of the Old Northwest came to an end.

Hamilton might have been captured, but the raiding and violence he inspired on either side of the Ohio River lived on. One of the last of these organized raids, and one of the last pitched battles of the Revolutionary War, took place at the Battle of Blue Licks, KY, on August 19, 1782.

White renegade Simon Girty and British Captain William Caldwell led 400 Ohio Native Americans south across the Ohio River into northern Kentucky. Their destination was Bryan's Station, one of the isolated southern American settlements whose fall Henry Hamilton had envisioned as far back as 1777. The British and Native American war party surrounded Bryan's Station, but a small cadre of 44 long-rifle armed sharpshooters successfully defended the besieged fort.

Meanwhile, the alarm had gone out to other northern Kentucky settlements that Bryan's Station was under attack, and militia companies began rushing to its aid. Girty and Caldwell learned that American forces were converging, and conducted a retrograde movement north toward the Licking River. The British and Indian war party was careful to leave full evidence of its retreat, even to the point of virtually blazing a trail, in the hope the untrained militia would rashly follow them into the trap Girty was formulating in his mind. At Blue Licks, Girty and Caldwell crossed the Licking River and concealed their army among brushy ravines in the hills beyond. Sure enough, the first American unit to answer the call and pursue Girty and Caldwell to the Licking River was a three-company strong (200-man) militia force under Lieutenant Colonel

John Todd. Heedless of the danger into which his militia was blindly rushing, Todd forced a crossing of the river and began climbing the hills on the far side. Girty's Native Americas burst from the concealed ravines and streamed into the ascending militia. In a violent five-minute battle, the Native American war party killed approximately 43 (possibly up to 77) Kentucky militiamen, including Daniel Boone's son, Israel, at minimal loss to themselves. A militia party arriving three days later buried the scalped and unrecognizable corpses at the battle site.

The struggle in the Northwest had taken on a decidedly barbaric cast. General George Rogers Clark surveyed the carnage from his base at Fort Washington (Cincinnati), and decided a punitive raid was needed – a raid against a significant target. The hostile Miami Nation was the strongest power in the Old Northwest at this time, and its capital was Kekionga at the confluence of the St. Marys, St. Joseph, and Maumee Rivers. In November, 1782 Clark gathered 1,050 mounted militiamen and headed northwest up the Great Miami River Valley, intent on the destruction of Kekionga. His November start made it impossible to reach Kekionga that fall. Clark made it as far as Loramie's Post (current Ft. Loramie, OH), settling for the destruction of this British/Indian trading enclave as payment for the defeat and death of Colonel Crawford and the butchery at Blue Licks.

1786: The War That Never Was

The Treaty of Paris was signed in 1783, officially ending the Revolutionary War between Britain and the United States. Yet, small-scale raids and counter-raids seesawed back and forth across the Ohio/Kentucky frontier during the mid-1780s. The British in Detroit maintained a baleful presence, arming and supplying their Native American allies in the hope of destabilizing American claims to the area west of the Appalachian Mountains. The American settlers in Kentucky and southern Ohio hung on to their territorial claims with the meager resources at their disposal. Each side in the struggle seemed intent on "one-upping" the other in the commission of horrific atrocities.

Southern Ohio and Northern Kentucky were still frequent destinations for raids perpetrated by Native Americans between 1782 and 1786. In the fall of 1786, the Kentucky militia decided to once again plunge north of the Ohio River in a two-pronged assault to chastise the Indians for losses visited upon Kentucky. George Rogers Clark, having lost his commission as brigadier general of Virginia (Kentucky district) militia in 1783 for unpaid debts to the state, agreed to lead the westernmost assault. This mission was to move northwest into what is now southern Indiana toward the complex of Native American villages on the upper Wabash River and its tributaries. The mission was plagued by a lack of food and other supplies, which caused the unruly militia to mutiny. The entire expedition ignominiously straggled back to the Ohio River, leaving Clark's shaky reputation in a permanent shambles.

Meanwhile, Clark's trusted lieutenant from the old days, Colonel Benjamin Logan, led the easternmost advance. In October 1786, the 700 to 800 troops of this assault force left the Maysville, KY-Aberdeen/Ripley, OH area, moving north up the now familiar Greater Miami and Mad River valleys. Its destination was the group of Shawnee villages in the Mac-o-chee highlands of west-central Ohio. This operation was quite successful in accomplishing its grisly work, as the militia destroyed seven Native American villages and the old English fort now utilized as Native American stronghold in the Mac-o-chee.

Even this operation was not without its atrocities. The aged Chief Moluntha readily submitted to arrest by the invading militia. However, rampaging militia Colonel McGary, acting on his own, crushed the old warrior's skull in cowardly, unprovoked fury. An angry and sympathetic Benjamin Logan raised Moluntha's young son as his own, naming him Johnny. As John Logan, this young man would subsequently play an active and varied role in the history of the Old Northwest.

The last militia action to be launched from Kentucky by non-Federal troops occurred in August 1789. Major John Hardin, later to be active in the Woodland Wars of 1790-'95, led a 220-man militia force toward the Wabash River region in order to chastise Native Americans who had raided Kentucky. Hardin's troops attacked a

Shawnee encampment, killing three warriors and five women and children. Federal authorities at Vincennes were not pleased with Hardin's raid, as it occurred in the midst of peace treaty negotiations with the northwestern tribes.

As one can see from this review of just the more organized operations (there were literally hundreds more small-scale skirmishes) in what was soon to become the Northwest Territory, the Revolutionary War never quite truly ended in the area west of the Appalachian Mountains. The incursions and atrocities continued with increasing frequency throughout the late-1780s, until the United States government was pressed into officially addressing the situation through military action. Both the stubbornly aggressive Americans and the entrenched Native Americans (backed by the British) rushed headlong toward the first of the conflicts that would decide the ultimate fate of the Old Northwest: The Woodland Wars of 1790-'95.

Appendix B: Revolutionary War "Battles and Raids" in the Eastern "Old Northwest."

Date	Year		Victor	# Soldiers
October	1774	General Andrew Lewis	U.S.	1,100
		Battle of Point Pleasant, WV: Attack on southern division of two-pronged "Lord Dunmore's War" campaign. Shawnees under Cornstalk attack American militia at the confluence of the Kanawha and Ohio Rivers. Americans hold the battlefield.		
September	1777	Fort Henry	U.S.	
		Dual sieges of the fort result in 41 settlers' deaths		
July	1778	General George Rogers Clark	U.S.	175
		Kaskaskia, Cahokia, & Vincennes captured in celebrated campaign from Kentucky		
September	1778	Lt. Colonel Daniel Boone	U.S.	
		Shawnees unsuccessfully lay siege to Boone's Northern Kentucky fort, Boonesborough		
October	1778	Governor Henry Hamilton	British	781
		-From Detroit, moved down the Maumee River -Crossed portage from Kekionga (Ft Wayne) to the Forks of Wabash, & on to conquer Vincennes.		
February	1779	General George Rogers Clark	U.S.	180
		Clark recaptures Vincennes after epic march from Kaskaskia over flooded prairie; Illinois area secured.		
	1779	Colonel John Bowman	Shawnees	
		-From Cincinnati, was defeated at Old Chillicothe		
May-June	1780	Captain Henry Bird	British	850-1,200
		-Raid from Detroit to Central Kentucky		
June 24		*--Captured Ruddle's Station, and*		
June 28		*--Martin's Station*		
August 8	1780	General George Rogers Clark	U.S.	1,100
		-From Cincy, defeated Shawnees at Pickawillany, OH, and burned village.		
November 5	1780	Colonel Auguste LaBalme	Miamis	100
		-From Vincennes, was defeated at Kekionga/Eel R.		
	1781	Colonel William Broadhead	U.S.	
		-Destroyed Goschochgung (Coshocton, OH) in raid up the Muskingum River.		
March	1782	Captain William Caldwell	British	"Several Hundred"
		-Staged raid from Detroit to Springfield, OH		
April	1782	Colonel David Williamson		200
		Massacred Moravian Indians in east -central Ohio		
May-June	1782	Colonel William Crawford	Senecas/ Wyandots	480
May 24		*-Staged raid from PA to Upper Sandusky, OH*		
June 5		*--Defeated at Battle Island, and*		
June 6		*--Battle of the Olentangy*		
August 19	1782	Simon Girty	Shawnees	400
		-Leads 400 Shawnees against Logan's Station, KY Draws out militia garrison, kills 43+ at Battle of Blue Licks		
November	1782	General George Rogers Clark	U.S.	1,050
		-From Cincy, destroyed Loramie's Post, OH		
October	1786	Colonel Benjamin Logan (Clark's 2nd-in-Com'd)	U.S.	700-800
		-From Maysville, KY /Aberdeen-Ripley OH, destroyed Mad River settlements - 7 villages and English fort @ current Zanesfield, OH.		
October	1786	General George Rogers Clark	Inconclusive	
		-Concurrently with Logan's raid, Clark moved up Southeast Indiana toward the Central Indiana villages. The attack accomplished no results.		

Appendix C

The Battle of Mississinewa

A Footnote to a Major Western Campaign in the War of 1812

A bright, glistening, crystal-clear day. A bustling Native American village situated on a frozen river. Children playing with dogs and toys beneath the skeletal sycamore and cottonwood trees, as their parents work at various tasks in the village.

Suddenly, from the east, a troop of U.S. Cavalry swoops and storms into the idyllic scene. The cavalry shatters and burns the village, forcing the Indians west toward an uncertain winter without adequate clothing and shelter.

Sound like something from the Old West – perhaps the Dakotas – circa 1873? Well, the Old West, certainly! Or perhaps the Old Northwest is more descriptive. Actually, the above action took place in Indiana Territory in 1812! Driving north on Indiana State Route 15, north of Marion, Indiana, you may notice a sign with directions to a historical marker which is located a few miles to the west of the highway. If you make a slight detour to follow those directions, you will come upon the site of the Battle of Mississinewa.

It was November 25, 1812, and the War of 1812 was in full swing. General William Henry Harrison, commander of the U.S. Second North Western Army, ordered Lieutenant Colonel John B. Campbell to gather a mounted force to destroy the Native American villages on the Mississinewa River. Campbell was to gather his force at Franklinton (Columbus), Ohio, and travel through Springfield, Xenia, and Dayton to Eaton. At Eaton, Campbell was to secure provisions for the final drive to the Mississinewa.

The size of Campbell's mounted troop has been disputed: the estimates range from 600 (the generally accepted total) to 781 soldiers. Campbell himself was a member of the 19th Infantry Regiment, and had a company of the Nineteenth with him. Major James V. Ball was second in command, at the head of the Second Dragoons. Lieutenant Colonel James Simrall and his four troops of Kentucky Dragoons, which had previous experience fighting the Indiana Miamis, were included in the force. Rounding out the mounted force were a militia company of Pennsylvania riflemen, an additional company known as the Pittsburgh Blues (under Captain James Butler), units of Ohio volunteers, and a company of spies and scouts.

Lieutenant Colonel Campbell picked up pack horses at Dayton and completed the final assembly of troops at Greenville. After a hard but steady march to the Mississinewa, Campbell's command arrived at the Native American villages early on the morning of December 17th, 1812. (The exact dates are disputed, variously given as the 12th, the 16th, or the 17th, but the date of December 17th seems most accepted.) Campbell believed he had reached the main Miami village of Silver Heel's Town, but instead, the mounted raiders had first come upon a minor village of the Munsee Indians (a branch of the Delawares). Immediately slashing in to attack, the mounted forces turned the village into a whirlwind of confusion. In a few minutes, the dragoons and mounted militia had killed eight braves and captured eight other braves plus 34 women and children. Despite the rapidity of the attack, some of the Native Americans escaped. The dragoons brought the prisoners back to an area where the infantry was building a fortified encampment, the protected area being roughly five hundred feet square.

After securing the prisoners in the control of the infantry, the mounted troops again loped to the west to attack Silver Heel's Town, approximately two miles further downstream. Finding the village deserted (the escapees had spread word of the attacking U.S. troops), the soldiers burned the town and destroyed all crops and livestock. As the day was growing later, and the dragoons didn't care to be caught in the deep woods in the midwinter gloom, the force headed back to the east to the fortified encampment for the night.

At four the next morning, the drummer sounded reveille. The officers met to determine their next move. Should they advance to the next large Miami village, Mississineway, twenty miles further down the river, or should they seek out the Miamis and Delawares from the destroyed villages who had eluded their net?

As they conferred in the predawn gloom, the shriek of a combined Miami and Delaware attack broke over them. Although they were not caught completely by surprise, the soldiers were not able to determine exactly from which direction the attack was coming or estimate the size of the attacking force (later determined to be approximately 300 attackers). In a savage, two-hour battle, Campbell's force repelled the attack. With the coming of dawn and an improvement in the gathering light, the fire from the regulars and the Pennsylvania riflemen improved accordingly, and the Indians retreated from the galling fire.

Campbell's men waited for a time, then crept out of their camp to examine the surrounding woods. The evidence they found there led them to estimate that at least 30 to 40 of the enemy had been killed in the attack. Campbell's own losses had been significant. The U.S. force had lost twelve men killed and 48 wounded in the two-day conflict.

The officers once more convened to take stock of their situation. Many of Campbell's men were suffering from frostbite, the wounded had to be tended and transported, and the prisoners had to be guarded. Furthermore, it was unclear whether the Indians were retreating or merely regrouping for a second attack. Intelligence gathered by the spies and scouts indicated there were additional Native American forces in the area, possibly led by the great Shawnee leader, Tecumseh.

The course was now clear. Campbell ordered a retreat to Greenville, to begin that afternoon, December 18th. With the burden of prisoners and wounded, and having lost over 100 horses in the campaign, the mounted command did not reach Greenville until Christmas Day, 1812.

General Harrison was pleased with the campaign. In his report of the battle, he issued the following commendation:

> "*The character of this gallant detachment exhibiting, as it did perseverance, patience, fortitude and bravery, would however, have been incomplete, if, in the midst of victory, they had forgotten*

the feelings of humanity. It is with the sincerest pleasure, that the general has heard, that the most punctual obedience was paid to his orders; not only in saving the women and children, but in sparing all the warriors who ceased to resist; and that even, when vigorously attacked by the enemy, the claims of mercy prevailed over every sense of their own danger; and this heroic band respected the lives of their prisoners. The general believes that humanity and true bravery are inseparable. The rigid rules of war may sometimes, indeed, make a severe retaliation necessary; but the advantages which attend a frequent recurrence of it, are very uncertain, and are not to be compared with the blessings which providence cannot fail to shed upon the efforts of the soldier, who is 'in battle a lion, but, the battle once ended, in mercy a lamb.' Let an account of the murdered innocence be opened in the records of Heaven against our enemies alone; the American soldier will follow the example of his government, and neither the sword of the one will be raised against the helpless or the fallen, nor the gold of the other paid for the scalp of a massacred enemy."

Many of the facts of the battle are well established. We can now consider more interesting and debatable questions. Why did a battle of significant magnitude take place between the U.S. Army and the Miami Nation during the War of 1812? Even more interestingly, why did it take place in the middle of the wilderness that was the Indiana Territory at that time – far from even the fringe of European/American civilization?

Background to the Battle.

To really understand the Battle of Mississinewa, we must travel back in time slightly more than one year from December 17th, 1812 – to the time of what many consider the true opening battle of the War of 1812. When we were in school and beginning our studies of American history, most of us were taught that the Battle of Tippecanoe (November 7, 1811) was the engagement that broke the back of Native American resistance in the Old Northwest Territory. However, I think it is significant that many accounts both then and now indicate it was much less final in its implications. Tecumseh, the prominent Midwestern Native American leader, was in the South at that time attempting to build a large confederation of Indian tribes to oppose white encroachment beyond established treaty lines. Tecumseh knew that by 1800 it was impossible to force the Americans back over the Appalachians. However, he envisioned a great confederacy of Midwestern and Southern Indian nations, concentrated above the various treaty lines in Ohio, Indiana Territory, and Illinois Territory, acting as a buffer state between the Americans in Kentucky and southern Ohio and the British in Canada.

While Tecumseh was in the South, William Henry Harrison, then governor of Indiana Territory, moved north to provoke the Native Americans living at the center of the confederacy movement, Prophet's Town, on the Tippecanoe River in west-central Indiana. Tecumseh's brother, Tenskwatawa (also known as "The Prophet") led a group of combined tribes against Harrison's army in a surprise pre-dawn attack. Harrison's Regular Army forces repelled the attack with significant losses to themselves (38 killed, 150 wounded). Thus, Tecumseh's dream of building a buffer state of Native American nations was destroyed by the defeat of the fledgling confederacy which was assembled at Prophet's Town.

There are two points of significance in evaluating this battle. First, in the passing of time, the legend has grown that Tippecanoe was the battle that crushed the Indian war movement in the Old Northwest. In reality, it only broke the Native Americans' ability to *win* the war, not to contest it strenuously. In this sense, it is much like the Battle of Midway in the Pacific Theater of World War II. Midway ended any hope of Japan conducting a negotiated peace and retaining possession of the substantial territorial gains it had acquired during the early phases of the war. However, Japan still possessed great forces which enabled it to continue the war for three more years, without a true hope for ultimate victory.

Tippecanoe was the "Native Americans' Midway" in the Old Northwest. The Indians still possessed enough manpower to strongly contest the increasing numbers of white settlers flooding into the Northwest Territories, but they no longer had a realistic chance of a negotiated peace as a buffer state between the Americans and the British. The only realistic possibility was an alliance with the British in the War of 1812.

Second, the Battle of Tippecanoe was far less "crushing" in the Americans' own eyes at that time than it now seems from our vantage point of history. Harrison held his lines for 36 hours after the battle, breathlessly awaiting a massive frontal attack that never came. Only after a day and a half did his men advance from their protected positions to find that the Indians had gone. The Indians must still have represented a significant offensive force in Harrison's mind as he left the Tippecanoe battle scene. Events in the War of 1812 would seem to validate Harrison's mindset.

The War of 1812 was declared by Congress on June 18th, 1812. One of the United States' goals was to invade and capture Canadian territory with a three-pronged attack. An eastern offensive was to be launched from the Lake Champlain area. In November, under the command of General Henry Dearborn, a drive was started from Plattsburg, New York, toward Montreal. This offensive failed when the New York militia refused to leave United States soil.

Another American attempt to invade Canada occurred along the Niagara River on October 13th, 1812. General Isaac Brock, the commander of the British forces in the area, had about 1,200 soldiers along the Niagara River. The Americans, under Generals Stephen Van Rensselaer and Alexander Smyth, had about 6,000 troops. During two attempts to cross the river and occupy Canada's Queenston Heights, the Americans achieved limited initial successes, but in each case those soldiers that crossed the river were counterattacked and either killed or captured. The Battle of Queenston Heights ended the second American attempt to invade Canada in 1812.

The third, western-most prong was to be launched from Detroit. Accordingly, General William Hull, governor of Michigan Territory, gathered a force and moved from Urbana in Ohio to Detroit to conduct the attack. Hull's position at Detroit was hopeless from the start. Quickly flanked and cut off from supplies, Hull was forced to surrender to the British on August 16th, 1812, with his entire army. One of the major reasons for Hull's defeat was Tecumseh, now a brigadier general in the British army, at the head of a powerful Native American force.

The fall of Detroit signaled the start of a series of sharp Indian raids in mid-1812. Almost simultaneously with the fall of Detroit,

Fort Dearborn (Chicago) fell to Indian attackers. A series of well-coordinated attacks took place in September – all bearing Tecumseh's "signature" as overall mastermind. The attacks included Pigeon's Roost (September 3), Fort Harrison (September 4), Fort Madison (September 5), and Fort Wayne (September 6).

The most serious was the attack on Fort Wayne. With the fall of Detroit and Fort Dearborn, Fort Wayne now became the U.S.'s northwestern-most outpost by far, and as such was very vulnerable to attack. For seven days, Native Americans laid siege to the small garrison. William Henry Harrison, recently named commander of the Second North Western Army, marched from the headwaters of the St. Marys River to relieve the besieged bastion. As holder of dual commissions (brigadier general in the United States Army and brevet major general of the Kentucky militia), he ordered General James Winchester's 1,500-man strong army of Kentuckians (originally assembled to relieve Hull at Detroit) to rendezvous with him at Fort Wayne. The Indians lifted the siege at the approach of General Harrison's army. After Winchester arrived, Harrison ordered him to move down the Maumee River and recapture Detroit.

Harrison now had an army in the field, headed for Detroit. His new problem was how to supply this force from his main commissaries at Cincinnati, Greenville, and Piqua. In examining the map, we see that he chose to construct a series of forts, each built one travel-day apart, running from Piqua in the south to Fort Meigs at the Maumee Rapids. These forts guarded the lines of communication and supply, and eventually the forts became the lifeline of the army operating in the Northwest.

A closer examination of a topical map shows what Harrison almost certainly must have seen as he pondered his strategic situation: a series of rivers running from southeast to northwest, all located just to the west of his line of new forts. The St. Marys, the Wabash, the Salamonie, and the Mississinewa Rivers pointed like arrows at his lower bases at Greenville, Piqua, Fort Loramie, and Fort Barbee (present-day St. Marys, Ohio). Even Fort Amanda on the upper reaches of the Auglaize River could not be considered safe from these avenues of attack. More ominously, situated on the lower reaches of the Mississinewa was the largest concentration of Native American villages in Indiana Territory, including Silver Heel's Town. Many of the inhabitants of these villages were thought to have participated in the September raids on Fort Harrison and Fort Wayne.

Given the sequence of events just related – the uncertainty of final victory at Tippecanoe, the fall of Detroit and Fort Dearborn to "British Indians," the sharp September raids, and the siege of Fort Wayne, William Henry Harrison almost certainly had to be asking himself the following questions: Where exactly was Tecumseh? How many warriors did he have? Where could Tecumseh strike to cause maximum damage, and which avenues could he use to make these attacks? What area could support a large number of warriors through the cold, dark winter months? Harrison, possessing a sharp military mind from his youthful study of strategy and tactics, was almost certainly aware of the old military axiom: *"Never march parallel to a strong enemy force on one's flank."*

William Henry Harrison certainly recognized the strategic importance of this Native American concentration in Indiana Territory. Robert Breckinridge McAfee quoted Harrison's rationale for the December, 1812 raid on the Mississinewa villages, in Harrsion's own words:

"The situation of this town, as it regards one line of operations… would render a measure of this kind highly proper…the Indians…will direct all their efforts against fort Wayne, and the convoys which are to follow the left wing of the army. Mississiniway will be their rendezvous, where they will receive provisions and every assistance they may require for any hostile enterprise. From that place they can by their runners ascertain the period, at which every convoy may set out from St. Marys, and with certainty intercept it on its way to the Miami Rapids."(I.e.: the Maumee Rapids – Author's note.) "But that place being broken up, and the provisions destroyed, there will be nothing to subsist any body of Indians, nearer than the Potawatamie towns on the waters of the St. Josephs of the Lake." Harrison.

Thus the raid which developed into the Battle of Mississinewa was born of sound strategic thinking on the part of General William Henry Harrison. The elimination of a potential enemy force on his western periphery secured his left flank well into 1813. Harrison certainly must have believed that Winchester's army would have recaptured Detroit well before the Miami Confederation forces could recover from the Mississinewa destruction. The campaign that would lead to the River Raisin massacre of Winchester's army was in place. Due to Winchester's defeat at Frenchtown (River Raisin), Harrison would have to remount his campaign against Detroit in 1813.

The Commanders' Subsequent Lives.

What became of the protagonists in this battle? Certainly at least partially due to Harrison's commendation for his execution of the Mississinewa raid, John B. Campbell obtained a brevet promotion to colonel. By 1814, Campbell had been promoted once again and was colonel and commander of the 11th Infantry Regiment on the north-central theater of the Canadian front. To retaliate for British destruction of Buffalo, New York, the previous winter, and perhaps forgetting the nature of the commendation for his conduct of the Battle of Mississinewa, Campbell loaded his command into boats, crossed Lake Erie, and destroyed Port Dover. His actions in destroying private property were censured by his own men, and he was reprimanded by the United State government. However, he was back in command of the 11th Infantry Regiment in July, 1814, and was badly wounded in the Battle of Chippewa on July 5th, 1814. Never fully recovering, Colonel John B. Campbell died on August 28th, 1814.

William Henry Harrison went on to fame as the eventual victor in the Northwestern Theater of the War of 1812, and he used this fame to become the ninth President of the United States. His organizational skills and supply efforts bulwarked the United States' defense of the Old Northwest in 1813, and were rewarded when Commodore Oliver Hazard Perry defeated the British fleet in the naval Battle of Lake Erie (also known as the Battle of Put-In-Bay). Quickly switching from the defensive to the offensive mode of operation and using Perry's warships as troop transports, Harrison crossed Lake Erie and pursued the fleeing British into Canada. (The British General Procter had been compelled to abandon Detroit after it became untenable with the loss of British control of Lake

Erie.) Harrison caught Procter at Moraviantown and defeated his forces in the Battle of the Thames River, ending the British threat to the Old Northwest. One of Harrison's adversaries in the Battle of the Thames was Tecumseh.

Tecumseh became a true "swords and roses" figure of the American West. After failing to dislodge the Americans from their western settlements and strong points, Tecumseh strengthened Native American forces at Detroit to fight beside the British. He participated in a series of unsuccessful offensives against the U.S.'s northern fortifications during 1813. After the British loss in the Battle of Lake Erie, Tecumseh reluctantly followed General Procter in his tactical retreat into Canada. Run down by his nemesis, General Harrison, at Moraviantown on the Thames River, Tecumseh commanded the British right flank in the ensuing battle. As the British left and center broke and began streaming backward, Tecumseh, on the right, held. Tecumseh led his warriors and fought bravely until killed at the height of the battle, forever passing into the pantheon of American legends as one of the greatest Native American leaders.

The Battle of Mississinewa – an almost forgotten footnote in an ultimately unsuccessful campaign in a little-known war. Yet, for students of military history, the battle provides an opportunity to study a major operational theater of a Nineteenth Century war. It also provides an opportunity to study the tactics of a commander who was successful in the field – Campbell; the strategies of a commander who would someday be the leader of his country – Harrison; and the politics of a leader who dreamed of becoming the father of his country – Tecumseh.

Appendix D: Battles of the Trans-Appalachian Wars, 1790-1818

State	Date	Woodland Wars	Victor	Theater
IN	10/19/1790	Eel River	Miami Confederation	NW
IN	10/22/1790	Kekionga (Harmar's Crossing)	Miami Confederation	NW
OH	11/04/1791	St. Clair's Defeat (Upper Wabash)	Miami Confederation	NW
OH	11/6/1792	Fort St. Clair	Americans	NW
OH	6/30-7/1/1794	Fort Recovery	Americans	NW
OH	8/20/1794	Fallen Timbers	Americans	NW
		War of 1812 - Old Northwest		
IN	11/7/1811	Tippecanoe	Americans	NW
MI	7/12/1812	Ft Michillimackinac	Brit/Shawnee Conf.	NW
MI	8/5/1812	Brownstown	Brit/Shawnee Conf.	NW
MI	8/9/1812	Monguagon	Draw/Adv Brit-Shaw	NW
IL	8/15/1812	Ft Dearborn	Brit/Shawnee Conf.	NW
MI	8/16/1812	Detroit	Brit/Shawnee Conf.	NW
IN	9/7-12/1812	Ft Wayne	Americans	NW
IN	Nov-Dec, 1812	North Indiana (KY Mounted Militia)	Americans	NW
IN	12/17-18/1812	Mississinewa	Draw/Adv American	NW
MI	1/18/1813	1st Raisin River (Frenchtown)	Americans	NW
MI	1/22/1813	2nd Raisin River (Frenchtown)	Brit/Shawnee Conf.	NW
OH	4/28-5/8/1813	1st Ft Meigs	Draw/Adv American	NW
OH	7/21-28/1813	2nd Ft Meigs	Americans	NW
OH	7/28-8/2/1813	Ft Stephenson	Americans	NW
OH	9/10/1813	Lake Erie	Americans	NW
MI	9/27-30/1813	Detroit evacuated and reoccupied	Americans	NW
CAN	10/2-5/1813	Thames (Moraviantown)	Americans	NW
		Creek War		
AL	6/15/1813	Tuckabatchee	Red Stick Creeks	SW
AL	7/27/1813	Burnt Corn Creek	Red Stick Creeks	SW
AL	8/30/1813	Ft Mims	Red Stick Creeks	SW
AL	Late Oct,1813	Black Warrior River (TN Mnted Militia)	Americans	SW
AL	11/3/1813	Tallushatchee	Americans	SW
AL	11/9/1813	Talladega	Americans	SW
AL	11/18/1813	Hillabee Towns	Americans	SW
AL	11/29/1813	Autosse	Draw/Adv Creeks	SW
AL	12/23/1813	Econochaca	Americans	SW
AL	1/22/1814	Emuckfau Creek	Draw/Adv Creeks	SW
AL	1/24/1814	Enitachopco Creek	Draw/Adv Creeks	SW
AL	1/27/1814	Calabee Swamp	Draw/Adv Creeks	SW
AL	3/27/1814	Horseshoe Bend	Americans	SW
		War of 1812 - Old Southwest		
AL	4/12-15/1813	1st Mobile	Americans	SW
AL	9/14-15/1814	2nd Mobile	Americans	SW
FL	11/07/1814	Pensacola	Americans	SW
LA	12/14/1814	Lake Borgne	British	SW
LA	12/23/1814	Villere Plantation	Draw/Adv American	SW
LA	12/28/1814	1st New Orleans	Americans	SW
LA	1/1/1815	2nd New Orleans	Americans	SW
LA	1/8/1815	3rd New Orleans	Americans	SW
AL	2/8-11/1815	3rd Mobile	British	SW
		Patriot/1st Seminole War		
FL	March, 1812	St. Augustine/Fernandia (Patriot War)	Spanish	SW
FL	Fall, 1812	North Florida (GA Mounted Militia)	Americans	SW
FL	Winter, 1813	Alachua Prairie (TN Mounted Militia)	Americans	SW
FL	5/5/1814	Elotchaway (Patriot War)	Seminoles	SW
FL	7/27/1816	Prospect Bluff	Americans	SW
GA	11/21/1817	Fowltown (1st Seminole War)	Americans	SW
FL	11/30/1817	Apalachicola River	Seminoles	SW
FL	12/23/1817	St. Augustine - Amelia Island	Americans	SW
FL	3/31/1818	Mikasukian Towns	Americans	SW
FL	4/7/1818	St. Marks	Americans	SW
FL	4/12/1818	Natural Bridge	Americans	SW
FL	4/15-16/1818	Bowlegs Towns	Americans	SW
FL	5/24-27/1818	Pensacola	Americans	SW

Biographical Notes

In commencing the writing of this book, I was amazed to find that there existed a wealth of information about American military struggles between 1790 to 1818. What drew me to the subject was that there did not seem to be a flowing narrative that knitted this information together under any particular theme, such as "empire building." Thus, I perceived a historical niche that I could fill. I would, however, be remiss to not recognize the work of research historians who developed the source information in this area. I owe a great debt of gratitude to their pioneering work, and wish to mention a few of the many sources of historical facts and information contained in this book.

The internet is typical of the phenomenon of "a wealth of facts, but no flowing commentary." I drew heavily on sources contained therein for the early chapters of the book. In particular, the archives of <u>Ohio History, the Scholarly Journal of the Ohio Historical Society</u> were invaluable as a source of information for Harmar's campaign – indeed, excerpts from his and Captain John Armstrong's personal logs of the campaign were contained there. "Arthur St. Clair's Biography" on the <u>Museum of History</u> website, as well as Linda Cunningham Fluharty's 1890 <u>History of the Upper Ohio Valley, Volume I.</u> provided a great amount of information on St. Clair's campaign. Dale Van Every's outstanding article, "President Washington's Calculated Risk" in <u>American Heritage</u> along with Paul O'Neil's <u>The Frontiersmen</u> were the base source documents for my account of "Mad Anthony" Wayne's triumphant march into the Old Northwest.

The book then moves ahead to the War of 1812. To say that David S. Heidler and Jeanne T. Heidler's outstanding work in creating and editing the <u>Encyclopedia of the War of 1812</u> was valuable would be an understatement. The encyclopedia was a bedrock source of information for the various accounts of the activities in Trans-Appalachia between 1812 and 1815 found in this book. This tremendous work is a veritable treasure house of information on the War of 1812, and certainly is the single greatest source for facts and accounts of the War (arranged by individual historical participant) that I have seen. I stand in awe of Heidler and Heidler's (and the contributing writers') monumental efforts in this area.

Another truly outstanding work on this time period is Alec Gilpin's The War of 1812 in the Old Northwest. This great commentary, zeroing in on the Northwest Theater, filled in the spaces that Heidler and Heidler's massive work of necessity had to leave out. Gilpin's thorough research supplied many pieces of valuable information.

The focus of the book then shifted to the Old Southwest. As I was "shelf-browsing" at the local library, I came upon a true gem of information: Robert Breckinridge McAfee's 1816 History of the Late War in the Western Country. McAfee was a participant in several of the actions in the west during the War, and his well-written work (in very readable prose) was a storehouse of information on the Battle of New Orleans, among other actions in the west and southwest. Another outstanding source of information for various military actions in the old Southwest is Frank W. Owsley's Struggle for the Gulf Borderlands: The Creek War and the Battle of New Orleans, 1812-1815

Robert Remini has spent many years studying Andrew Jackson, and his outstanding knowledge of his subject shows through. As I moved to the post-War of 1812 phase of the book (particularly the "First Seminole War" area) Remini's Andrew Jackson and his Indian Wars became the foundation for the accounts contained therein.

To develop the thesis that the Miami Valley / Great Black Swamp Corridor moved from a military thoroughfare to an economic thoroughfare, I sought information from Frank Wilcox's The Ohio Canals. This well-written and heavily illustrated work was priceless in developing the flow of ideas in final chapters of the book.

Many years ago, I found a 1905 railroad map, printed by the State of Ohio Department of Transportation, in my great-grandmother's attic. This source was invaluable in tracing the courses of the local railroads that further developed the Miami Valley / Great Black Swamp Corridor.

I have, of course, only touched on the main sources of information for the completion of this book. I would love to mention them all.

I encourage you to review the Chapter Endnotes and Bibliography to note and review all sources of information. To those whose work I have mentioned, as well as the scores of others not mentioned, thank you for your developmental work on the early history of Trans-Appalachia. This book would not be possible without your tireless efforts.

John Eric Vining

Chapter Endnotes

Introduction

"...interest in a war..." Byron Farwell, <u>The Great War in Africa, 1914-1918.</u> New York: W.W. Norton & Company, 1986.

Chapter 1 – Prologue

What is an *empire?* <u>New Webster's Dictionary</u>, 1990 ed., s.v. "empire."
...negative connotation...*exploitation*... Ibid., s.v. "exploitation."
To *exploit* **is...** Ibid., s.v. "exploit."
"What happened was inevitable..." Joel B. Michaels, prod., Tab Murphy, Dir/ Writer, <u>Last of the Dogmen</u> (Hollywood, CA: Savoy Pictures/Carolco Pictures, Inc., 1995), Videocassette. 118 minutes.

Chapter 2

"Only a handful of..." Allan W. Eckert, <u>Wilderness Empire</u> (New York: Bantam Books, 1971), 1.
"I hereby take possession..." Ibid., 1-2. (This paragraph and one subsequent paragraph.)
"Year 1749" Ibid., 134.
"The journey up the Great Miami..." Ibid., 154 (This paragraph and one subsequent paragraph.)
"Following the rough map..." Ibid., 156.
"Located here was Fort Miamis..." Ibid., 156-57.
She had been ceded... Dale Van Every, "President Washington's Calculated Risk," <u>American Heritage</u>, IX, No, 4 (June 1958), 57.
...England made the stunning cession... Ibid., 59.
"...Dutchman's Point, Point-au-Fer, Oswegatchie..." Paul O'Neil, <u>The Frontiersmen</u> (Alexandria, VA: Time Life Books, Inc., 1977), 128.
Spain refused to recognize... Van Every, 59.
"...to hold the West at every risk..." Ibid., 57.
"Only one road..." Ibid.
The new United States Congress... O'Neil, 128.
"...most famous leaders...advocated..." Van Every, 59.
"James Winchester had taken..." Ibid., 60.
Dr. James O'Fallon... Ibid.
George Rogers Clark contemplated... Ibid.
"...Shawnee-Delaware-Wyandot-Miami confederacy..." Ibid., 57.

...Creeks and Cherokees... Ibid.
In 1780, '82, and...'86... O'Neil, 128.
"A war department was organized." Van Every, 60.
...to compel the Indian tribes... Ibid.
"Arthur St. Clair...was authorized..." Ibid., 61.

Chapter 3

"...tradition in U.S. military history..." Max Boot, <u>The Savage Wars of Peace:</u>
<u>Small Wars and the Rise of American Power</u> (New York: Basic Books.,
2002), xiv.
"These are the non wars..." Ibid., xiv-xv.
"...fascinating stories - tales of blunders..." Ibid., xv.
"...the many wars against Native Americans..." Ibid., xvi.
"...Fort McIntosh, January 20th, 1785..." "Virtual American Biographies: Josiah
Harmar," <u>Edited Appleton's Encyclopedia</u>, Virtualology, 2001. Internet Site:
http://famousamericans.net/josiahharmar/
"...Fort Finney...January 3rd, 1786..." Basil Meek, "General Harmar's
Expedition," <u>Ohio History, The Scholarly Journal of the Ohio Historical</u>
<u>Society</u>, 20, No. 1 (January, 1911), 76. Internet Site: http://publications.
ohiohistory.org/ohstemplate.cfm?action=detail&Page=002076.html&Star
tPage=74&EndPage=108&volume=20-es=&newtitle=Volume%2020%20
Page%2074
"...and Fort Harmar...January 9th, 1789." Ibid.
...approximately 400 soldiers... Ibid., 78.
"...700 Virginia/Kentucky and 500 Pennsylvania militia..." Ibid.
"Amongst the militia were..." Ibid., 97.
"Kentucky seemed as if..." Ibid., 103.
"They were boys, old men, drunkards..." Howard H. Peckham, "Josiah
Harmar and His Indian Expedition," <u>Ohio History, The Scholarly</u>
<u>Journal of the Ohio Historical Society</u>, 55, No.3 (July-September, 1946),
236. Internet Site: http://publications.ohiohistory.org/ohstemplate.
cfm?action=detail&Page=0055227.html&StartPage=227&EndPage=241&v
olume=55-es=&newtitle=Volume%2055%20Page%20227
"...Kekionga..." Otho Winger, "The Indians Who Opposed Harmar," <u>Ohio</u>
<u>History, The Scholarly Journal of the Ohio Historical Society</u>, 50, No. 1
(January-March, 1941), 55. Internet Site: http://publications.ohiohistory.
org/ohstemplate.cfm?action=detail&Page=05055.html&StartPage=55&End
Page=59&volume=50-es=&newtitle=Volume%2050%20Page%2055
...seven Miami, Shawnee, and Delaware villages... Ibid., 56.
The manuscript journal of Captain John Armstrong... Ibid., 79-89.
...as well as that of General Harmar... Ibid., 89-96.
(Biographical Note: The author drew heavily on the above two references
for the description of the route to the headwaters of the Maumee and

the two battles at that location. These are two excellent contemporary accounts of the march and battles, and the author strongly recommends readers to consult these original texts.)

"The motive which I conceived…" Ibid., 102.

"…intending to surprise any parties…" Ibid., 107.

The plan of battle… Ibid., 85-7.

"…trail of blood…" "Historic Fort Wayne: The Great American Outpost." Internet Site: http://geocities.com/Heartland/Valley/7029/fortwayne.html

…demanded an official Court of Inquiry… Meek, 88-9.

"…common cause with the Miamis." Ibid., 88.

Chapter 4

"Fine weather. The detachment…" Meek, 93.

St. Clair was a Major General… Richard Battin, "Early America's Bloodiest Battle," The News Sentinel , 1994. Internet Site: http://earlyamerica.com/review/summer/battle.html 2 / 5.

…won a seat in the transitional… Ibid.

…on March 4th, 1791… "Arthur St. Clair Biography," Museum of History, Virtualology, 2000. Internet Site: http://www.arthurstclair.com/1. arthurstclair.com/ 2 / 11.

The Secretary of War…stole $55,000 of the $75,000… "Did You Know…?" Internet Site: http://www.noacsc.org/ohiohist/regional/fort/facts.htm 1 / 2.

…newly appointed Army Quartermaster… U.S. Army Quartermaster Corps Historian, "This Week in Quartermaster History, 4-10 November." Internet Site: http://www.qmmuseum.lee.army.mil/historyweek/Nov4-10.htm 1 / 2.

Duer sent stale… Battin, 3 / 5.

"…musket balls bounced off…" Ibid.

"…15 hatchets, 18 axes, 12 hammers, and 24 handsaws…" Ibid.

"…horsemaster…'had never been in the woods…'" Ibid.

A second Regular Army regiment… Peckham, 238.

The First was considered… "Arthur St. Clair Biography," 3 / 11.

"…the prisons, wheelbarrows, and brothels…" Ibid., 2 / 11.

"…the worst and most dissatisfied troops…" Ibid.

"…badly clothed, badly paid, and badly led…" Ibid.

On September 17th, 1791, St. Clair marched… "St Clair's Defeat," Ohio History Central, Ohio Historical Society. Internet Site: http://www.ohiohistorycentral. org/ohc/history/h_indian/events/stclrdft.shtml 1 / 2.

"…Fort Jefferson…" Linda Cunningham Fluharty, History of the Upper Ohio Valley, Vol. 1 (Madison, WI: Brant & Fuller, 1890), 21. Internet Site: http://www.rootsweb.com/~wvmags/chap7.txt 21 / 26.

…with freezing rain and snow. "St. Clair's Defeat," 1 / 2.

…flour and beef…60 militia reinforcements…more food and reinforcements… Fluharty, 22 / 26.

...Chief Payomingo... Ibid., 21 / 26.

...20 Chickasaw warriors... "Arthur St. Clair Biography," 3 / 11.

On October 29ᵗʰ, St. Clair detached... Fluharty, 22 / 26, and "Arthur St. Clair Biography," 3 / 11.

"...a young Shawnee warrior named Tecumseh..." "Arthur St. Clair Biography," 3 / 11.

"...60 of the militia deserted..." Fluharty, 22 / 26.

"...300 officers and men of the First American Regiment..." "Arthur St. Clair Biography," 3 / 11.

"...most able soldiers..." Ibid.

...approximately 1400 soldiers. "This Week in Quartermaster History," 1 / 2, "Arthur St. Clair Biography," 3 / 11, Batten, 3 / 5, and Fluharty, 14 / 26.

...1,000... Batten, 3 / 5.

...1,040... "Arthur St. Clair Biography," 3 / 11.

...St. Clair...stated that he had reached the St. Marys... Fluharty, 22-23 / 26.

...General St. Clair chose *not* to build breastworks... "Arthur St. Clair Biography," 3 / 11.

...second-in-command, Major General Richard Butler... Ibid.

...encamping a large portion of militia. Fluharty, 14 / 26.

...Butler...chose not to correspond with... Ibid.

...General St. Clair had reveille beaten... Ibid., 14 / 26 and 23 / 26.
Biographical Note: An outstanding description of the battle (from which the passages on these two pages are developed) is included in Fluharty, pages 14 / 26 and 23-25 / 26. The author strongly suggests the reader review this text for a detailed account of the battle.

"...618..." Fluharty, 16 / 26.

"...630..." O'Neil, 131.

"...637..." James Hanna, "Ohio Town Recalls 1791 Battle," The Journal Gazette (Ft. Wayne, IN) 3 November 1991, 17A.

"...39..." O'Neil, 132.

"...68 officers..." Fluharty, 16 / 26.

"...500..." "This Week in Quartermaster History," 2 / 2.

"Over 65% of the..." "Did You Know...?" 1 / 2.

...three quarters of the Second American Regiment. "Arthur St. Clair Biography," 3 / 11.

"...virtually without an army for two years." "Did You Know...?" 1 / 2.

"...150 women..." Fluharty, 16 / 26.

"Fifty-six were killed..." Ibid.

"...21..." Hanna, 17a.

"...37..." Fluharty, 16 / 26.

"...40..." "Arthur St. Clair Biography," 3 / 11.

"...eight cannon, 1,200 muskets..." Battin, 1 / 5.

"...$33,000..." "Arthur St. Clair Biography," 3 / 11.

...the worst defeat... Battin, 1 / 5.

"...March 27, 1792..." "Arthur St. Clair Biography," 4 / 11.

"**...April 7, 1792...**" "St.Clair's Defeat," 1 / 2.

Chapter 5

"**Great generals do not repeat...**" Bevin Alexander, <u>How Great Generals Win</u> (New York: W.W, Norton & Company, 2002), 21.

"**On the contrary...**" Ibid.

"**...the key to victory...**" Ibid., 23.

"**...point that is vital...**" Ibid.

"**...to 'mystify, mislead, and surprise...'**" Ibid.

"**The great captain of arms...will move...**" Ibid.

"**Practically all...moves...**" Ibid.

"**It is only the unusual...**" Ibid., 29.

"**...the purpose of war...**" Ibid., 30.

"**...the purpose of military strategy...is to diminish...**" Ibid., 31.

"**The successful general...chooses...**" Ibid., 32.

"**The Miami Indians...**" Battin, 4 / 5.

"**Washington feared...Wayne's...rashness...in battle...**" O'Neil, 131-'33.

"**...at Pittsburgh...**" Ibid., 133.

"*The offscourings of large cities and towns...*" Ibid.

"**...Legionville...**" Ibid.

"**...instruction in the use of the bayonet...**" Ibid.

"**...80 yards...**" Michael Glover, <u>The Napoleonic Wars</u> (New York: Hippocrene Books, 1978), 16.

"**General Charles Scott['s]...1500...**" O'Neil, 139.

"**...3000...**" Van Every, 110.

...Indian congress at the Sandusky Peninsula. Alan D. Gaff, <u>Bayonets in the Wilderness – Anthony Wayne's Legion in the Old Northwest</u> (Norman, OK: University of Oklahoma Press, 2004), 105, 129.

(Biographical Note: There is some question as to the exact location of this congress. Dale Van Every states that it occurred "...at the forks of the Auglaize and Maumee rivers in Ohio..."("President Washington's Calculated Risk," p. 110). A historical marker at Roche de Beouf, a rock outcropping/island in the Maumee River, implies the Indians met there before facing Wayne. However, the most recent research by Alan D. Gaff states the gathering took place on the Sandusky Peninsula, current Port Clinton, OH. It is safe to generalize that the Native Americans met in what is now northern Ohio, considered the American peace proposal, and communicated their rejection of it to the American government during the winter of 1793-'94.)

"**...as far away as the Gulf of Mexico, the Great Plains...**" Ibid.

In July, a separate commission... Ibid.

"**...53-acre stronghold...Fort Greeneville...**" O'Neil, 133.

"**...eight companies of troops...**" Ibid., 134.

"...satellite...Fort Recovery..." Ibid.

"Children, from the manner..." Ibid., 137.

"...Dorchester...Governor Simcoe...foot of the Maumee Rapids..." Ibid.

"...a storehouse...for rifles, gunlocks..." Ibid.

"...1,500..." "Battle of Fallen Timbers," Ohio History Central, Ohio Historical Society. Internet Site: http://www.ohiohistorycentral.org/ohc/history/h_indian/events/bfallen.shtml 1 / 2.

"...drivers had been ...allowed..." O'Neil, 137.

"...140...1000 feet..." "Fort Recovery" Ohio History Central, Ohio Historical Society. Internet Site: http://www.ohiohistorycentral.org/ohc/history/h_indian/places/frecover.shtml 1 / 2.

"...21 officers and [soldiers]..." O'Neil, 137.

"...360 pack horses..." Ibid.

"...250..." "Fort Recovery," 1 / 2.

"...40 dead and wounded..." Ibid.

"...22..." Ibid.

Wayne ordered the construction... O'Neil, 139.

"The Delaware scouts..." Ibid.

"...Fort Defiance..." Ibid., 140.

...Blue Jacket, now war faction leader... "Blue Jacket," Ohio History Central, Ohio Historical Society. Internet Site: http://www.ohiohistory.org/ohc/history/h_indian/people/bluejack.shtml 1 / 2.

...Little Turtle having fallen... "Little Turtle" Ohio History Central, Ohio Historical Society. Internet Site: http://www.ohiohistorycentral.org/ohc/history/h_indian/people/lturtle.shtml 1 / 2.

"...their sharpened ends toward..." Elroy M. Avery, A History of the United States and Its People, (1910), cited in Dale Van Every, "President Washington's Calculated Risk," American Heritage, IX, No. 4, (June 1958), 58.

"...1300..." Richard Battin, "'Mad Anthony' Wayne at Fallen Timbers," The News Sentinel, (Fort Wayne, IN), copywrite 1994-1996. Internet Site: http://earlyamerica.com/review/fall96/anthony.html 1 / 6, and O'Neil, 140.

"...proximity..." Van Every, 111.

Captain Robert MisCampbell... Gaff, 304.

...400... O'Neil, 135 and 139.

Biographical Note: The figure of 400 cavalry is derived from O'Neil. O'Neil reports "2,500, with mounted dragoons..." on page 139 and "2,100 men..." on page 135, thus the derived figure of 400 cavalry.

"...1500..." O'Neil, 139.

"...2100..." Ibid., 135.

...attack with bayonets only... Ibid., 140.

"...into the backs of..." Ibid., 140-41.

...40-minute battle... Ibid., 135.

"...33..." "Battle of Fallen Timbers," 2 / 2.

"...44..." Avery, cited in Van Every, 58.

"...100 wounded..." "Battle of Fallen Timbers," 2 / 2.

"cannon...loopholes...empty..." O'Neil, 141.

"...pistol range...burned..." Ibid.

"...two months..." Ibid.

"On August 3rd, 1795..." "Treaty of Greenville," Ohio History Central, Ohio Historical Society. Internet Site: http://www.ohiohistorycentral.org/ohc/history/h_indian/document/tgreenev.shtml 1 / 2.

Chapter 6

"...Cuyahoga River...Fort Laurens...Fort Loramie...Fort Recovery...Ohio River." "Treaty of Greeneville," 1 / 2.

"...north and west...$20,000...$9,500..." Ibid.

"Fort Wayne (June 7th, 1803), Vincennes (August 18th and 27th, 1804), Grouseland (August 21st, 1805), and...Fort Wayne (September 30th, 1809)." Alameda McCollough, ed., The Battle of Tippecanoe: Conflict of Cultures, (Lafayette, IN: The Research and Publication Committee of the Tippecanoe County Historical Association, 1973), 5.

"...August, 1810..." David S. Heidler and Jeanne T. Heidler, eds., Encyclopedia of the War of 1812 (Santa Barbara, CA: ABC-CLIO, Inc., 1997), s.v. "Harrison, William Henry," by David S. Heidler and Jeanne T. Heidler.

"...July, 1811..." Ibid.

...1000 soldiers... Ibid.

...Tenskwatawa assured his warriors... Ibid., s.v. "Tenskwatawa," by Heidler and Heidler.

"...1,200 Ohio militiamen..." Ibid., s.v. "Hull, William," by Malcolm Muir, Jr.

"...800..." Ibid.

...fortified with blockhouses... Heidler and Heidler, eds., xxix, and James Huston, Counterpoint: Tecumseh vs. William Henry Harrison (Lawrenceville, VA: Brunswick Publishing Company, 1987, endpaper.

...valuable intelligence...Heidler and Heidler, eds., "Hull, William," by Muir.

"...Hull reached Detroit on..." Walter R. Borneman, 1812: The War that Forged a Nation. (New York: Harper Collins Publisher, 2004), 61.

...concerned about his...supplies...Heidler and Heidler, eds., "Hull, William," by Muir.

"...Brownstown...200..." David S. Heidler and Jeanne T. Heidler, eds., Encyclopedia of the War of 1812 (Santa Barbara, CA: ABC-CLIO, Inc., 1997), s.v. "Brownstown, Battle of," by Heidler and Heidler.

...Monguagon... David S. Heidler and Jeanne T. Heidler, eds., Encyclopedia of the War of 1812 (Santa Barbara, CA: ABC-CLIO, Inc., 1997), s.v. "Monguagon, Battle of," by Heidler and Heidler, and Ibid., s.v. "Miller, James," by Robert J. Holden.

...600... Borneman, 63.

"...month's...rations...33 cannon...2,500 muskets..." Ibid., "Hull, William," by Muir.

"...(24-pounders)..." David S. Heidler and Jeanne T. Heidler, eds., <u>Encyclopedia of the War of 1812</u> (Santa Barbara, CA: ABC-CLIO, Inc., 1997), s.v. "Detroit, Surrender of," by Heidler and Heidler.

"...**Pigeon's Roost...Fort Harrison...Fort Madison...Fort Wayne...**" Alec R. Gilpin, <u>The War of 1812 in the Old Northwest</u> (East Lansing, MI: The Michigan State University Press, 1958), 139.

"...**Potawatomi chief Winnemac...**" David S. Heidler and Jeanne T. Heidler, eds., <u>Encyclopedia of the War of 1812</u> (Santa Barbara, CA: ABC-CLIO, Inc., 1997), s.v. "Wayne, Fort," by Robert J. Holden.

"...**2,200...**" Murray Holliday, The Battle of Mississinewa, 1812. (Marion, IN: Grant County Historical Society, 1964. Second Printing, 1991), 7.

...**Winchester...mixed force of Kentucky militia and Regulars...** David S. Heidler and Jeanne T. Heidler, eds., <u>Encyclopedia of the War of 1812</u> (Santa Barbara, Ca: ABC-CLIO, Inc., 1997), s.v. "Winchester, James," by Heidler and Heidler.

"...**effective September 17th, 1812...**" Ibid., "Harrison, William Henry," by Heidler and Heidler.

"...**melted away...**" Ibid., "Wayne, Fort," by Holden.

...**ordered Winchester to march...** Ibid., "Winchester, James," by Heidler and Heidler.

...**approximately 1,250...Fort Harrison...November 11, 1812...** David S. Heidler and Jeanne T. Heidler, <u>Encyclopedia of the War of 1812</u> (Santa Barbara, CA: ABC-CLIO, Inc., 1997, s.v. "Indiana Territory," by Robert S. Holden, and Ibid., s.v. "Hopkins, Samuel," by Heidler and Heidler.

...**Trimble...500...** David S. Heidler and Jeanne T. Heidler, eds., <u>Encyclopedia of the War of 1812</u> (Santa Barbara, CA: ABC-CLIO, Inc., 1997), s.v. "Trimble, Allen," by Heidler and Heidler.

...**John B. Campbell...Mississinewa...** Holiday, 10.

...**to the Maumee Rapids...** Heidler and Heidler, eds., "Winchester, James," by Heidler and Heidler.

"...**including an outbreak of typhoid fever...**" Ibid.

...**supplies had slowly dwindled...** Ibid.

...**January 8th, 1813...Frenchtown...30 miles...** Ibid.

...**on January 13th...** Ibid.

...**Colonel Henry Procter...** David S. Heidler and Jeanne T. Heidler, eds., <u>Encyclopedia of the War of 1812</u> (Santa Barbara, CA: ABC-CLIO, Inc., 1997), s.v. "Frenchtown, Battles of," by David Curtis Skaggs.

...**Roundhead...** Brian Blodgett, "Tecumseh: His Role in the Cause and Conduct of the War of 1812." Internet Site: http://members.tripod.com/ Brian_Blodgett/Tecumthe.html 7 / 12, and Heidler and Heidler, eds., s.v. "Frenchtown, Battles of," by Skaggs.

"...**600...**" David S. Heidler and Jeanne T. Heidler, eds., <u>Encyclopedia of the War of 1812</u> (Santa Barbara, CA: ABC-CLIO, Inc., 1997), s.v. "Lewis, William," by Heidler and Heidler.

"...healthiest and best-..." Ibid., s.v. "Winchester, James," by Heidler and Heidler.

...January 17th, 1813... Ibid., s.v. "Lewis, William," by Heidler and Heidler.

...afternoon of January 18th... Ibid.

"...small force of British and Indians..." Ibid.

"...convinced him..." Ibid.

"...remainder...January 20th..." Ibid.

Biographical note: The figure of 334 soldiers advancing to Frenchtown on January 20th is derived from two numbers quoted in Heidler and Heidler's Encyclopedia of the War of 1812. Under "Lewis, William," they quote a total of 600 soldiers that moved forward on January 17th. Under "Frenchtown, Battles of" a figure of Winchester's total force at Frenchtown is quoted at 934 soldiers, hence the calculation of 334 moving up on the 20th.

...security...lax... Ibid., s.v. "Winchester, James," by Heidler and Heidler.

"...dispersed...throughout the village..." Ibid., s.v. "Frenchtown, Battles of," by Skaggs.

"...their backs to the river..." Office of the Chief of Military History, United States Army, "The War of 1812." (Extracted from: American Military History; Army Historical Series, Chapter 6). Internet Site: http://www.army.mil/cmh-pg/books/amh/AMH-06.htm 9 / 24.

"...597 British...800 Indians..." David S. Heidler and Jeanne T. Heidler, eds., Encyclopedia of the War of 1812 (Santa Barbara, CA: ABC-CLIO, Inc., 1997), s.v. "Hart, Nathaniel Gray Smith," by Harry M. Ward.

"Between 4:00 and 5:00..." Heidler and Heidler, eds., s.v. "Lewis, William," by Heidler and Heidler.

...100 killed...500 captured... Office of the Chief of Military History, 9 / 24.

...60... Heidler and Heidler, eds., s.v. "Winchester, James," by Heidler and Heidler.

"...only 33 escaped death or capture." Heidler and Heidler, eds., s.v. "Frenchtown, Battles of," by Skaggs.

...between 30 and 60... Ibid.

Chapter 7

"...Ensign Hugh Brady..." David S. Heidler and Jeanne T. Heidler, eds., Encyclopedia of the War of 1812 (Santa Barbara, CA: ABC-CLIO, Inc., 1997), s.v. "Brady, Hugh," by Heidler and Heidler.

"...Major Henry Burbeck..." David S. Heidler and Jeanne T. Heidler, eds., Encyclopedia of the War of 1812 (Santa Barbara, CA: ABC-CLIO, Inc., 1997), s.v. Burbeck, Henry," by David T. Zabecki.

"...1st Lieutenant Ferdinand L. Claiborne..." David S. Heidler and Jeanne T. Heidler, eds., Encyclopedia of the War of 1812 (Santa Barbara, CA: ABC-CLIO, Inc., 1997), s.v. "Claiborne, Ferdinand L.," by Heidler and Heidler.

"**...Captain Leonard Covington...**" David S. Heidler and Jeanne T. Heidler, eds., <u>Encyclopedia of the War of 1812</u> (Santa Barbara, CA: ABC-CLIO, Inc., 1997), s.v. "Covington, Leonard," by Heidler and Heidler.

"**...Captain Moses Porter...**" David S. Heidler and Jeanne T. Heidler, eds., <u>Encyclopedia of the War of 1812</u> (Santa Barbara, CA: ABC-CLIO, Inc., 1997), s.v. "Porter, Moses," by David T. Zabecki.

"**...Cornet Solomon Van Rensselear...**" David S. Heidler and Jeanne T. Heidler, eds., <u>Encyclopedia of the War of 1812</u> (Santa Barbara, CA: ABC-CLIO, Inc., 1997), s.v. "Van Rensselear, Solomon," by John K. Mahon.

...Governor Isaac Shelby... David S. Heidler and Jeanne T. Heidler, eds., <u>Encyclopedia of the War of 1812</u> (Santa Barbara, CA: ABC-CLIO, Inc., 1997), s.v. "Shelby, Isaac," by Lowell H. Harrison.

...ten-acre timber and earth palisaded... David S. Heidler and Jeanne T. Heidler, eds., <u>Encyclopedia of the War of 1812</u> (Santa Barbara, CA: ABC-CLIO, Inc., 1997), s.v. "Meigs, Fort," by William E. Fischer, Jr.

"**...Colonel William Russell...**" David S. Heidler and Jeanne T. Heidler, eds., <u>Encyclopedia of the War of 1812</u> (Santa Barbara, CA: ABC-CLIO, Inc., 1997), s.v. "Illinois Territory," by Robert J. Holden, and Ibid., s.v. "Indiana Territory," by Holden.

On March 18th, 1813, Major Tipton... David S. Heidler and Jeanne T. Heidler, eds., <u>Encyclopedia of the War of 1812</u> (Santa Barbara, CA: ABC-CLIO, Inc., 1997), s.v. "Tipton. John," by Heidler and Heidler.

"**...in March, 1813...between 300 and 400 militia volunteers...17 small forts.**" Ibid., s.v. "Illinois Territory," by Holden.

...1,200 British...1,200 Indians...
Biographical Note: The British figure is derived from Alec Gilpin's <u>The War of 1812 in the Old Northwest</u>, pages 182-'83. Gilpin states the British force had "a total of 984, not including various Indian Department officials...a few volunteers, a few men at River Raisin, and the Marine Department."... "The 1,200 Indians (making a probable total force of nearly 2,400) led by Tecumseh and Roundhead..." While other sources vary as to the number of soldiers investing Fort Meigs, this total seems most probable.

"**...2,000...**" Gilpin, 180.

...on April 28th...enemy columns and gunboats were in sight... Ibid.

The British completed positioning their artillery by dawn, April 30th... Ibid., 183.

...shelled for two days...the heaviest...on May 1st. Ibid., 184.

...General Green Clay...about 1,200 Kentucky militia. Heidler and Heidler, eds., s.v. "Fort Meigs," by Fischer, and David S. Heidler and Jeanne T. Heidler, eds., <u>Encyclopedia of the War of 1812</u> (Santa Barbara, CA: ABC-CLIO, Inc., 1997), s.v. "Clay, Green," by Heidler and Heidler.

...800 men...left wing... Gilpin, 184-85, and Heidler and Heidler, eds., s.v. "Clay, Green," by Heidler and Heidler.

...right wing of 400... Ibid., and Ibid.

"...Lt Colonel William Dudley...Captain Leslie Combs...600 killed or captured..." David S. Heidler and Jeanne T. Heidler, eds., Encyclopedia of the War of 1812 (Santa Barbara, CA: ABC-CLIO, Inc., 1997), s.v. "Combs, Leslie," by Larry L. Nelson.

"...the smaller right (south) wing...fought its way...and entered the fort." Ibid., s.v. "Clay, Green," by Heidler and Heidler.

...350-man raid...Colonel John Miller... David S. Heidler and Jeanne T. Heidler, eds., Encyclopedia of the War of 1812 (Santa Barbara, CA: ABC-CLIO, Inc., 1997), s.v. "Miller, John," by Heidler and Heidler.

"...40 prisoners..." Ibid.

...Native Americans...drifted away...divide...and parade... Gilpin, 189-90.

...strike...at Presque Isle... Ibid., 202.

...Fort Meigs...renewed attack... Ibid.

...General Green Clay in charge of Fort Meigs... Heidler and Heidler, eds., s.v. "Clay, Green," by Fischer.

"...3,000 and 4,000..." Ibid.

...arrived at the Rapids on July 20th... Robert Breckinridge McAfee, History of the Late War in the Western Country (Lexington, KY: Worsley & Smith, 1816. Reprinted by Readex Microprint Corporation, 1966), 317.

...began the second seige...on July 21st. Heidler and Heidler, eds., s.v. "Clay, Green." by Fischer.

...mock attack... Gilpin, 204-05.

...July 26th... Ibid., 204.

...Clay, resisting the pleas... Heidler and Heidler, eds., s.v. "Clay, Green," by Fischer.

...had been informed by courier... Gilpin, 205.

...Fort Stephenson, like Fort Meigs...professionally designed by...Captain Eleaser D. Wood. David S. Heidler and Jeanne T. Heidler, eds., Encyclopedia of the War of 1812 (Santa Barbara, CA: ABC-CLIO, Inc., 1997), s.v. "Wood, Eleaser Derby," by David Curtis Skaggs.

...July 29th – 31st... David S. Heidler and Jeanne T. Heidler, eds., Encyclopedia of the War of 1812 (Santa Barbara, CA: ABC-CLIO, Inc., 1997), s.v. "Stephenson, Fort," David Curtis Skaggs, and McAfee, 322-24.

...August 1st... Heidler and Heidler, eds., s.v. "Stephenson, Fort," by Skaggs; Gilpin, 206; and McAfee, 324.

...Harrison had grave doubts... McAfee, 322.

...its one 6-pounder... Gilpin, 206-07.

...160-man garrison... David S. Heidler and Jeanne T. Heidler, eds., Encyclopedia of the War of 1812 (Santa Barbara, CA: ABC-CLIO, Inc., 1997), s.v. "Groghan, George," by Heidler and Heidler.

...could not convince their Indian allies... Gilpin, 207.

...the weakest point of the fort... McAfee, 326.

...Old Betsy...double-shotted...with canister...Heidler and Heidler, eds., s.v. "Stephenson, Fort," by Skaggs.

...on August 1st, 1813...Procter ...demanded the surrender... Gilpin, 206.

...**August 2ⁿᵈ...500 balls...** Heidler and Heidler, eds., s.v. "Stephenson, Fort," by Skaggs.

At 4:00...on August 2ⁿᵈ...115 officers and men... Ibid.

...**dull axes...** Ibid.

...**over by 4:30 PM...** Ibid.

...**26 officers and men died...** Gilpin, 207.

...**41 were wounded...** Ibid.

...**29 officers and men captured...** Ibid.

...**Americans lost 1 dead and 7 wounded.** Heidler and Heidler, eds., s.v. "Stephenson, Fort," by Skaggs.

Chapter 8

...**3,000 Regular Army troops and 5,000 militia...** Bil Gilbert, "The Battle of Lake Erie," <u>Smithsonian</u>, 25, No. 10 (January 1995), 27.

"...**5,000...**" Ibid., 32.

...**another 1,000 in the Maumee River Valley...** David S. Heidler and Jeanne T. Heidler, eds., <u>Encyclopedia of the War of 1812</u> (Santa Barbara, CA: ABC-CLIO. Inc., 1997), s.v. "Thames, Battle of the," by Sandor Antal.
Biographical Note: The figure of "another 1,000 in the Maumee River Valley" is derived from Bil Gilbert, who states, "...at the mouth of the Sandusky River...Harrison...had 5,000 men...camped 20 miles downriver..." (page 32), and Sandor Antal, who states, "In Northern Ohio, Harrison was poised...massing upwards of 6,000 fighters." From this I infer that the difference was the garrison in and around Fort Meigs in the Maumee Valley.

...**all within 20 miles of Lake Erie...** Gilbert, 32.
Biographical note: Fort Meigs is also within 20 miles of Lake Erie.

...**American naval activities on Lake Ontario...** David S. Heidler and Jeanne T. Heidler, eds., <u>Encyclopedia of the War of 1812</u> (Santa Barbara, CA: ABC-CLIO, Inc., 1997), s.v. "Lake Ontario," by Richard V. Barbuto.

...**This meant that for all practical purposes...** David S. Heidler and Jeanne T. Heidler, eds., <u>Encyclopedia of the War of 1812</u> (Santa Barbara, CA: ABC-CLIO, Inc., 1997), s.v. "Procter, Henry," by Sandor Antal, and David S. Heidler and Jeanne T. Heidler, eds., <u>Encyclopedia of the War of 1812</u> (Santa Barbara, CA: ABC-CLIO, Inc., 1997), s.v. "Barclay, Robert Heriot," by Frederick C. Drake, and Ibid., s.v. "Thames, Battle of the," by Antel.

"...**plan for an amphibious raid...**" Gilbert, 30.

...**allowed to use the fleet as a blockading squadron...** Ibid.

...**260-ton brigs** *USS Lawrence* **(20 guns) and** *USS Niagara* **(20).** David S. Heidler and Jeanne T. Heidler, eds., <u>Encyclopedia of the War of 1812</u> (Santa Barbara, CA: ABC-CLIO, Inc., 1997), s.v. "Lake Erie Campaign," by Stanley D.M. Carpenter.

...*Caledonia* (3)...*Somers* (2)...*Trippe* (1)... David Curtis Skaggs and Gerald T. Altoff, <u>A Signal Victory: The Lake Erie Campaign, 1812-1813</u>. (Annapolis, MD: Bluejacket Books/ Naval Institute Press, 1997), 110.

...*Tigress*...*Porcupine*...*Scorpion*...and *Ariel*, **collectively carrying 8 cannon**... Ibid.

"...**200-ton corvette** *Queen Charlotte* **(17 guns)**..." **et. al.** Heidler and Heidler, eds., s.v. "Lake Erie Campaign," by Carpenter.

...*Detroit* **(19 guns)**...Gilbert, 31.

...**mixed caliber...differently prepared gunpowder charges**... Heidler and Heidler, eds., s.v. "Lake Erie Campaign," by Carpenter.

...**lesser numbers of 32-pounder carronades**... Ibid.

...**short-range weapons..."smashing effect"**... Gilbert, 32.

...**Number of ships...9...6**... Heidler and Heidler, eds., s.v. "Lake Erie Campaign," by Carpenter, and Ibid., s.v. "Barclay, Robert Heriot," by Drake.

...**Number of Men...553...440**... Gilbert, 32.

...**Number of Artillery Weapons...54...63**... Heidler and Heidler, eds., s.v. "Lake Erie Campaign," by Carpenter, and Gilbert, 32.

...**Total Weight of Fire...1,536...887**... Heidler and Heidler, eds., s.v. "Barclay, Robert Heriot," by Drake.

...**Weight of Broadside Fire...936...496**...Ibid., and Gilbert, 32.

...**Weight of Long-Range Cannon...304...208**... Heidler and Heidler, eds., s.v. "Barclay, Robert Heriot," by Drake.

...**Weight of Short-Range Carronades...632...288**... Ibid.

...**Sunday, August 1st, 1813. Lookouts reported**... Gilbert, 31.

...**fear of incoming storms**... Heidler and Heidler, eds., s.v. "Lake Erie Campaign," by Carpenter.

...**the need to aid the completion**... Ibid.

...**desire to visit and attractive widow**... Gilbert, 31.

...**shifted his smaller ships**... Ibid.

...**nudged the lightened big ships**... Ibid.

...**small ships sailing directly**... David S. Heidler and Jeanne T. Heidler, eds., <u>Encyclopedia of the War of 1812</u> (Santa Barbara, CA: ABC-CLIO, Inc., 1997), s.v. "Perry, Oliver Hazard," by John K. Mahon.

...**12 cannon**... Gilbert, 31.

"...**entire...American fleet...**" Ibid.

...**anchoring at the mouth of the Sandusky River on August 16th...conferring**... Heidler and Heidler, eds., s.v. "Lake Erie Campaign," by Carpenter.

"**By early September, the...situation...**" Ibid.

"**Only a few days' supply of flour remained...**" Ibid.

...**while supplies piled up at Long Point, 150 miles**... Ibid., s.v. "Perry, Oliver Hazard," by Mahon.

At dawn on September 10th... Ibid., s.v. "Lake Erie Campaign," by Carpenter.

...**only possible advantage: to stay at a distance**... Gilbert, 32.

...**wind shifted to the southeast**...Skaggs and Altoff, 121.

At 11:45 AM, *USS Lawrence* **came into range**... Ibid., 128.

...Elliott...backed off his main topsail and declined to engage... Gilbert, 32.

...for two-and-one-half hours... Ibid., 32-34.

By 2:30 PM, the last of her cannon... Ibid.

...Captain Perry directed four sailors...Skaggs and Altoff, 141

...lost their senior officers to death or injury. Heidler and Heidler, eds., s.v. "Lake Erie Campaign," by Carpenter, and Ibid., s.v. "Barclay, Robert Heriot," by Drake.

...junior officers struggled...the big British corvettes collided... Ibid., s.v. "Lake Erie Campaign," by Carpenter.

...double-shotted rounds...effect was devastating...Gilbert, 34.

...fifteen minutes... Heidler and Heidler, eds., s.v. "Perry, Oliver Hazard," by Mahon.

"Lake Erie was now an American pond." Gilbert, 34.

...narrow isthmus between the Portage and Sandusky Rivers... Gilpin, 218.

...80 bateaux... David S. Heidler and Jeanne T. Heidler, eds., Encyclopedia of the War of 1812 (Santa Barbara, CA: ABC-CLIO, Inc., 1997), s.v. "Put-in Bay, Ohio," by David Curtis Skaggs.

"...strategic withdrawal..." Ibid., s.v. "Thames, Battle of the," by Antal.

"neither Procter nor Tecumseh was familiar..." Ibid.

...withdrawal up the Thames...September 26th, 1813... Gilpin, 217.

He landed a large portion...September 27th... Ibid., 219.

...large Kentucky mounted force, under Richard Johnson... Ibid., 218.

...the force...united with the...invasion force... Ibid., 220.

...approximately 3,500 soldiers...Heidler and Heidler, eds., s.v. "Put-in-Bay, Ohio," by Skaggs.

...Indians retreated...on the south side...British moved up the north... Gilpin, 223.

...sickness, exhaustion, and desertion...Heidler and Heidler, eds., s.v. "Thames, Battle of the," by Antal.

...Native American families...stringing...far to the rear... Ibid.

...October 4th...at the rapids...Ibid.

...three ships loaded... Gilpin, 222, and McAfee, 386.

...stands of small arms...Ibid., and Ibid.

Moraviantown was defensible... Gilpin, 223.

...Procter had purchased the village as his army's winter quarters... Heidler and Heidler, eds., s.v. "Thames, Battle of the," by Antal.

...430 British Regulars and 600 Native Americans...Ibid., and Ibid., s.v. "Procter, Henry," by Antal.

...two miles west... Gilpin, 224.

...to the south, the Thames... William Francis Freehoff, "Tecumseh's Last Stand," Military History (Military.com) Internet Site: http://www.military.com/Content/MoreContent?files=PRthames 4 / 4.

...limited the width of the area...Heidler and Heidler, eds., s.v. "Thames, Battle of the," by Antal.

"...Backmetack Marsh..." Ibid.

...6-pounder cannon... Ibid.

...120-man corps... William Francis Freehoff, "Tecumseh's Last Stand," Part 2, Military History (Military.com) Internet Site: http://www.military.com/Content/MoreContent?files=PRthames2 1 / 4.

...Colonel William Johnson's thousand-man regiment... Heidler and Heidler, eds., s.v. "Thames, Battle of the," by Antal.

...three brigades...under Major General William Henry... Freehoff, Part 2, 2 / 4.

,..American left...Major General Joseph Desha... Ibid.

...3,000 soldiers... Heidler and Heidler, eds., s.v. "Thames, Battle of the," by Antal.

...drawn up in open formation... Gilpin, 224.

...launch a mounted infantry charge... Freehoff, Part 2, 2 / 4.

...Colonel Johnson...second crucial command decision... Gilpin, 225.

...horses...became frightened... Heidler and Heidler, eds., s.v. "Thames, Battle of the," by Antal.

...a volley or two... Gilpin, 225

...three minutes of battle time... Heidler and Heidler, eds., s.v. "Thames, Battle of the," by Antal.

...half hour pitched battle... Ibid.

...Colonel Richard Johnson...fired the lethal... David S. Heidler and Jeanne T. Heidler, eds., Encyclopedia of the War of 1812 (Santa Barbara, CA: ABC-CLIO, Inc., 1997), s.v. "Johnson, Richard Mentor," by Frederick C. Drake.

...British lost 18 killed and 22 wounded... Freehoff, Part 2, 4 / 4.

...Indians lost at least 33 killed... Ibid.

...Americans had 15 killed and 30 wounded... Ibid.

...capturing 601 prisoners... Heidler and Heidler, eds., s.v. "Thames, Battle of the," by Antal.

...William Henry Harrison to resign... Heidler and Heidler, eds., s.v. "Harrison, William Henry," by Heidler and Heidler.

Chapter 9

...to the east were the Cherokees... David S. Heidler and Jeanne T. Heidler, eds., Encyclopedia of the War of 1812 (Santa Barbara, CA: ABC-CLIO, Inc., 1997), s.v. "Cherokee Indians," by Thomas S. Martin.

"...Seminoles...refused to register..." Robert M. Utley and Wilcomb E. Washburn, Indian Wars (New York: American Heritage, 1997; reprint; Boston: Houghton Mifflin company, 1987), 135. (page reference is to reprint edition).

...Lower Creeks...western Georgia border area... Davis S. Heidler and Jeanne T. Heidler, eds., Encyclopedia of the War of 1812 (Santa Barbara, CA: ABC-CLIO, Inc., 1997), s.v. "Creek War," by Heidler and Heidler.

To the west... Ibid

The relationship between Great Britain and Spain... Frank Lawrence Owsley, Jr., <u>Struggle for the Gulf Borderlands: The Creek War and the Battle of New Orleans, 1812-1815.</u> (Gainesville, FL: University Presses of Florida, 1981), 18.

(Biographical Note: The political relationship between Great Britain, Spain, the United States, and the various Native American nations in the geographical area of the Gulf Coast during the period of 1811 to 1818 was very complicated. It is beyond the scope of this book to engage in an in-depth analysis of this situation. However, Frank L. Owsley, Jr. completed an outstanding analysis in his book, <u>Struggle for the Gulf Borderlands</u>. The author strongly recommends the reading of Chapter 2, "The Role of Britain and Spain in the War in the South," (p. 18-29), and Chapter 9, "British Arrival on the Gulf," (p. 95-105) to that student interested in this complex political combination.)

Chapter 10

...particularly with Scottish traders... David S. Heidler and Jeanne T. Heidler, eds., <u>Encyclopedia of the War of 1812</u> (Santa Barbara, CA: ABC-CLIO, Inc., 1997), s.v. "McQueen, Peter," by John M. Keefe.

...a religious revival swept... Heidler and Heidler, eds., s.v. "Creek War," by Heidler and Heidler.

...the visit of Shawnee leader Tecumseh... Owsley, 11.

...deliberately rejected it...O'Brien, Sean Michael. <u>In Bitterness and In Tears: Andrew Jackson's Destruction of the Creeks and Seminoles</u>. (Westport, CT: Lyons Press/Greenwood Publishing Group, Inc., 2003, 2005), 24.

...known...for their practice... Davis S. Heidler and Jeanne T. Heidler, eds., <u>Encyclopedia of the War of 1812</u> (Santa Barbara, CA: ABC-CLIO, Inc., 1997), s.v. "Red Sticks," by Rory T. Cornish.

...returned to the northwest...took part... Owsley, 14

...a series of bloody massacres... Robert V. Remini, <u>Andrew Jackson and His Indian Wars</u>. (New York: Viking Pinguin, Inc., 2001), 55.

...a series of murders within... Heidler and Heidler, eds., s.v. "Creek War," by Heidler and Heidler.

..."law menders" to execute... Ibid.

...surrender Big Warrior in retribution... Owsley, 17.

"...summer of 1813..." David S. Heidler and Jeanne T. Heidler, eds., <u>Encyclopedia of the War of 1812</u> (Santa Barbara, CA: ABC-CLIO, Inc., 1997), s.v. "Tuckabatchee," by Thomas S. Martin.

...200 warriors...O'Brien, 40.

...escape that village before... Heidler and Heidler, eds., s.v. "Tuckabatchee," by Martin.

...rampaged...the surrounding countryside... O'Brien, 40.

"...4,000..." Heidler and Heidler, eds., s.v. "Red Sticks," by Cornish.

"...350..." David S. Heidler and Jeanne T. Heidler, eds., <u>Encyclopedia of the War of 1812</u> (Santa Barbara, CA: ABC-CLIO, Inc., 1997), s.v. "Burnt Corn, Battle of," by Peter R. Faber.

"...July, 1813..." Ibid.

...a half-ton of gunpowder...O'Brien, 40.

...five rounds per warrior... Heidler and Heidler, eds., s.v. "McQueen, Peter," by Keefe.

"...July 27th...80 miles north of Pensacola..." Ibid.

"...180..." Heidler and Heidler, eds., s.v. "Burnt Corn, Battle of," by Faber.

"...200..." Heidler and Heidler, eds., s.v. "McQueen, Peter, " by Keefe.

...Colonel James Caller... Owsley, 30.

...plunder the wagons...Ibid., 31.

"...100..." Heidler and Heidler, eds., s.v. "Burnt Corn, Battle of," by Faber.

...Red Sticks lost about 20 men and most of their supplies... Heidler and Heidler, eds., s.v. "McQueen, Peter," by Keefe.

...hastily erected wooden stockades...O'Brien, 43.

...Fort Mims...Alabama River... Ibid.

"...white, [Lower] Creeks, and mixed blood..." David S. Heidler and Jeanne T. Heidler, eds., <u>Encyclopedia of the War of 1812</u> (Santa Barbara, CA: ABC-CLIO, Inc., 1997), s.v. "Mims, Attack on Fort," by Heidler and Heidler.

"...120 Mississippi Territorial Militia..." Ibid.

"...Major Daniel Beasley..." O'Brien, 45.

"...few...scouting...not very vigilant..." Heidler and Heidler, eds., s.v. "Mims, Attack on Fort," by Heidler and Heidler.

...gate propped open...sand drifted against it... Owsley, 36.

"...whipped for giving a false alarm..." Ibid.

"...750..." Heidler and Heidler, eds., s.v. "Mims, Attack on Fort," by Heidler and Heidler.

"...13 towns..." Heidler and Heidler, eds., s.v. "McQueen, Peter," by Keefe.

"...the sentries...quickly...shot..." Owsley, 36.

"...still struggling..." Heidler and Heidler, eds., s.v. "Mims, Attack on Fort," by Heidler and Heidler.

...led by Paddy Welsh... Owsley, 37.

"...portholes...four feet above the ground..." Heidler and Heidler, eds., s.v. "Mims, Attack on Fort," by Heidler and Heidler.

"...remainder...rushed into the fort..." Ibid.

...destroying efforts to mount a unified defense... Ibid.

...they no longer could load their weapons... Ibid.

...cut their way through... Ibid.

"...247..." Owsley, 36.

"...100..." Ibid.

"News of the massacre...rapidly..." Heidler and Heidler, eds., s.v. "Mims, Attack on Fort," by Heidler and Heidler..

Chapter 11

Two states and one territory... Remini, <u>Jackson</u>, 43.

...raised a total of four armies... Heidler and Heidler, eds., s.v. "Creek War, " by Heidler and Heidler.

...virtually no communication...coordination...was almost nonexistent... Ibid.

...they did not have the supplies... David S. Heidler and Jeanne T. Heidler, eds., <u>Encyclopedia of the War of 1812</u> (Santa Barbara, CA: ABC-CLIO, Inc., 1997), s.v. "Pinckney, Thomas," by Heidler and Heidler.

...a characteristic...*short terms of enlistment*... Ibid., and Ibid.

...Sixth Military District...North Carolina, South Carolina, and Georgia... O'Brien, 52.

Command...Thomas Pinckney... Heidler and Heidler, eds., s.v. "Pinckney, Thomas," by Heidler and Heidler.

...Seventh Military District...Louisiana, Tennessee, and Mississippi Territory... David S. Heidler and Jeanne T. Heidler, eds., <u>Encyclopedia of the War of 1812</u> (Santa Barbara, CA: ABC-CLIO, Inc., 1997), s.v. "Flournoy, [John] Thomas," by Junius P. Rodriguez

Command...Thomas Flournoy... O'Brien, 52.

...no way to communicate... Heidler and Heidler, eds., s.v. "Flournoy, [John] Thomas," by Rodriquez.

...coordination...impossible... Heidler and Heidler, eds., s.v. "Red Sticks," by Cornish.

...virtually ignorant militarily... Heidler and Heidler, eds., s.v. "Flournoy, [John] Thomas," by Rodriquez.

He got along with almost no one... Ibid.

...command to Major General Thomas Pinckney... Heidler and Heidler, eds., s.v. "Pinckney, Thomas," by Heidler and Heidler.

...Flournoy originally send the Third and Seventh U.S. Regular Infantry... Owsley, 45.

...recalled the Regulars and dismissed the Mississippi Dragoons... Ibid, 46.

"...Flournoy reprimanded him..." Heidler and Heidler, eds., s.v. "Claiborne, Ferdinand," by Heidler and Heidler.

"...even...the Third Infantry to [re]join the campaign." Ibid.

...November 13th, 1813...1,200 regulars and militia... Owsley, 46-47.

"...up the Alabama River..." Heidler and Heidler, eds., s.v. "Claiborne, Ferdinand," by Heidler and Heidler.

...100 miles up the Alabama River to Econochaca... David S. Heidler and Jeanne T. Heidler, eds., <u>Encyclopedia of the War of 1812</u> (Santa Barbara, CA: ABC-CLIO, Inc., 1997), s.v. "Econochaca, Battle of," by John M. Keefe.

...the farther...the weaker... Heidler and Heidler, eds., s.v. "Claiborne, Ferdinand," by Heidler and Heidler.

"...an invisible barrier..." Owsley, 47.

...Carson...right...Russell...center...Cassells...left... Heidler and Heidler, eds., s.v. "Econochaca, Battle of," by Keefe.

Many...immediately fled. Heidler and Heidler, eds., s.v. "Claiborne, Ferdinand," by Heidler and Heidler.

...leaping...30-foot cliff...Alabama River... David S. Heidler and Jeanne T. Heidler, eds., Encyclopedia of the War of 1812 (Santa Barbara, CA: ABC-CLIO, Inc., 1997), s.v. "Weatherford, William," by John M. Keefe.

"...33 killed..." Owsley, 47.

...Americans lost one...and 20 wounded. Ibid.

...Brigadier... David S. Heidler and Jeanne T. Heidler, eds., Encyclopedia of the War of 1812 (Santa Barbara, CA: ABC-CLIO, Inc., 1997), s.v. "Georgia," by Heidler and Heidler.

...(later Major) General John Floyd... Heidler and Heidler, eds., s.v. "Creek War," by Heidler and Heidler.

...2,000...at Fort Hawkins... Ibid.

...a shortage of food and ammunition, plus a miserable logistics system... O'Brien, 93-94.

...20-day supply... Ibid., 95.

"...950 soldiers..." Owsley, 54.

"...Fort Mitchell..."O'Brien, 95.

"...400 allied [Lower] Creeks..." Heidler and Heidler, eds., s.v. "Georgia," by Heidler and Heidler.

"...20 miles north of its confluence..." David S. Heidler and Jeanne T. Heidler, eds., Encyclopedia of the War of 1812 (Santa Barbara, CA: ABC-CLIO, Inc., 1997), s.v. "Autosse, Battle of," by John M. Keefe.

...approached in three columns... Ibid.

...plan was to envelop... Owsley, 54.

...devolved into fierce hand-to-hand fighting... Heidler and Heidler, eds., s.v. "Georgia," by Heidler and Heidler.

...ended by 9:00AM. Heidler and Heidler, eds., s.v. "Autosse, Battle of," by Keefe.

...200 dead and 400 dwellings destroyed... Ibid.

"...11 killed and 54 wounded..." Owsley, 54.

"General Floyd was among those wounded." Heidler and Heidler, eds., s.v. "Georgia," by Heidler and Heidler.

...forced to return to Fort Mitchell... Heidler and Heidler, eds., s.v. "Creek War," by Heidler and Heidler.

...Red Sticks...attack the rearguard... Heidler and Heidler, eds., s.v. "Georgia," by Heidler and Heidler.

...recurring problems of supplies and recruits... Owsley, 55.

"...1,300 Georgia and Carolina volunteers..." David S. Heidler and Jeanne T. Heidler, eds., Encyclopedia of the War of 1812 (Santa Barbara, CA: ABC-CLIO, Inc., 1997), s.v. "Calabee, Battle of," by Brigitte F. Cole.

...McIntosh's 400 warriors... Ibid.

…**February 22, 1814**… Heidler and Heidler, eds., s.v. "Creek War," by Heidler and Heidler.

…**40 miles…Fort Hull**… Ibid.

"…**1,800**…" Heidler and Heidler, eds., s.v. "Calabee, Battle of," by Cole.

…**approximately 30 minutes before sunrise on January 27th, 1814**… Ibid.

"…**completely surprised**…" Ibid.

"…**general…hand-to-hand**…" Ibid.

"…**capture the cannon**…" Ibid.

"…**Floyd…led a charge**…" Ibid.

…**70 dead and 132 wounded**… Owsley, 58.

…**22 dead and 147 wounded**… Heidler and Heidler, eds., s.v. "Calabee, Battle of," by Cole.

…**1,500 militia**… David S. Heidler and Jeanne T. Heidler, eds., Encyclopedia of the War of 1812 (Santa Barbara, CA: ABC-CLIO, Inc., 1997), s.v. "Blount, Willie," by Thomas H. Winn.

…**additional 3,500 militia**… David S. Heidler and Jeanne T. Heidler, eds., Encyclopedia of the War of 1812 (Santa Barbara, CA: ABC-CLIO, Inc., 1997), s.v. "Cocke, John," by Heidler and Heidler.

…**West Tennessee Militia…Major General Andrew Jackson**… Owsley, 43.

…**East Tennessee Militia…Major General John Cocke**… Ibid.

…**turn command over**… Heidler and Heidler, eds., s.v. "Creek War," by Heidler and Heidler.

…**glory and political value**…Owsley, 66.

…**Fort Armstrong…70 miles east**… Heidler and Heidler, eds., s.v. "Cocke, John," Heidler and Heidler.

96 "…**Hillabee Towns**…" David S. Heidler and Jeanne T. Heidler, eds., Encyclopedia of the War of 1812 (Santa Barbara, CA: ABC-CLIO, Inc., 1997), s.v. "Hillabee Massacre, Creek Territory," by Robert Saunders, Jr.

…**thoroughly beaten…sued for peace**… Ibid.

…**granted on November 17th, 1813**… Ibid.

…**General James White…cavalry…allied Cherokees under Colonel Gideon Morgan**… Ibid.

…**Little Oakfusky and Genalga**… Owsley, 66.

"…**were caught completely by surprise**…" Ibid., 67.

"…**64…killed, 29 were wounded, and 237 captives**…" Ibid.

…**to fight to the death**… Heidler and Heidler, eds., s.v. "Hillabee Massacre, Creek Territory," by Saunders.

"…**some of the last**…" Ibid.

…**ordered Cocke and the soon-to-be-discharged militia north**… Ibid.

Chapter 12

...**46-year-old...** David S. Heidler and Jeanne T. Heidler, eds., <u>Encyclopedia of the War of 1812</u>. Santa Barbara, CA: ABC-CLIO, Inc., 1997), s.v. "Jackson, Andrew," by Rory T. Cornish.
Biographical Note: In this book, the background for Andrew Jackson's life and career up to the Creek War was drawn from Cornish's entry on Andrew Jackson in Heidler and Heidler's <u>Encyclopedia of the War of 1812</u>, noted above. The author strongly suggests the reader review this excellent entry in the encyclopedia.

...**militia to concentrate at Fayetteville, Tennessee, on October 10ᵗʰ...** Ibid.

...**planned to link with his cavalry...at Huntsville...**Remini, <u>Jackson</u>, 62.

...**Fort Deposit...20 miles south of Huntsville...** David S. Heidler and Jeanne T. Heidler, eds., <u>Encyclopedia of the War of 1812</u> (Santa Barbara, CA: ABC-CLIO, Inc., 1997), s.v. "Strother, Fort," by John M. Keefe.

...**detached...Coffee...with 600 men...**Owsley, 64.

...**900 to 1,000...** David S. Heidler and Jeanne T. Heidler, eds., <u>Encyclopedia of the War of 1812</u> (Santa Barbara, CA: ABC-CLIO, Inc., 1997), s.v. "Tullushatshee, Battle of," by Phillip E. Koerper.

...**morning of November 3ʳᵈ, 1813...** Owsley, 64.

...**the left under Colonel Newton Cannon...** O'Brien, 73.

The central force under Lieutenants E. Hammond and Andrew Patterson... Ibid.

...**fired only once, then reverted to bows and arrows...** Heidler and Heidler, eds., s.v. "Tullashatshee, Battle of," by Koerper.

...**186 warriors killed (and probably more...)** Ibid.

...**5 killed and 40 wounded...** Ibid.

On November 7ᵗʰ, Jackson received a message... David S. Heidler and Jeanne T. Heidler, eds., <u>Encyclopedia of the War of 1812</u> (Santa Barbara, CA: ABC-CLIO, Inc., 1997), s.v. "Talladega, Battle of," by Heidler and Heidler.

...**believing General John Cocke was soon to arrive...** Heidler and Heidler, eds., s.v. "Creek War," by Heidler and Heidler.

...**2,000 troops to Talladega...**Owsley, 65, and Remini, <u>Jackson</u>, 65.

Jackson was only a short distance... Heidler and Heidler, eds., s.v. "Talladega, Battle of," by Heidler and Heidler.

Jackson positioned...infantry in the middle... Heidler and Heidler, eds., s.v. "Jackson, Andrew," by Cornish.

...**Red Sticks...attacked a gap...** Owsley, 66.

...**Jackson's army inflicted 299 deaths...** Ibid.

...**William Weatherford and...700...escaped.** Heidler and Heidler, eds., s.v. "Jackson, Andrew," by Cornish.

...**95 casualties...** Heidler and Heidler, eds., s.v. "Talladega, Battle of," by Heidler and Heidler.

…supply limitations and the unilateral action… Heidler and Heidler, eds., s.v. "Jackson, Andrew," by Cornish.

General Cocke…arrive…December 12th, 1813…Owsley, 70.

Jackson…ordered Cocke back to Tennessee… O'Brien, 88.

"…150 soldiers…" Heidler and Heidler, eds., s.v. "Creek War," by Heidler and Heidler.

Most wanted to abandon… Remini, Jackson , 69-74.

"…January 14th… Ibid.

…650 new 60-day recruits…200 allied Lower Creeks…

> Biographical Note: The figure of 650 is derived from several sources. Remini, Jackson, quotes "850 raw recruits…sent by Governor Blount." Keefe quotes "…200 friendly Indians…" [David S. Heidler and Jeanne T. Heidler, eds., Encyclopedia of the War of 1812 (Santa Barbara, CA: ABC-CLIO, Inc., 1997), s.v. "Emuckfau Creek, Battle of," by John M. Keefe.] Cornish quotes "…new 60-day recruits under Col. William Carroll." From my reviews, the figure of 850 seems to include the 200 allied Native Americans. However, depending on interpretations, there could have been 850 Tennessee recruits and 200 allied Native Americans arriving at Fort Strother on January 14th, 1814. One fact is certain: Jackson received enough reinforcements to feel justified to swing to the offensive against the Creeks shortly after the arrival of this contingent.

…having gotten wind of Major General John Floyd's offensive… Owsley, 75

…1,000 men and one cannon… Heidler and Heidler, eds., s.v. "Emuckfau Creek, Battle of," by Keefe.

By the evening of January 21st, 1814… Ibid.

"At 6:00 AM…about 900…" Ibid.

…General Coffee charged… Owsley, 75.

…retreat toward Fort Strother. Remini, Jackson, 73.

…Jackson had been alert for a Red Stick attack on his rearguard. David S. Heidler and Jeanne T. Heidler, eds., Encyclopedia of the War of 1812 (Santa Barbara, CA: ABC-CLIO, Inc., 1997), s.v. "Enitachopco Creek, Battle of," by Heidler and Heidler.

…waited until…the…cannon was in the creek… O'Brien, 121.

…right and left flanks to pivot… Ibid, 122 .

…rearguard gave way… Remini, Jackson, 74.

…pincers became…assault columns… Ibid.

…cannon…filled with grapeshot… Heidler and Heidler, eds., s.v. "Enitachopco Creek, Battle of," by Heidler and Heidler.

Twenty Americans killed and 75 wounded… Remini, Jackson, 74.

…two hundred Red Sticks… Ibid.

…General Coffee arriving with a contingent… David S. Heidler and Jeanne T. Heidler, eds., Encyclopedia of the War of 1812 (Santa Barbara, CA: ABC-CLIO, Inc., 1997), s.v. "Horseshoe Bend, Battle of," by Donald S. Frazier.

More Cherokee warriors and Lower Creeks… Ibid.

…Pinckney…stepped in…with crucial assistance… Heidler and Heidler, eds., s.v. "Pinckney, Thomas," by Heidler and Heidler.

"…600-man 39ᵗʰ U.S. Infantry…" Heidler and Heidler, eds., s.v. "Horseshoe Bend, Battle of," by Frazier.

"…well-drilled infantry assisted… Heidler and Heidler, eds., s.v. "Creek War," by Heidler and Heidler.

"…rigid discipline…" Ibid.

"…teen-aged private…executed…" Ibid.

"…4,000…" Heidler and Heidler, eds., s.v. "Horseshoe Bend, Battle of," by Frazier.

"…5,000…" Remini, 75.

…loop…nearly enclosed… Ibid.

"…350 yard neck…" Ibid.

…log and tree trunk… Ibid.

"…five to eight feet…" Ibid.

…zig-zagging…cleverly placed loopholes… Ibid.

…a steep cliff… Ibid.

…approximately 1,000 warriors… Owsley, 79.

…2,000…700…500…100… Remini, Jackson, 75.

…stopping only to build Fort Williams… Heidler and Heidler, eds., s.v. "Jackson, Andrew," by Cornish.

"…10:00 AM…" Remini, Jackson, 76.

…March 27ᵗʰ, 1814… Heidler and Heidler, eds., s.v. "Creek War," by Heidler and Heidler.

"It is impossible to conceive…" Remini, Jackson, 76.

"…*penned themselves up for slaughter…*" Ibid.

…Brigadier General John Coffee, 700 soldiers, and 600 allied Indians… O'Brien, 141.

"…one six-pounder…and one 3-pounder…" Remini, Jackson, 76.

"…10:30 AM…" Ibid.

…cross it and destroy a line of canoes… Owsley, 80.

…scaled the cliff… Remini, Jackson, 76.

…burned several buildings there… Heidler and Heidler, eds., s.v. "Horseshoe Bend, Battle of," by Frazier.

…Reds Sticks…were distracted… Remini, Jackson, 76.

…firing through the loopholes… Ibid., 76-77.

…the determined soldiers were up and over the wall… Ibid., 77.

…swim the Tallapoosa… Heidler and Heidler, eds., s.v. "Horseshoe Bend, Battle of," by Frazier.

"…850…" Remini, Jackson, 79.

…49 dead and 154 wounded… Ibid.

…Major General Thomas Pinckney…and Benjamin Hawkins… David S. Heidler and Jeanne T. Heidler, eds., Encyclopedia of the War of 1812 (Santa Barbara, CA: ABC-CLIO, Inc., 1997), s.v. "Fort Jackson, Treaty of," by Peter R. Faber.

…Jackson continued his rampage… Remini, <u>Jackson</u>, 80-81.

…erected Fort Jackson… Ibid., 81.

…William Weatherford walked boldly… Ibid., 82-83.

…the security of the United States against European intervention or invasion… Ibid., 85.

…all Native Americans must be removed…above Fort Williams… Ibid., 84.

…22 million acres… Heidler and Heidler, eds., s.v. "Fort Jackson, Treaty of," by Faber.

…(including 2.2 million acres of the allied Cherokees' lands…) Heidler and Heidler, eds., s.v. "Cherokee Indians," by Martin.

"…August 9th, 1814…" Ibid., s.v. "Fort Jackson, Treaty of," by Faber.

…the vast majority…were allied Lower Creek leaders! Remini, <u>Jackson</u>, 86-93.

Chapter 13

…to first Brigadier… Remini, <u>Jackson</u>, 86.

…then Major General…June 18th, 1814… Heidler and Heidler, eds., s.v. "Jackson, Andrew," by Cornish.

…earned him the appellation *Sharp Knife*… Remini, <u>Jackson</u>, 81.

"Command of the Seventh Military District…" Ibid., 86.

…conversion from state control… David S. Heidler and Jeanne T. Heidler, eds., <u>Encyclopedia of the War of 1812</u> (Santa Barbara, CA: ABC-CLIO, Inc., 1997), s.v. "Carroll, William," by Thomas S. Winn.

…Jackson initially believed Mobile was the target… Heidler and Heidler, eds., s.v. "Jackson, Andrew," by Cornish.

…Major William Lawrence and 160 men to Fort Bowyer… David S. Heidler and Jeanne T. Heidler, eds., <u>Encyclopedia of the War of 1812</u> (Santa Barbara, CA: ABC-CLIO, Inc., 1997), s.v. "Bowyer, Fort," by Gene A. Smith.

On September 12th, 1814…British…130 marines… David S. Heidler and Jeanne T. Heidler, eds., <u>Encyclopedia of the War of 1812</u> (Santa Barbara, CA: ABC-CLIO, Inc., 1997), s.v. "Lawrence, William," by Heidler and Heidler.

…180 Indians… O'Brien, 172.

…land assault (September 14th) that got within 800 yards… Ibid.

…and naval bombardment… Owsley, 110.

"…27 killed…45 wounded…" David S. Heidler and Jeanne T. Heidler, eds., <u>Encyclopedia of the War of 1812</u> (Santa Barbara, CA: ABC-CLIO, Inc., 1997), s.v. "Mobile, Battles of," by Gene A. Smith.

…4 killed and 5 wounded… Ibid.

…900 Creek refugees… David S. Heidler and Jeanne T. Heidler, eds., <u>Encyclopedia of the War of 1812</u> (Santa Barbara, CA: ABC-CLIO, Inc., 1997), s.v. "Pensacola, West Florida," by Henry S. Marks.

…100 to 200 Royal Marines… David S. Heidler and Jeanne T. Heidler, eds., <u>Encyclopedia of the War of 1812</u> (Santa Barbara, CA: ABC-CLIO, Inc., 1997), s.v. "Pensacola, Battles of," by Eric Jarvis.

...**Captain George Woodbine...Prospect Bluff...** David S. Heidler and Jeanne T. Heidler, eds., Encyclopedia of the War of 1812 (Santa Barbara, CA: ABC-CLIO, Inc., 1997), s.v. "Prospect Bluff, West Florida," by Gene A. Smith.

... **in May, 1814...** David S. Heidler and Jeanne T. Heidler, eds., Encyclopedia of the War of 1812 (Santa Barbara, CA: ABC-CLIO, Inc., 1997), s.v. "Seminole Indians," by Heidler and Heidler.

"**...2,000 stands of arms and 300,000 ball cartridges...**" Remini, Jackson, 94.

...**one thousand pistols, one thousand carbines, five hundred rifles, and greater than a million rounds of ammunition...** Ibid.

...**more than 4,000 Seminoles and refugee Creeks...** Ibid.

...**Jackson asked permission...** Ibid., 94-95.

"**...without waiting...**" Ibid., 95.

...**4,000 soldiers...**O'Brien, 178.

"**...as early as November, 1812...**" Heidler and Heidler, eds., s.v. "Pensacola, West Florida," by Marks.

...**on November 6th, 1814.** Owsley, 113..

"**...Fort San Carlos de Barrancas...**" Heidler and Heidler, eds., s.v. "Pensacola, Battle of," by Jarvis

...**seven ships...** McAfee, 498.

...**Spanish garrison of approximately 500 men...**O'Brien, 178.

...**Fort San Miguel, located directly inside the city...** Heidler and Heidler, eds., s.v. "Pensacola, West Florida," by Marks.

...**500 men on the west side...**O'Brien, 179.

...**3,500 men.**
Biographical Note: The number of 3,500 men who circled Pensacola to the north is a derived figure. Marks states that "...in early November he [Jackson] took the initiative to advance on the town [Pensacola] with about 4,000 men." Jarvis concurs with the 4,000 figure, then continues: " Jackson then used 500 of his men to attack the town [Pensacola] from the west as a feint..."

...**eluding pickets...** Heidler and Heidler, eds., s.v. "Pensacola, Battle of," by Jarvis.

...**rounds...into the dock area...** Ibid.

...**spiked the cannon...** Heidler and Heidler, eds., s.v. "Pensacola, West Florida," by Marks.

...**sailed to Prospect Bluff...** David S. Heidler and Jeanne T. Heidler, eds., Encyclopedia of the War of 1812 (Santa Barbara, CA: ABC-CLIO, Inc., 1997), s.v. "Nicholls, Edward," by Heidler and Heidler.

...**unofficial intelligence...merchant captains...** David S. Heidler and Jeanne T. Heidler, eds., Encyclopedia of the War of 1812 (Santa Barbara, CA: ABC-CLIO, Inc., 1997), s.v. "New Orleans, Battle of," by Heidler and Heidler.

...**took...Tennessee Mounted Infantry...Mississippi Dragoons... 44th U.S. Infantry Regiment...** McAfee, 503.

...**the 7th U.S. Infantry...** Ibid., 510.

...2,000 man...under General Taylor... Ibid., 503.

...2,500-strong Georgia Militia... Ibid., 491.

...under Major General John McIntosh... Ibid., 503.

...(second-in-command being Brigadier General Blackshear)... Ibid.

The overall commander...General James Winchester...Owsley, 126.

...Kentucky...2,500-man...Major General John Thomas...Brevet Brigadier General John Adair... McAfee, 502.

...Major General William Carroll...Tennessee Militia... 3,000...Brigadier General Byrd Smith. Ibid.

...Louisiana...several local militia units... Ibid., 503.

...Major General Villere, who commanded the militia between the Mississippi River and Lake Borgne... Ibid., 509.

...General D.B. Morgan...Robert V. Remini, The Battle of New Orleans: Andrew Jackson and America's First Military Victory. (London: Viking Press, 1999), 86.

...Baratarian pirates...Jacques Laffite... Heidler and Heidler, eds., s.v. "New Orleans, Battle of," by Heidler and Heidler.

...two relatively powerful U.S. warships... David S. Heidler and Jeanne T. Heidler, eds., Encyclopedia of the War of 1812 (Santa Barbara, CA: ABC-CLIO, Inc., 1997), s.v. "Lake Borgne, Battle of," by Spencer S. Tucker.

...(Carolina [15 guns] and Louisiana [16])... Ibid.

...St. Phillip, and St. Leon... Remini, New Orleans, 25.

...English Turn, an S-shaped twist in the river... David S. Heidler and Jeanne T. Heidler, eds., Encyclopedia of the War of 1812 (Santa Barbara, CA: ABC-CLIO, Inc., 1997), s.v. "Louisiana," by Gene A. Smith

...5 gunboats (Nos. 5, 12, 156, 162, and 163) and two small schooners (Sea Horse and Alligator)... Heidler and Heidler, eds., s.v. "Lake Borgne, Battle of," by Tucker.

...Mobile...4,500 militia...

Biographical Note: This figure is derived from McAfee. He quotes the Georgia Militia at Mobile (p. 527) under Major General John McIntosh (p. 503) at 2,500 (p. 491). He also quotes the Tennessee Militia under General Taylor (pgs. 503 and 527) at 2,000 (p. 503).

...Fort Bowyer...about 350 men...

Biographical Note: The figure of "about 350" is derived from several sources. McAfee reports "360 prisoners" surrendered on February 11th, 1815. Heidler and Heidler note a garrison of "375 men" (s.v. "Lawrence, William"). Smith notes the "fort's compliment" of "almost 400" men (Heidler and Heidler, eds., s.v. "Mobile, Battles of," by Smith). A figure of "about 350 men" seems conservative.

...several large cannon... Heidler and Heidler, eds., s.v. "Lawrence, William," by Heidler and Heidler.

...important because they bought...time... Heidler and Heidler, eds., s.v. "Lake Borgne, Battle of," by Tucker.

...British arrived at Ship Island...December 12th, 1814... McAfee, 504.

Lake Borgne was too shallow... Heidler and Heidler, eds., s.v. "Lake Borgne, Battle of," by Tucker.

...7,000-man assault force... Ibid.

...transferred...to shallow draft vessels... Ibid.

Master Commandant Daniel Todd Patterson...subordinate commander...Lt. Thomas ap Catesby Jones. Ibid.

...1,200 to 83 advantage in men; a 42 to 23 advantage in cannon... McAfee, 505.

...forced by calm winds...Malheureux Islands... Ibid.

...December 24th, 1814... Ibid.

...Villere Plantation...9 miles...southeast... David S. Heidler and Jeanne T. Heidler, eds., Encyclopedia of the War of 1812 (Santa Barbara, CA: ABC-CLIO, Inc., 1997), s.v. "Villere Plantation," by Junius P. Rodriguez.

...Louisiana militia General Jacques Villere... Owsley, 142.

...General Robert Ross was to have commanded...Remini, New Orleans, 17.

...Major General John Keene...Lieutenant General Edward Pakenham... Heidler and Heidler, eds., s.v. "New Orleans, Battle of," by Heidler and Heidler.

...2,000 troops... Heidler and Heidler, eds., s.v. "Villere Plantation," by Rodriguez.

...Coffee's Tennessee Mounted Infantry, Hind's Mississippi Dragoons...local militia...7th and 44th U.S. Infantry... McAfee, 510.

...Patterson brought the Carolina down... Ibid.

...about 8:30... Ibid.

"...Night Battle of New Orleans..." Heidler and Heidler, eds., s.v. "Villere Plantation," by Rodriguez.

...Coffee assaulting the British right and Jackson...the left... McAfee, 511.

...a thick fog around 10:00 PM... Ibid.

...American army...lost 215 men...British lost 275 men... Heidler and Heidler, eds., "Villere Plantation," by Rodriguez.

...General Keene decided to wait until General Pakenham arrived... McAfee, 512.

...General Carroll...arrived...on the 22nd... McAfee, 510.

...7th and 44th Infantries... Ibid., 517.

...Patterson's warship Louisiana... Heidler and Heidler, eds., s.v. "New Orleans, Battle of," by Heidler and Heidler.

...Coffee's steady Tennessee Mounted Militia occupied the right... McAfee, 517.

...Jackson had erected four artillery batteries... Heidler and Heidler, eds., s.v. "New Orleans, Battle of," by Heidler and Heidler.

...Pakenham arrived on December 25th... Remini, New Orleans, 87.

He determined to attack...on December 28th... Ibid., 94.

...tremendous barrage from the British artillery... McAfee, 513.

...one column came close to breaking through... Heidler and Heidler, eds., s.v. "New Orleans, Battle of," by Heidler and Heidler.

...**120 casualties**... McAfee, 514.

...**used many scarce cannonballs**... David S. Heidler and Jeanne T. Heidler, eds., Encyclopedia of the War of 1812 (Santa Barbara, CA: ABC-CLIO, Inc., 1997), s.v. "Dickson, Alexander," by David T. Zabecki.

...**three days**... Heidler and Heidler, eds., s.v. "New Orleans, Battle of," by Heidler and Heidler.

...**January 1ˢᵗ, 1815**... Ibid.

"**...batteries from four to eight...**" Ibid.

...**repulsed with heavy casualties**... McAfee, 515.

...**January 4ᵗʰ, the Kentucky Militia arrived**... Ibid.

...**between 2,250**... Heidler and Heidler, eds., s.v. "New Orleans, Battle of," by Heidler and Heidler.

...**2,500 effectives**... McAfee, 502.

...**arrived...carrying rifles**... David S. Heidler and Jeanne T. Heidler, eds., Encyclopedia of the War of 1812 (Santa Barbara, CA: ABC-CLIO, Inc., 1997), s.v. "Adair, John," by Heidler and Heidler.

...**New Orleans was scoured for weapons**... McAfee, 515.

"**...800...**" Heidler and Heidler, eds., xxxvii.

...**to 1,000**... McAfee, 516.

Major General Thomas...had taken ill... Remini, New Orleans, 87

...**command...by Brigadier General Adair**... Ibid.

...**reserve behind General Carroll**... McAfee., 517.

...**Choctaw Indians...Captain Pierre Jugeat...along the river**... David S. Heidler and Jeanne T. Heidler, eds., Encyclopedia of the War of 1812 (Santa Barbara, CA: ABC-CLIO, Inc., 1997), s.v. "Choctaw Indians," by Thomas S. Martin.

...**Patterson to land several...naval cannon**... McAfee, 515.

...**500-man unit of the Louisiana Militia**... Ibid., 519.

...**under Major General D.B. Morgan**... Ibid., 515.

...**200 additional Kentucky militia...west flank**... Ibid., 516.

...**under Colonel Davis**... Ibid., 519.

Major General Samuel Gibbs... Heidler and Heidler, eds., s.v. "New Orleans, Battle of," by Heidler and Heidler.

...**commanded the stronger British right**... McAfee, 517.

...**800 yard front**... Ibid.

...**breastwork 4 to 5 feet high**... Ibid., 512.

...**wet ditch 4 feet deep and 8 feet wide**... Ibid.

...**left, a smaller British column...Major General Keene**... Ibid., 517.

...**Colonel William Thornton led**... Heidler and Heidler, eds., s.v. "New Orleans, Battle of," by Heidler and Heidler.

...**85ᵗʰ Regiment across the Mississippi River**... McAfee, 519.

The plan was...to capture...and sweep... Heidler and Heidler, eds., s.v. "New Orleans, Battle of," by Heidler and Heidler.

...**Thornton ...captured...but not until**... Ibid.

Twice they rallied...three times they charged... Ibid., 517-18.

...**Pakenham and 300...died...** Heidler and Heidler, eds., s.v. "New Orleans, Battle of," by Heidler and Heidler.

...**1262 lay wounded...484 captured...** Ibid.

...**5,500 British soldiers (3,600...actually engaged)...** Heidler and Heidler, eds., xxxvii.

...**2,046 never returned...**
Biographical Note: 300 killed, 1,262 wounded, 484 captured per Heidler and Heidler, eds., s.v. "New Orleans, Battle of," by Heidler and Heidler.

...**finalized the Treaty of Ghent on December 24th, 1814...** David S. Heidler and Jeanne T. Heidler, eds., Encyclopedia of the War of 1812 (Santa Barbara, CA. ABC-CLIO, Inc., 1997), s.v. "Ghent, Treaty of," by Blaine T. Browne.

...**news...did not reach...until February 13th, 1815...** Heidler and Heidler, eds., s.v. "Mobile, Battles of," by Smith.

...**ratified...February 15th, 1815...** Heidler and Heidler, eds., s.v. "Ghent, Treaty of," by Browne.

...**officially ended until 11:00 AM on February 17th, 1815...** Ibid.

...**Lambert...called off the offensive...** Heidler and Heidler, eds., s.v. "New Orleans, Battle of," by Heidler and Heidler.

...**General James Winchester...formally exchanged...** McAfee, 517.

...**about 400...** Heidler and Heidler, eds., s.v. "Mobile, Battles of," by Smith.

...**British General Lambert gathered nearly 5,000 soldiers...** Heidler and Heidler, eds., s.v. "Lawrence, William," by Heidler and Heidler.

...**landed 1,400 on the landward side of Fort Bowyer...** Heidler and Heidler, eds., s.v. "Mobile, Battles of," by Smith.

By February 11th, Lambert was ready... Ibid.

General Winchester was fully appraised... McAfee, 527-28.

...**delayed sending reinforcements until after the seige had begun...** Ibid., 528.

...**surrendered...360 men...** Ibid.

...**reinforcements arrived 24 hours after Fort Bowyer fell...** Ibid.

...**British lost 30 to 40 men...** Ibid.

...**February 13th...word reached the Gulf Coast...** Heidler and Heidler, eds., s.v. "Mobile, Battles of," by Smith.

Chapter 14

...**struggles with Napoleon in Europe.** David S. Heidler and Jeanne T. Heidler, eds., Encyclopedia of the War of 1812 (Santa Barbara, CA: ABC-CLIO, Inc., 1997), s.v. "Florida," by Eric Jarvis.

...**on their own to meet their own needs...** Ibid.

...**constant turmoil by arming them...** Ibid.

...**St Augustine...Castillo de San Marcos...** David S. Heidler and Jeanne T. Heidler, eds., Encyclopedia of the War of 1812 (Santa Barbara, CA: ABC-CLIO, Inc., 1997), s.v. "St. Augustine, Florida," by George E. Frakes.

...West Florida, the capital city of Pensacola... Heidler and Heidler, eds., s.v. "Florida," by Jarvis.

...Fort San Miguel... Heidler and Heidler, eds., s.v. "Pensacola, West Florida," by Marks.

...Fort San Carlos De Barrancas... Remini, Jackson, 160.

...between 400 and 500 soldiers...governor...Don Mateo Gonzales Manrique... Heidler and Heidler, eds., s.v. "Pensacola, West Florida," by Marks.

...Governor Jose Masot... O'Brien, 218.

...interpreted the *Louisiana Purchase* to include... David S. Heidler and Jeanne T. Heidler, eds., Encyclopedia of the War of 1812 (Santa Barbara, CA: ABC-CLIO, Inc., 1997), s.v. "Patriot War," by John K. Mahon.

Between January and June, 1811, Madison slid through...
Biographical Note: Two references support this statement. Frakes states: "Congress, meeting in a secret session on 11 January 1811 – nearly 16 months prior to the declaration of war – passed a bill, which President Madison signed, authorizing him to purchase or militarily occupy East Florida." (Heidler and Heidler, eds., s.v. "St. Augustine, Florida," by Frakes.) Mahon states: "Accordingly, he [President Madison] pushed through Congress on 15 June 1811 a secret resolution to absorb Florida if some responsible authority willingly transferred it." (Heidler and Heidler, eds., s.v. "Patriot War," by Mahon.)

"...if some responsible authority willingly..." Heidler and Heidler, eds., s.v. "Patriot War," by Mahon.

...General George Matthews, a respected veteran of the American Revolutionary War... Ibid.

...Madison strongly hinted...but specific...assurances were never uttered... Ibid.

...gathered a group of people with vested interests... Ibid.

...organized as the "Patriots." Ibid.

...an "army" of approximately 79 Patriots...St. Augustine... Heidler and Heidler, eds., s.v. "St. Augustine, Florida," by Frakes

"...Fernandia on Amelia Island." Heidler and Heidler, eds., s.v. "Patriot War," by Mahon.

...two American gunboats, one brig, and 150 U.S. soldiers... Ibid.

"...siege to the Castillo de San Marcos..." Heidler and Heidler, eds., s.v. "Florida," by Jarvis.

"...camped just outside cannon range..." Heidler and Heidler, eds., s.v. "St. Augustine, Florida," by Frakes

"...declared the independence of East Florida...Fernandia as their capital..." Heidler and Heidler, eds., s.v. "Patriot War," by Mahon.

...elected John Huston McIntosh...as director... Ibid.

"...offered the area between the St. Marys and the St. Johns Rivers to General Matthews..." Ibid.

"...Federalists in the Senate...British diplomatic pressure..." Heidler and Heidler, eds., s.v. "St. Augustine, Florida," by Frakes

On April 4th…Madison…repudiated… Heidler and Heidler, eds., s.v. "Patriot War," by Mahon, and Ibid., s.v. "St. Augustine, Florida," by Mahon.

"…commendable zeal…" Heidler and Heidler, eds., s.v. "Patriot War," by Mahon.

…Matthews…began…but died in route on August 30, 1812. Ibid.

…stayed on Spanish soil near the St. Marys River. Heidler and Heidler, eds., s.v. "Florida," by Jarvis.

One day after war was declared…the House…considered… Heidler and Heidler, eds., s.v. "Patriot War," by Mahon.

"…Senate disagreed…" Ibid.

…remove…U.S. troops…ignore…wishes. Ibid.

"…the troops stayed…" Ibid.

…in early 1813…another attempt… Ibid.

"…once again refused." Ibid.

…the troops must go. Ibid.

…the fall of 1813…Buckner Harris… Ibid.

…deep into Seminole country… Ibid.

…raiding parties to loot and steal… Ibid.

…Seminoles attacking what were still U.S. citizens… Heidler and Heidler, eds., s.v. "Seminole Indians," by Heidler and Heidler.

…United States refused to recognize… Heidler and Heidler, eds., s.v. "Patriot War," by Mahon.

…150… Ibid.

…defeated in battle by…escaped slaves and Seminole warriors… Heidler and Heidler, eds., s.v. "St. Augustine, Florida," by Frakes

…Harris…killed…May 5th, 1814. Heidler and Heidler, eds., s.v. "Patriot War," by Mahon.

…made their way back to the United States. Ibid.

…Lieutenant Colonel Edward Nicholls remained… Heidler and Heidler, eds., s.v. "Nicholls, Edward," by Heidler and Heidler.

…in June, 1815, he left… Heidler and Heidler, eds., s.v. "Florida," by Jarvis.

…the fort was well stocked… Heidler and Heidler, eds., s.v. "Nicholls, Edward," by Heidler and Heidler.

"…General Edmund Pendleton Gaines…" Remini, Jackson, 130.

…fort on a cliff… O'Brien, 192.

"…120 feet in circumference…" Heidler and Heidler, eds., s.v. "Prospect Bluff, West Florida," by Smith.

…18 feet thick, and 15 feet high… O'Brien, 192.

"…moat…14 feet wide and 4 feet deep…" Heidler and Heidler, eds., s.v. "Prospect Bluff, West Florida," by Smith

"…octagonal-shaped powder magazine constructed of earth…" Ibid.

"…one 32-pounder, three 24-pounders, two 9-pounders, two 6-pounders…a howitzer." Ibid.

"…6,000 stands of rifles…" Ibid.

"…three hundred 'negros' lived in the fort…" Remini, Jackson, 130.

"…wore red coats…" Ibid.

…50 miles…north and south… O'Brien, 192.

"…400…500…'Negro Colonial Marines' …" Heidler and Heidler, eds., s.v. "Prospect Bluff, West Florida," by Smith.

"…organized a government and …a military leader…" Ibid.

…ordered Gaines to construct a fort just north of the Georgia/Florida border… Remini, Jackson, 130.

…Colonel Duncan Clinch…200…Creeks under William McIntosh… David S. Heidler and Jeanne T. Heidler, eds., Encyclopedia of the War of 1812 (Santa Barbara, CA: ABC-CLIO, Inc., 1997), s.v. "McIntosh, William," by Charles H. McArver, Jr.

…squadron of gunboats… Remini, Jackson, 131.

…Clinch and McIntosh…laying waste… Heidler and Heidler, eds., s.v. "McIntosh, William," by McArver, Jr.

…July 10th…mouth of the Apalachicola River… Remini, Jackson, 131.

…July 27th…ready to begin assault… Ibid.

"On the very first volley…" Ibid.

…hit the large powder magazine… Ibid.

…a tremendous explosion…killing 270…and wounding 61 more… Ibid.

…asked the Seminoles for help… Heidler and Heidler, eds., s.v. "Seminole Indians," by Heidler and Heidler.

…Seminoles declared…neutral…a conflict between…whites. Ibid.

…Patriots…threatened the Seminoles… Ibid.

…Seminoles…began raiding…in the summer of 1812. Ibid.

In the fall of 1812…Georgia militia… McAfee, 455-456.

…more powerful one by Tennessee militia under…Colonel John Williams… winter of 1812-1813… Remini, Jackson, 131, and McAfee, 456.

…penetrated…Alachua prairie…destroyed…food supply… Heidler and Heidler, eds., s.v. "Seminole Indians," by Heidler and Heidler.

…1817…Seminoles at the mouth of the Apalachicola River… Remini, Jackson, 132.

…welcomed Red Stick refugees… Ibid.

…Neamathla…Fowltown…the Flint River was the dividing line… O'Brien, 198.

…communicated to General Jackson… Remini, Jackson, 133.

Twiggs and 250 … O'Brien, 198.

…morning of November 21st, 1817… Ibid.

…killing five Seminoles … Ibid.

On November 30th, 1817…Seminoles…attacked a boat… Ibid.

…forty soldiers, seven women…four children… Remini, Jackson, 133.

…six soldiers…escaped…four…wounded… Ibid.

…Secretary of War John C. Calhoun… O'Brien, 199.

…December 26th, 1817, Calhoun ordered Jackson to take command… Remini, Jackson, 134.

...chastise the Seminoles... Heidler and Heidler, eds., s.v. "Jackson, Andrew," by Cornish.

...challenge Spanish control of the Floridas... Ibid.

"...reported 2,700 Seminoles..." Remini, Jackson, 134.

On December 23rd, General Gaines captured Amelia Island... Ibid., 137.

...contradictory orders...whether Jackson...confront Spanish... Ibid., 137-40.

...Nashville to Fort Scott on January 22nd, 1818... O'Brien, 203.

...eight officers...1,000 Tennessee riflemen... Remini, Jackson, 140.

...800 regular army soldiers... Ibid., 141.

...4th and 7th Regiments... O'Brien, 202.

...William McIntosh...2,000 allied Indians... Heidler and Heidler, eds., s.v. "'McIntosh, William," by McArver, Jr., and Remini, Jackson, 142-43.

...5,000 soldiers... Remini, Jackson, 142.

...46 days...450 miles...Nashville to Fort Scott... Ibid., 141-42.

...army in danger of starvation... Ibid., 142.

...supply ships had left New Orleans... Ibid.

...March 10th...three-day supply of food... O'Brien, 205.

...March 15th...Jackson reached...destroyed Fort Apalachicola... Remini, Jackson, 143.

"...boatload of food..." Ibid.

...Jackson ordered the rebuilding... O'Brien, 205.

...named the...bastion Fort Gadsden. Ibid.

On March 26th...march...St. Marks... Remini, Jackson, 146.

...march to the northeast...Mikasukian towns... Ibid., 147.

...advanced companies ran into hostile Indians...small but heated battle... O'Brien, 207.

...outreaching columns to encircle... Remini, Jackson, 147.

...Indians saw...and...retreated. Ibid.

...to these Red Sticks, the current struggle... Ibid.

...burned nearly 300 houses... O'Brien, 208.

"...arrived at St. Marks..." Remini, Jackson, 148.

...late in the day on April 6th... Ibid.

...armed hostile Creeks and Seminoles... Ibid.

...companies of Jackson's 4th and 7th Regular Army regiments... O'Brien, 208.

...without a fight on April 7th, 1818. Remini, Jackson, 149.

...Bowlegs Town, around 100 miles to the east... O'Brien, 211.

...eight days rations...start of the march... Remini, Jackson, 151.

"On the morning of April 12th..." O'Brien, 212.

"...Natural Bridge on the Ecofina River..." Remini, Jackson. 151.

...massed on the edge of a swamp... Ibid.

...Native Americans plus 50 Tennesseans...routed... O'Brien, 213.

...37 warriors killed, six warriors wounded, and 97 women and children captured... Ibid.

On the morning of April 15th, 1818... Remini, Jackson, 152.

"...approximately 12 miles..." Ibid.

…killing one warrior, and capturing 4… Ibid.

…hard march of 16 miles…large pond at 3:00 PM…still six miles… Ibid.

…Seminoles…discovered… Ibid.

…reaching the outskirts at sunset… Ibid.

…left under Colonel Thomas Williamson…2nd Regiment, Tennessee volunteers… Ibid.

Jackson…center…U.S. Regulars, the Georgia Militia, a unit of Kentucky and Tennessee guards. O'Brien, 214.

…Allied Creeks under Colonel Noble Kinnard. Ibid.

…right… 1st Regiment, Tennessee Volunteers…allied Creeks under Brig. General William McIntosh. Remini, Jackson, 152.

The right…cut off the escape… O'Brien, 214.

…11 bodies… Remini, Jackson, 152.

"…a large quantity of corn…" Ibid., 153.

…about 30 cattle, and a large number of horses… Ibid.

"…three hundred houses…" Ibid.

…led his army the 107 miles back to St. Marks in 5 days. Ibid., 154.

…Spanish governor in Pensacola… Ibid., 157.

…Jackson would take his army west to Pensacola… O'Brien, 218.

…morning of April 29th…1,200 soldiers departed St. Marks for Fort Gadsden… Remini, Jackson, 158.

…May 24th…Pensacola… Ibid. 160.

"…already retreated to Fort…Carlos de Barrancas…" Ibid.

Jackson called…for surrender… Ibid., 160-61.

…morning of May 27th…one 9-pounder and one eight-inch howitzer… Ibid., 161.

…ladders in hand and in full view of the fortress… Ibid.

…a white flag appeared…the 300-man garrison surrendered… Ibid.

…Colonel William King as governor…Spanish laws would remain in effect… properly respected… Ibid.

…Spain had been weakened by the war against Napoleon… Heidler and Heidler, eds., s.v. "Florida," by Jarvis.

…Adams-Onis Treaty…signed on February 22, 1819. Ibid.

"…Florida…became…U.S. territory in July, 1821." Ibid.

Chapter 15

…sent agents to Scandinavia… Stewart H. Holbrook, "The Legend of Jim Hill," American Heritage, IX, No. 4 (June 1958), 98.

…sold them land…for $2.50 an acre. Ibid.

"…feeder lines…" Ibid.

"…peasant(s) from Europe…for $25…" Ibid.

…42% of Montana's area was settled by homesteaders… Ibid., 99.

"…Greatly Reduced One-Way *Colonist* Rates…" Ibid., 12.

"The Great Northern's number one...train... *The Empire Builder*..." Ibid., 101.

...Hill himself was...nicknamed the Empire Builder. Ibid., 10.

"Jim Hill hitched...places and things together..." Ibid., 101.

In 1818...Ethan Allen Brown...proposed... Wendy J. Adkins, Ohio Canals, Copywrite, 1997. Internet Site: http://www.geocities.com/Heartland/Prairie/6687 1 / 7.

In 1822, a canal act was passed... Ibid.

By early 1823, preliminary reports and surveys... Ibid.

...the safest, easiest, and cheapest mode of transportation. Ibid.

...February 4th, 1825, a bill...passed... Ibid., 2 / 7.

Ground was broken...Miami and Erie Canal...July 21st, 1825... Wendy J. Adkins, Miami & Erie, Copywrite, 1997. Internet Site: http://www.geocities/Heartland/Prairie/6687/miami.htm 2 / 4.

...67 miles from Cincinnati to Dayton... Frank Wilcox, William A. McGill, ed., The Ohio Canals (Kent, OH: The Kent State University Press, 1969), 66.

...reaching Middletown on November 28, 1827. Ibid., 66.

...1828-'29, boats...from Cincinnati to Dayton. Ibid., 66-7.

...work...continued until 1834. Adkins, Ohio Canals, 3 / 7.

...Miami Extension...begun in 1833... Adkins, Miami & Erie, 2 / 4.

...first boat...Cincinnati to Toledo...June 27th, 1845. Wilcox, 69.

...specification...1) 4 foot...2) 40 feet...3) 26 feet...4) towpath 10 feet... T. Deitsch, Miami and Erie Canal Tour Internet Site: http://www.bright.net/~dietsch/grandlake/canal.htm 2 / 4.

...5) locks 90 feet...by 15 feet... Adkins, Ohio Canals, 3 / 7.

...there were 103 of them... Adkins, Miami & Erie, 1 / 4.

...most were approximately 78 feet long... Adkins, Ohio Canals, 5 / 7.

"...13 to 14 feet wide..." Ibid.

...drew 3 feet of water... Wilcox, 23.

...handle 50 to 80 tons... Ibid.

...6-horse team... Adkins, Ohio Canals, 5 / 7.

...4 miles per hour...faster speeds...damaged the canal walls. Ibid., 6 / 7, and Wilcox, 23.

"Passenger fees...were 2 to 3 cents per mile..." Deitsch, 1 / 2.

...some packets...charged 4 to 5 cents... Wilcox, 23.

Freight rates...2 cents per mile...going down to 1.5 cents...over 100 miles. Deitsch, 1 / 2.

...from Cincinnati to Toledo...249 miles... Ibid.

...64 hours... Adkins, Miami & Erie, 1 / 4.

For 25 years...Miami and Erie Canal...principal means... Adkins, Ohio Canals, 4 / 7.

"...581,295 in 1820 to 1,980,329 in 1850..." Ibid., 5 / 7.

"...68%...between 1830 and 1840..." Deitsch, 1 / 2.

"In 1832, 1,000..." Adkins, Ohio Canals, 5 / 7.

"In 1842...52,922..." Ibid.

...the cost to move a ton of freight...$125. Ibid., 4 / 7.

After the advent...$25. Ibid.

...price of a bushel of wheat...from $.50 to $.75... Deitsch, 2 / 2.

Between 1833 and 1850...between 18,000 and 35,000 bushels... Adkins, <u>Ohio Canals</u>, 4 / 7.

Cincinnati...shipped sugar and molasses... Ibid.

...refined commodities...pork, flour, and whiskey... Ibid.

...Toledo, Michigan, and...Northwestern Ohio...Mexican War. Wilcox, 69.

...officers by packet...enlisted soldiers...on freight barges. Ibid.

...important military conduit...until 1856. Ibid.

"...third most populous state in the Union." Adkins, <u>Ohio Canals</u>, 5 / 7.

"...mills, machine shops, foundries, distilleries, wool..." Ibid.

Management skills from the operation... Ibid.

The cash paid... Ibid.

...freighters...hired to carry rails and ties... Wilcox, 8.

Chapter 16

...toll revenue...1840...$532,688... Adkins, <u>Ohio Canals</u>, 6 / 7.

By 1851...$799,024... Ibid.

In 1848...the first railroad... Ibid.

In 1851...Cincinnati, Columbus, and Cleveland... Ibid.

...operated more economically... Ibid.

...due to frozen canals. Ibid.

...1850 to 1860...railway miles...375 miles to 2,946 miles... Deitsch, 1 / 2.

...*Niagara*, was built in 1845... Wilcox, 69.

...eroded the side banks... Ibid., 70, and Adkins, <u>Ohio Canals</u>, 6 / 7.

...transportation of passengers...discontinued... Wilcox, 73.

By 1856, expenditures...exceeded...revenues. Adkins, <u>Ohio Canals</u>, 6 / 7.

...(as late as 1903, ...$700,000)... Adkins, <u>Miami & Erie</u>, 1 / 4.

In 1906, only the mainline... Wilcox, 95.

The last revenue-generating cargo boat...in 1912. Adkins, <u>Miami & Erie</u>, 1 / 4.

...the disastrous 1913 floods... Ibid.

The Miami and Erie Canal officially closed in 1929. Ibid., 4 / 4.

The railroad most closely following the path of the canal...

> Biographical Note: The descriptions of the paths of the four "local" lines contained on pages 144 to 146 were derived from a 1905 railroad map (J.C. Morris, <u>Railroad Map of Ohio</u> [Columbus, OH: The Columbus Lithograph Co., 1905]), plus maps and details in the following referenced sources.

...the Cincinnati Northern... John A. Rehor, <u>The Nickel Plate Story</u> (Milwaukee, WI: Kalmbach Publishing Co., 1965), 140.

...the original mainline of the Wabash Railroad. Bill Stephens, "Automotive Artery," <u>Trains</u> 56, No. 1 (January 1996), 46-47.

...The Clover Leaf Railroad. Rehor, 119.
...Decatur...Willshire... Ibid., 472-73.
...intersected the Miami and Erie Canal at Delphos... Ibid., 122,123.
...an errant course toward Toledo... Ibid., 140, 173.

Appendix A

...initial battle of the Revolutionary War (1775-'83). "The Dunmore War, 1774." Historical Marker, 18 Locust Street, Gallipolis, OH 45631, 1992.
The 1768 Treaty of Fort Stanwix, NY... James K. Swisher, "War for the Ohio," Military Heritage, 5, No. 3 (August 2003), 74.
...alliance...Shawnee, Miami, Ottawa, Delaware, and Mingo nations... Ibid.
...John Murray...received authority... Ibid.
...advance on the Native American villages... Ibid., 75.
The northern 1,500-man force... Ibid.
This southern, 1,100-man force... "The Dunmore War, 1774." Marker # 7-27;Historical Marker, 18 Locust Street, Gallipolis, OH 45631, 1992.
With between 800 and 1,000 warriors... Swisher, 76.
...in the early morning hours of October 10, 1774... Ibid.
...an hour before dawn to an hour before dark... Ibid., 77.
...at the cost of 75 dead and 140 wounded... Ibid., 78.
...the loss of between 35 and 75 warriors killed. Ibid.
..."The Year of the Bloody Sevens"... O'Neil, 54.
...two sieges of Fort Henry... Ibid.
...approximately 41 settlers... Ibid., 55.
...Daniel Boone captured...January, 1778. Ibid., 53.
...traveling 160 miles in 4 days and 4 nights... Ibid., 57.
...30 grown men and 20 older boys... Ibid.
...approximately 450-man attack force... Ibid.
In November, 1778...General Lachlan McIntosh and 1,200 troops... "The Great Trail: The Ohio County in the Revolution." Marker # 2-10; Historical Marker, 600 W. Canal Street, Malvern, OH 44644, 2001.
"It was the only Continental Army fort..." Ibid.
In late-1777, Clark...went to Virginia Governor Patrick Henry... O'Neil, 113.
...commissioned Clark a colonel. Ibid.
"...175... May 12, 1778..." Ibid.
"...171..." "The Forks of the Wabash." Historical Marker; Intersection, U.S. Route 24 and Indiana State Route 9, Huntington, IN
"...60..." Bruce Lancaster, History of the American Revolution (New York: American Heritage, Inc., 1971; 2003), 300.
"...200 additional..." Lancaster, 302; 315.
...January 29th, 1779. O'Neil, 116.
...180 militia soldiers... Lancaster, 301.
...February 5th... O'Neil, 119.

...marched his soldiers again and again... Lancaster, 302.

...February 25th... O'Neil, 125.

...Colonel John Bowman... "Ohio Revolutionary Trails System." Ohio County Info: Pioneer Migration Routes through Ohio. Internet Site: http://homepages. rootsweb.com/~maggieoh/trails.html 1-2 / 11.

...150...Colonel George Slaughter... Maude Ward Lafferty, "Destruction of Ruddle's and Martin's Forts in the Revolutionary War." From the Register of the Kentucky Historical Society. Vol. 54, October, 1956, No. 189. Internet Site: http://www.military.state.ky.us.kyngemus/Destruction%20of%20Ruddle's%20 and%20m...11 / 38.

...Captain Henry Bird...850 soldiers... "Redcoats in Shelby County, Ohio." 1780 Redcoats; Shelby County Historical Society. Internet Site: http://www. shelbycountyhistory.org/schs/indians/1780redcoats.htm 1 / 1.

...between 1,000 and 1,200 men... Lafferty, 7 / 38.

...capture Ruddle's Station on June 24th. Ibid., 18 / 38.

...Martin's Station, capturing it June 28th. Ibid., 30 / 38.

"...470 prisoners..." Ibid., 12 / 38.

...arriving on August 4th. Ibid.

...Clark...100 Regulars and 1,000 Kentucky volunteers... "Ohio Revolutionary Trails System," 2 / 11.

...Pickawillany and on August 8th... Ibid.

"...19 dead..." Ibid.

...(Autumn, 1780), Colonel Auguste La Balme... "Colonel Augustin de La Balme's Defeat – Indiana Revolutionary War Battle." La Balme's Defeat – Indiana Society Sons of the American Revolution. Internet Site: http:// inssar.org/sar_labalme.htm 1/3.

...only 100 militiamen... Sarah A. Meisch, "Miami Indians Victorious in Revolutionary War Fight." Historical Society Whitley County Indiana Genealogical Purchasers of Land Patents... Internet Site: http://historical. whitleynet.org/lebalme.htm 2/4.

...left about 20 men... "Colonel Augustin de La Balme's Defeat – Indiana Revolutionary War Battle." 1/3.

"...November 5th, 1780..." Ibid.

Indeed, in the 1780... Henry Howe, Historical Collections of Ohio, Volume I. (Cincinnati, OH: C.J. Krehbiel & Co., Printers and Binders, 1900), 480.

...to 1781 timeframe... "Ohio Revolutionary Trails System," 10/11.

...Captain William Caldwell...Ibid., 9/11.

...Mac-o-chee (Shawnee for "Smiling Valley") highlands... "The Smiling Valley." Welcome to West Liberty Est. 1817 History. Internet Site: http:// www.westliberty.com/history.htm 1/3.

...to raid Springfield... "Ohio Revolutionary Trails System." 9/11.

In March, 1782... O'Neil, 93.

...commanded by militia Colonel David Williamson... Ibid., 93, 96.

...about 90 Moravian Delawares... Ibid., 93.

...Washington sent his trusted subordinate, Colonel William Crawford... "Colonel William Crawford: The 1782 Sandusky Campaign." Marker # 1-88, Historical Marker. Wyandot County Historical Society, Patriotic Citizens of Wyandot County, and the Ohio Historical Society.

...about 480 soldiers... "Crawford's Expedition, 1782." Marker # 3-17, Historical Marker. Crawford County Historical Foundation, Inc., and the Ohio Historical Society, 1976. Also, Henry Howe, Historical Collections of Ohio, Volume II. (Cincinnati, OH: C.J. Krehbiel & Co., Printers and Binders, 1900) 886.

...current Steubenville, OH, on May 25ᵗʰ... Howe, Volume II, 886.

...Battle Island, June 5ᵗʰ...

(The exact date of this battle is not unequivocally established. Howe [Volume II, page 886] states the march continued "the next morning" after "the sixth of June," the battle commencing "about 2 o'clock," while Historical Marker # 3-17 says "June 4-5." A monument to Colonel Crawford in Upper Sandusky, OH states that Crawford "met his defeat at Battle Island, June 5ᵗʰ, 1782..." The battle took place between June 4 and 7, 1782, with June 5ᵗʰ as the most likely date.)

...Crawford was gruesomely burned at the stake on June 11ᵗʰ... Historical Markers # 1-88 and # 3-17. Also, Howe, Volume II, pages 888 to 890, describes Crawford's execution, then states, "Next morning, being June 12..." Thus, the date of Crawford's execution was fixed by an eye witness as June 11ᵗʰ, 1782.

...the Battle of Blue Licks, August 19, 1782. O'Neil, 60.

...400 Ohio Native Americans... O'Neil, 60.

Estimates vary widely on the number of British and allies that actually took part in the siege of Bryan's Station and subsequent Battle of Blue Licks. All the battles and skirmishes during the Revolutionary War in what would become the Old Northwest Territory and Kentucky were very under-documented. Blue Licks, one of the better known battles, multiplies the problem by having many anecdotal accounts and statistics. Compounding this was the fact that many Native American bands joined or left the British during the course of the expedition. Theodore P. Savas and J. David Dameron, A Guide to the Battles of the American Revolution. (New York: Savas Beatie LLC, 2006), 337, state that 300 British and 1,000 Indians took part in the battle. Neal O. Hammond and Richard Taylor, Virginia's Western War, 1775-1786. (Mechanicsburg, PA: Stackpole Books, 2002), 155, report that "...British agents Capts. Alexander McKee and William Caldwell had assembled 'eleven hundred Indians on the ground and three hundred within a day's march'...with the intention of going on the offensive...many of the Indians left for home...McKee and Caldwell convinced the remainder, 'upwards of three hundred Hurons and Lake Indians, a few Delawares, Shawnese [sic] or Mingos to march to the Ohio'...the remainder crossed the river, march to the heart of the Bluegrass, and surrounded Bryan's Station (now a part of Lexington)." O'Neil, as noted above, states that there was "a raid into

Kentucky by a force of more than 400 Ohio Indians under the notorious Simon Girty. The renegade white man's target was Bryan's Station, north of Boonesborough." It seems relatively clear that while the British and Native American force at one point may have numbered upwards of 1,300 to 1,400 combatants, not all crossed the Ohio River, and the effective force on August 19th, 1782 may have been in the 300-to-450-man range.

...44 long-rifle armed sharpshooters... O'Neil, 60-61, and Hammond and Taylor, 156.

...(200-man) militia force... O'Neil, 61. Savas and Dameron quote "181" on page 337. Hammond and Taylor quote "182" on page 158.

...approximately 43... O'Neil, 62.

...(possibly up to 77) Kentucky militiamen... Hammond and Taylor, 164, and Savas and Dameron, 341.

In November, 1782, Clark gathered 1,050 mounted militia... "Ohio Revolutionary Trails System," 3 / 11. Once again, statistical accounts vary as to the size of Clark's force. Hammond and Taylor, page 167, note that Clark "...thought he could collect 950 men, including the 100 regular Virginia troops he thought he could spare." On page 169, they further note that "... Clark succeeded in collecting an army of 1,128 men."

...Clark made it as far as Loramie's Post... "Ohio Revolutionary Trails System," 3 / 11. Hammond and Taylor note that Clark marched only as far as "...(t) he first objective...the Shawnee town of New Chillicothe, or Standing Stone, on the Miami River." In general, all that can be established is that during this time period, Clark led a punitive raid up the Miami Valley and burned British and Indian possessions in retribution of the slaughter at Blue Licks and the execution of Colonel William Crawford.

In the fall of 1786... Hammond and Taylor, 194-198.

"...700 to 800..." "Ohio Revolutionary Trails System, 3 / 11.

...Clark's trusted lieutenant... Hammond and Taylor, 198.

...seven Native American villages... Ibid., 199.

...and the old English fort... "Zanesfield." Historical Marker C 362. Zanesfield, OH; Ohio Revolutionary Memorial Commission, 1930.

...the aged Chief Moluntha... Hammond and Taylor, 200.

...August 1789... Ibid, 202.

...Major John Hardin...220-man... Ibid.

...three warriors and five women and children... Ibid.

...Federal authorities... Ibid., 203.

Appendix C

"...November 25th, 1812..." Gilpin, 153.

"...Franklinton...Springfield...Xenia...Dayton...Eaton..." Ibid.

...Eaton...secure provisions... Ibid.

...600...to 781...

Biographical Note: The total of 600 soldiers is the most cited total, being quoted by Gilpin (p. 154), Huston (p. 539), Holden (Heidler and Heidler, eds., p. 254), and McAfee (p. 178). However, the author has seen the number of 773 quoted, and a total of 781 was observed on a historical marker at the battle site circa 1992 (although this marker too has been amended to 600).

...Campbell...a company of the 19th... Gilpin, 154, and McAfee, 178.

...Ball...Second Dragoons... Gilpin, 154.

Lieutenant Colonel James Simrall...four troops of Kentucky dragoons... Gilpin, 139, 154.

"...a militia company of Pennsylvania riflemen..." Gilpin, 154.

"...Pittsburgh Blues...under Captain James Butler..." Ibid.

...units of Ohio volunteers... Gravestones at the battle site.

"...a company of spies...scouts..." Gilpin, 154.

...Dayton...pack horses... Ibid.

...early on the morning of December 17th, 1812.

Biographical Note: December 17th, 1812, is the most accepted date of the battle. The marker from the early 1990s at the battle site had "December 12th, 1812," but this has subsequently been changed to the 17th. Holden states, "16 December" (Heidler and Heidler, eds., p. 254). The text in both Huston (p. 539) and McAfee (p. 178) can be construed to indicate the date of December 17th, 1812. Gilpin unequivocally states December 17th, 1812 (p. 154).

Campbell believed...Silver Heels' Town... Gilpin, 154.

...Munsee...(a branch of the Delawares). Huston, 539-40.

...killed eight...captured eight, plus 34... Gilpin, 154, and McAfee, 179.

...some Native Americans escaped. Gilpin, 154, and McAfee, 178.

...Silver Heels' Town...two miles further... Gilpin, 154.

At four in the morning...reveille... Sign at the battle site.

Biographical note: Gilpin notes "Just before dawn..." and McAfee states, "About half an hour before day..." in reference to the beginning of this battle.

"...300..." Huston, 539.

"two-hour battle..." Sign at the battle site.

Biographical note: Both Gilpin (p. 154) and McAfee (p. 180) quote the battle's duration at about an hour.

...at least 30... Gilpin, 154.

...to 40...

Biographical note: A marker at the battle site states, " December 17-18, 1812: Approximately 48 Miami and Delaware gave their lives in defense of their lands." Both Gilpin (p. 154) and McAfee (p. 178) state that 8 Native Americans were killed on December 17th, 1812. Thus, 48 minus 8 equals 40 Native Americans killed on December 18th, 1812.

...frostbite... Gilpin, 154, McAfee, 181, and Huston, 540.

…additional Native American forces…Tecumseh. McAfee, 181, and Heidler and Heidler, eds., s.v. "Campbell, John B.," by Heidler and Heidler.

…retreat to Greenville…that afternoon, December 18th. Sign at the battle site, and McAfee, 181.

"The character of this gallant detachment…" Huston, 540, and McAfee, 181-82.

…(38 killed, 150 wounded)… O'Neil, 98.

"…for 36 hours…" Ibid.

"The situation of this town…" McAfee, 177-78.

"…obtained a brevet promotion to colonel."

Biographical note: The description of Campbell's subsequent career contained on page 156 is drawn from Heidler and Heidler, eds., s.v. "Campbell, John B.," by Heidler and Heidler (p. 80). The author recommends a full review of the entry in the original text.

William Henry Harrison went on to fame…

Biographical note: The description of Harrison's subsequent career contained on page 156 is drawn from Heidler and Heidler, eds., s.v. "Harrison, William Henry," by Heidler and Heidler (p. 230-32). The author recommends a full review of the entry in the original text.

Tecumseh became a true…

Biographical note: The description of Tecumseh's subsequent career contained on page 157 is drawn from David S. Heidler and Jeanne T. Heidler, eds., Encyclopedia of the War of 1812 (Santa Barbara, CA: ABC-CLIO, Ind., 1997), s.v. "Tecumseh," by Reginald Horsman (p. 504-05). The author recommends a full review of the entry in the original text.

BIBLIOGRAPHY

Books

Alexander, Bevin. <u>How Great Generals Win</u>. New York: W.W. Norton & Company, 2002.

Boot, Max. <u>The Savage Wars of Peace: Small Wars and the Rise of American Power</u>. New York: Basic Books, 2002.

Borneman, Walter R. <u>1812: The War That Forged a Nation</u>. New York: Harper Collins Publisher, 2004.

Eckert, Allan W. <u>Wilderness Empire</u>. New York: Bantam Books, 1971.

Farwell, Byron. <u>The Great War in Africa, 1914-1918</u>. New York: W.W. Norton & Company, 1986.

Fluharty, Linda Cunningham. <u>History of the Upper Ohio Valley, Vol. I</u>. Madison, WI: Brant & Fuller, 1890.

Gaff, Alan D. <u>Bayonets in the Wilderness: Anthony Wayne's Legion in the Old Northwest.</u> Norman, OK: University of Oklahoma Press, 2004.

Gilpin, Alec R. <u>The War of 1812 in the Old Northwest</u>. East Lansing, MI: The Michigan State University Press, 1958.

Glover, Michael. <u>The Napoleonic Wars</u>. New York: Hippocrene Books, 1978.

Hammon, Neal O, and Richard Taylor. <u>Virginia's Western War, 1775-1786.</u> Mechanicsburg, PA: Stackpole Books, 2002.

Holliday, Murray. <u>The Battle of Mississinewa, 1812</u>. Marion, IN: Grant County Historical Society, 1964. Second Printing, 1991.

Howe, Henry. <u>Historical Collections of Ohio, Volume I</u>. Cincinnati, OH: C.J. Kiehbiel & Co., Printers and Binders, 1900.

Howe, Henry. <u>Historical Collections of Ohio, Volume II</u>. Cincinnati, OH: C.J. Kiehbiel & Co., Printers and Binders, 1900.

Huston, James.   Counterpoint: Tecumseh vs. William Henry Harrison. Lawrenceville, VA: Brunswick Publishing Company, 1987.

Lancaster, Bruce. History of the American Revolution. New York: American Heritage, Inc., 1971, 2003.

McAfee, Robert Breckinridge. History of the Late War in the Western Country. Lexington, KY: Worsley & Smith, 1816; Reprinted by Readex Microprint Corporation, 1966.

McCollough, Alameda, ed., The Battle of Tippecanoe.   Lafayette, IN: The Research and Publication Committee of the Tippecanoe County Historical Association, 1973.

O'Brien, Sean Michael. In Bitterness and In Tears: Andrew Jackson's Destruction of the Creeks and Seminoles.   Westport, CT: Lyons Press/Greenwood Publishing Group, Inc. 2003, 2005.

O'Neil, Paul. The Frontiersmen. Alexandria, VA: Time-Life Books, Inc., 1977.

Owsley, Frank Lawrence, Jr. Struggle for the Gulf Borderlands: The Creek War and the Battle of New Orleans. Gainesville, FL: University Presses of Florida, 1981.

Rahor, John A. The Nickel Plate Story. Milwaukee, WI: Kalmbach Publishing Co., 1965.

Remini, Robert V.   Andrew Jackson and His Indian Wars.   New York: Viking Penguin, Inc., 2001.

------------ The Battle of New Orleans: Andrew Jackson and America's First Military Victory. London: Viking Press, 1999.

Savas, Theodore P. and J. David Dameron. A Guide to the Battles of the American Revolution. New York: Savas Beatty LLC, 2006.

Skaggs, David Curtis and Gerald T. Altoff.   A Signal Victory: The Lake Erie Campaign, 1812-1813. Annapolis, MD: Bluejacket Books/ Naval Institute Press, 1997.

Utley, Robert M. and Wilcomb E. Washburn. Indian Wars. New York: American Heritage, 1977: Reprint, Boston: Houghton Mifflin Company, 1987.

Wilcox, Frank; William A McGill, ed. The Ohio Canals. Kent, OH: The Kent State University Press, 1969.

Encyclopedias

Edited Appleton's Encyclopedia. 2001 Virtualology, S.v. "Virtual American Biographies: Josiah Harmar."

Heidler, David S. and Jeanne T. Heidler, eds., Encyclopedia of the War of 1812. Santa Barbara, CA: ABC-CLIO, Inc., 1997.

Dictionary

New Webster's Dictionary. 1990 Edition.

Historical Markers

"Colonel William Crawford: The 1782 Sandusky Campaign." Marker #1-88 (Ohio). Wyandot County Historical Society, Patriotic Citizens of Wyandot County, and the Ohio Historical Society, 1996.

"Crawford's Expedition, 1782."Marker #3-17 (Ohio). Crawford County Historical Foundation and the Ohio Historical Society, 1976.

"The Dunmore War." Marker # 7-27 (Ohio). 18 Locust Street, Gallipolis, OH 45631, 1992.

"The Great Trail: The Ohio Country in the Revolution." Marker # 2-10 (Ohio). 600 W. Canal Street, Malvern, OH 44644, 2001.

"Zanesfield."Marker # C362 (Ohio). Ohio Revolutionary Memorial Commission, 1930.

Internet

Adkins, Wendy J. Ohio Canals. Copywrite, 1997. Internet Site: http://geocities. com/Heartland/Prairie/6687/

Adkins, Wendy J. Miami & Erie. Copywrite, 1997. Internet Site: http://geocities.com/Heartland/Prairie/6687/miami.htm

"Arthur St. Clair Bibliography." <u>Virtualology</u>, 2000. Internet Site: http://www. arthurstclair.com/1.arthurstclair.com/

"Battle of Fallen Timbers." <u>Ohio History Central</u>. Ohio Historical Society. Internet Site: http://www.ohiohistorycentral.org/ohc/history/h_indian/ events/bfallen.shtml.

Blodgett, Brian, <u>Tecumseh: His Role in the Cause and Conduct of the War of 1812</u>. Internet Site: http://members.tripod.com/Brian_Blodgett/Tecumthe. html

"Blue Jacket." <u>Ohio History Central</u>. Ohio Historical Society. Internet Site: <u>http://ohiohistorycentral.org/ohc/history/h_indian/people/bluejack.shtml</u>

"Colonel Augustin de LaBalme's Defeat – Indiana Revolutionary War Battle." <u>LaBalme's Defeat – Indiana Society Sons of the American Revolution</u>. Internet Site: <u>http://inssar.org/sar_labalme.htm</u>

"Did You Know…?" Internet Site: <u>http://www.noacsc/ohiohist/regional/fort.facts. htm</u>

Dietsch, T. <u>Miami and Erie Canal Tour</u>. Internet Site: <u>http://www.bright. net/~dietsch/grandlake/canal.htm</u>

"Fort Recovery." <u>Ohio History Central</u>. Ohio Historical Society. Internet Site: http://www.ohiohistorycentral.org/ohc/history/h_indian/places/frecover. shtml

Freehoff, William Francis. "Tecumseh's Last Stand." <u>Military History</u>. (<u>Military.com</u>) Internet Site: http://www.military.com/Content. MoreContent?file=PRthames

Freehoff, William Francis. "Tecumseh's Last Stand." <u>Military History, Part 2</u>. (<u>Military.com</u>) Internet Site: <u>http://www.military.com/Content.More Content?file=Prthames2</u>

"<u>Historic Fort Wayne: The Great American Outpost</u>." Internet Site: http://www. geocities.com/Heartland/Valley/7029/fortwayne.htm/

"Little Turtle." <u>Ohio History Central</u>. Ohio Historical Society. Internet Site: <u>http://ohiohistorycentral.org/ohc/history/h_indian/people/lturtle.shtml</u>

Meisch, Sarah A. "Miami Indians Victorious in Revolutionary War Fight." <u>Historical Society Whitley County Indiana Genealogical Purchasers of Land Patents…</u> Internet Site: <u>http://historical.whitleynetorg/labalme.htm</u>

Office of the Chief of Military History, United States Army. "The War of 1812."
Extracted from American Military History: Army Historical Series, Chapter
6. Internet Site: http://www.army.mil/cmh-pg/books/amh/AMH-o6.htm

"Ohio Revolutionary Trails System." Ohio County Info: Pioneer Migration Routes
through Ohio. Internet Site: http://homepages.rootsweb.com/~maggieoh/
trails.html

"Redcoats in Shelby County, Ohio." 1780 Redcoats: Shelby County Ohio
Historical Society. Internet Site: http://www.shelbycountyhistory.org/schs/
indians/1780redcoats.hym

"St. Clair's Defeat." Ohio History Central. Ohio Historical Society. Internet Site:
http://ohiohistorycentral.org/ohc/history/h_indian/people/stcldft.shtml

"The Smiling Valley" Welcome to West Liberty, Est. 1817 History. Internet Site:
httm://www.westliberty.com/history.htm

"Treaty of Greenville" Ohio History Central. Ohio Historical Society. Internet
Site: http://ohiohistorycentral.org/ohc/history/h_indian/document/tgreenev.
shtml

U.S. Army Quartermaster Corps Historian. "This Week in Quartermaster
History, 4 – 10 November." Internet Site: http://www.qmmuseum.lee.army.
mil/historyweek/Nov4-10.htm

Map

Morris, J. C. Railroad Map of Ohio. Columbus, OH: the Columbus Lithograph
Co., 1905.

Newspaper

Hanna, James. "Ohio Town Recalls 1791 Battle." The Journal Gazette, 3 November
1991, 17A and 18A.

Periodical

Avery, Elroy M. A History of the United States and Its People. (1910), cited
in Dale Van Every, "President Washington's Calculated Risk," American
Heritage, IX, No. 4 (June 1958), 56-61 and 109-11.

Battin, Richard. "Early America's Bloodiest Battle." <u>The News-Sentinel</u>, Copywrite 1994.

------------. "'Mad Anthony' Wayne at Fallen Timbers." <u>The News-Sentinel</u>, Copywrite 1994-1996.

Gilbert, Bil. "The Battle of Lake Erie." <u>Smithsonian</u>. 25, No. 10. (January 1995), 24-34.

Holbrook, Stewart H. "The Legend of Jim Hill." <u>American Heritage</u>. IX, No. 4 (June 1958), 10-13 and 98-101.

Lafferty, Maude Ward. "Destruction of Ruddle's and Martin's Forts in the Revolutionary War." <u>Register of the Kentucky Historical Society</u>, Vol. 54, October 1956, No. 189.

Meek, Basil. "General Harmar's Expedition." <u>Ohio History, The Scholarly Journal of the Ohio Historical Society</u>. 20, No.1 (January 1911), 74-108.

Peckham, Howard H. "Josiah Harmar and His Indian Expedition." <u>Ohio History, The Scholarly Journal of the Ohio Historical Society</u>. 55, No. 3. (July-September 1946), 227-241.

Stephens, Bill. "Automotive Artery." <u>Trains</u>. 56, No. 1 (January 1996), 42-55.

Swisher, James K. "War for the Ohio." <u>Military Heritage.</u> 5, No 3. (August 2003), 79-79, 90.

Van Every, Dale. "President Washington's Calculated Risk." <u>American Heritage</u>. IX, No. 4 (June 1958), 56-61 and 109-11.

Winger, Otho. "The Indians Who Opposed Harmar." <u>Ohio History, The Scholarly Journal of the OhioHistorical Society</u>. 50, No. 1 (January-March 1941), 55-59.

Videocassette

Michaels, Joel B., prod., Tab Murphy, dir./writer. <u>Last of the Dogmen</u>. Hollywood, CA: Savoy Pictures/Carolco Pictures, Inc., 1995. Videocassette. 118 minutes.

Recommended Reading List
(In historical chronological order)

Meek, Basil. "General Harmar's Expedition." Ohio History, The Scholarly Journal of the Ohio Historical Society. 20, No.1. (January 1911), 74-108.

Peckham, Howard H. "Josiah Harmar and His Indian Expedition." Ohio History, The Scholarly Journal of the Ohio Historical Society. 55, No. 3. (July-September 1946), 227-241.

Williams, John Hoyt. "Shame With No Name." Great Battles: American Commanders' Defining Moments. Leesburg, VA: Primedia Enthusiast Publications, (2004), 24-30.

Niderost, Eric. "Fallen Timbers." Military Heritage. 6, No. 1. (August 2004). Herndon, VA: Sovereign Media Company, Inc., (2004), 40-48.

Gaff, Alan D. Bayonets in the Wilderness: Anthony Wayne's Legion in the Old Northwest. Norman, OK: University of Oklahoma Press, 2004.

Encyclopedia of the War of 1812. Santa Barbara, CA: ABC-CLIO, Inc., 1997. S.v. "Tippecanoe, Battle of," by Reginald Horsman.

Gilpin, Alec R. The War of 1812 in the Old Northwest. East Lansing, MI: The Michigan State University Press, 1958.

Gilbert, Bil. "The Battle of Lake Erie." Smithsonian. 25, No. 10. (January 1995), 24-34.

Skaggs, David Curtis, and Gerard T. Altoff. A Signal Victory: The Lake Erie Campaign, 1812-1813. Annapolis, MD: Bluejacket Books/Naval Institute Press, 1997.

Encyclopedia of the War of 1812. Santa Barbara, CA: ABC-CLIO, Inc., 1997. S.v. "Thames, Battle of the," by Sandor Antel.

McAfee, Robert Breckinridge. History of the Late War in the Western Country. Lexington, KY: Worsley & Smith, 1816; Reprinted by Readex Microprint Corporation, 1966.

Owsley, Frank Lawrence, Jr., Struggle for the Gulf Borderlands: The Creek War and the Battle of New Orleans. Gainesville, FL: University Presses of Florida, 1981.

Fleming, Thomas. "Old Hickory's Finest Hour" <u>Great Battles: Monumental Clashes of the 19<u>th</u> Century</u>. Leesburg, VA: Primedia Enthusiast Publications, Inc., (2004), 18-27, 90.

Remini, Robert V. <u>The Battle of New Orleans: Andrew Jackson and America's First Military Victory</u>. New York: Viking Penguin, Inc. 1999.

Remini, Robert V. <u>Andrew Jackson and His Indian Wars</u>. New York: Viking Penguin, Inc., 2001.

Wilcox, Frank; William A McGill, ed. <u>The Ohio Canals</u>. Kent, OH: The Kent State University Press, 1969.